The Chinese Kitchen

The Chinese Kitchen

A Traditional Approach to Eating

Yong Yap Cotterell

Weidenfeld and Nicolson . London

First published in Great Britain by
George Weidenfeld & Nicolson Limited
91 Clapham High Street, London SW4 7TA
1986

Map drawn by Richard Natkiel
Technical illustrations by Joy Fitzsimmons

ISBN 0 297 78702 0

Photoset by Deltatype, Ellesmere Port
Printed and bound in Great Britain by
Butler & Tanner Ltd
Frome and London

In memory of a very dear brother – Yong Soo

Contents

Map of Chinese Provinces ix
Preface xi

Introduction 1
  An Historical Perspective 1
Food and Health 12
Tea and Wine 22
  Recipes for Medicinal Wines 33
Chinese Cooking and Eating 36
Ingredients 46
Preliminary Preparations 88
  Cutting the Ingredients 88
  Utensils in the Chinese Kitchen 91
Cooking Methods 95
Selection of Recipes 111
  Cold Hors d'Oeuvres 111
  Meat Dishes 121
  Poultry and Game 144
  Fish and Seafood 159
  Egg Rolls 174
  Vegetables 176
  Soups 187
  Cakes and Desserts 204
  Savoury Snacks 216
Preparation of Some Chinese Ingredients 222

Chronology 230
Guide to Pinyin 231
Index 233

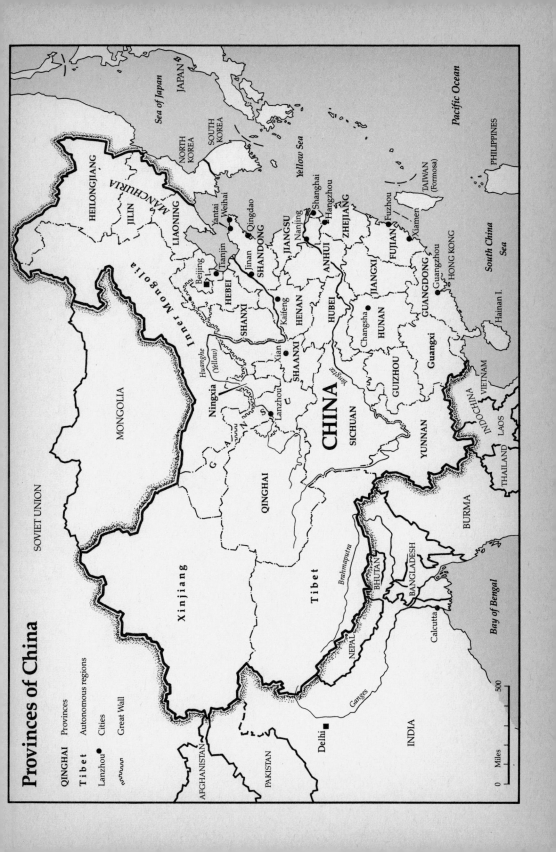

Provinces of China

QINGHAI Provinces
T i b e t Autonomous regions
●Lanzhou Cities
〰〰〰 Great Wall

SOVIET UNION

HEILONGJIANG

JILIN

MANCHURIA

LIAONING

NORTH KOREA

SOUTH KOREA

JAPAN

Sea of Japan

Inner Mongolia

MONGOLIA

Yantai
Weihai
Beijing
Tianjin
HEBEI
SHANXI
Jinan
Qingdao
SHANDONG

JIANGSU
Nanjing
Shanghai
Hangzhou
ANHUI
ZHEJIANG

Yellow Sea

Pacific Ocean

PHILIPPINES

TAIWAN (Formosa)

Fuzhou
FUJIAN
Xiamen

JIANGXI

GUANGDONG
Guangzhou
HONG KONG

South China Sea

Hainan I.

Kaifeng
HENAN
Xian
SHAANXI
HUBEI

Huanghe (Yellow)
Ningxia
Lanzhou

G
A
N
S
U

QINGHAI

CHINA

SICHUAN

Changsha
HUNAN

GUIZHOU

Yangtze

GUANGXI

YUNNAN

Xinjiang

Tibet

INDOCHINA
VIETNAM
LAOS

BURMA

THAILAND

Brahmaputra

BHUTAN
BANGLADESH

NEPAL

Calcutta

Ganges

Bay of Bengal

INDIA

Delhi

PAKISTAN

AFGHANISTAN

500

Miles

0

Preface

This book attempts to explain something of Chinese ways of cooking and eating. But in such a limited space it is impossible to deal with every aspect of the Chinese diet, which is after all a tradition already five thousand years old. The recipes included are intended to indicate the remarkable range of dishes available today; they also reveal the two prime concerns of the Chinese cook, taste and health.

The preoccupation of China's inhabitants with cookery is very ancient indeed. Excavation of tombs has shown how much care was taken over food preparation from earliest times, and how important a proper diet was considered to be for this life as well as the afterlife. Good food and good health have always been seen to go together. The attitude was summed up in the poem:

> Is he a chef or a doctor?
> Is this a pharmacy or a restaurant?
> Fish, meat, vegetables, spring onions and leeks:
> Delicious dishes banish tablets and pills,
> Nourishing food is the drug for all ills.

Because of lack of space only notable provincial recipes appear. However, they include typical meals taken in the home, since restaurant cooking is but one aspect of the Chinese diet. The fact that both women and men work in the kitchen makes cooking a family affair, just as eating a meal together is one of the chief events of social life. While the Chinese are of all people in the world the most conscious of their diet, they are also great connoisseurs of the culinary arts.

Introduction
An Historical
Perspective

Cereals and vegetables today form the basis of the Chinese diet, along with moderate consumption of meat and fish. The origins of this distinctive approach to cookery and eating can be traced as far back as the prehistoric period, when the first farmers settled in villages, grew millet as the staple crop, raised the newly domesticated pig, and supplemented food supplies by hunting and fishing. Sometime after 5000 BC they also started to manufacture clay pots for the preparation of their meals. Two particular vessels they devised were to remain in use for thousands of years. The first, the *ding*, three pots joined as a tripod, marked an enormous advance in terms of using heat, with its hollow legs both providing support and presenting a greater surface to the fire, while the internal division allows the cooking of several things at once. The second was the *hsien*, in which a lower vessel similar to a *ding* was surmounted by another one with a perforated bottom and a cover, in which food could be steamed. Even at this early stage of development we can observe some of the characteristics of Chinese cookery: sophisticated methods and fuel economy.

The archaeological record tells us that the Chinese have always been an agricultural people. They never seem to have passed through a pastoral phase. Milk and milk products are still largely absent from their diet, while their language is rich in agricultural metaphor. Then, as now, the chief crop in northern China was millet and in the central and southern provinces rice held sway. Both grains remain the chief ingredients of the Chinese meal; when cooked they are called *fan*, and vegetables *cai*. By the Chou period, 1027–256 BC, written documents refer to the culinary arts as 'cut and cook', a not inaccurate description of modern Chinese cookery. The cutting and mincing of the ingredients, and the blending of flavours, whether sweet, sour, bitter, hot or salty, had been already mastered. Both wild and domesticated animals and plants were boiled, steamed, roasted, simmered, pickled and dried; almost every cooking method except stir frying.

Since Chou times the Chinese way of eating has not greatly changed. Food is regarded as the means to a healthy life; in some places it is also

1

offered to the ancestral dead in order to secure family prosperity. And alcoholic beverages are restricted to feasts and ceremonial occasions.

If under the Chou kings the foundations of the Chinese cuisine were laid, however, the period of early empire known as the Han (202 BC–AD 220) saw what can only be termed a quiet revolution in taste and technique. The Han emperors expanded the borders of China, especially westwards, and as a result opened up the country to foreign influences. From Central Asia came exotic foods and drinks: grapes, grape wine, alfalfa, pomegranates, walnuts, sesame, onions, caraway seeds, peas, coriander, cucumbers. We can glimpse the rich and varied diet enjoyed by the Han upper classes in the elaborate dishes found in 1974 within a woman's tomb at Mawangdui, near Changsha in Hunan province. Set out for the deceased were forty-eight bamboo baskets of prepared meats and fruit as well as fifty-one pots containing cereals, vegetables and cakes. On small bamboo slips were recorded for each the details of preparation methods and ingredients. From the finds at Mawangdui, and other Han tombs, it is possible to list some of the main foods consumed in China prior to the era of expansion under Emperor Han Wudi (140–87 BC).

Cereals: millet, glutinous millet, rice, wheat, barley
Vegetables: soya, kidney beans, mustard seed, hemp seed, rape, bamboo shoots, taro, chives, lotus roots, lentils, ginger, melon, gourd, shallot, garlic, water chestnuts
Fruit: pears, plums, peaches, oranges, jujubes, persimmons
Meat: beef, mutton, pork, dog, horse, hare, venison, boar, chicken, pheasant, duck, wild goose, quail
Fish: carp, bream, perch
Beverages: wines made from rice, millet and wheat, plus fruit juices.

The favourite dish at Mawangdui was *geng*, a kind of stew that might contain cereals, pieces of meat or fish, and vegetables. It is first recorded in Chou times.

Sumptuous foods were served at Han feasts. The art of blending fine flavours and of slicing ingredients into the thinnest slivers was looked upon as the hallmark of fine cuisine, as indeed they are today. A Han feast began with wine, then came a stew, followed by a series of dishes culminating in grain, and followed by fruit. The same pattern persists in a present-day banquet, where fried rice or noodles are invariably the penultimate dish. From the first century BC the Chinese started to make noodles, steamed bread and wheat-flour cakes. And just as continued drinking after a Han feast was always accompanied by savoury snacks, so the modern Chinese never drink without eating.

Pigs were slaughtered on the eve of the New Year, as they still are for festivities in the rural areas. Throughout the rest of the year the Han Chinese preferred to eat chicken, a meat whose superiority is evident in

Food and drink at a literary gathering to collate books, Northern Qi (550–589)

the custom of serving it to guests. The poor in Han times ate wheat and soya beans, which were considered to be coarse grains by the well-to-do who liked millet and rice. In the same way boiled food was thought to be inferior and was eaten by the peasants, though on journeys or expeditions dried boiled grains were the normal fare, even for the Emperor. The invention of noodles, however, improved the diet of the ordinary people, who seem to have taken advantage of the importation of large-scale flour milling. Even the imperial kitchens succumbed to the noodle craze, the usurper Wang Mang enjoying the novel dish during his brief reign (AD 9–23).

Yet the Tang, more than any other dynasty, is identified with new developments in cookery. Under the Tang emperors (618–906), China was the largest and most populous state in the world, and its tolerance of foreign ideas and ways seems positively modern. Migrants and travellers brought new ingredients and new techniques to enhance the traditional cuisine. A bewildering variety of vegetables, nuts, fruit and spices from

3

Samarkand, Turkestan, Persia, the West, Indochina, South-East Asia, became known for the first time, with the result that some old favourites were relegated to the status of famine foods.

Of great importance in this change was the attitude of the palace, which did much to propagate new plants, investigate their value and experiment with their preparation. In particular, the advice of pharmacists was heeded when they pronounced on diet and health, sexual power, youthfulness or longevity. Besides chefs and assistants, the imperial kitchens contained eight dietitians, or *shihyu*, whose task it was to prescribe menus for banquets. Tonic foods, rejuvenators such as myrobalan and ginseng, and medicinal spices were employed, so that there was no division between feasting and eating for good health. Salt, as well as other salts obtained from plants, were regarded as essentials in the diet. And there was even a special method of cooking pork, mutton or eggs on natural sulphur hot springs, which was thought to be beneficial for invalids.

Tang Chinese regarded their domestic animals as valuable beasts of burden rather than sources of protein, and their diet was supplemented by the abundance of wild game with some fish and seafood. However, contact with the nomadic peoples beyond the Great Wall led to the upper classes eating veal and mutton as well as drinking milk. Occasionally camels were eaten, and to this day in certain provinces camel's hump remains a speciality. Fermented, curdled or soured milk was preferred, along with imported Persian dairy confections.

The Tang Chinese had a passion for cakes, especially foreign cakes, *hubing*. Persian vendors of *hubing* thronged the streets of the capital Chang-an, present-day Xian. Another foreign speciality was *pilo*, a fruity and aromatic fancy pastry of Western Asian origin. Frying or stir frying also became popular cooking methods at this time, especially for the preparation of fried sweet yeast cakes, a kind of doughnut. Food was strikingly decorative, with elaborate shapes, textures and tints; this upsurge of interest in the visual appearance of dishes has never been lost, as a visit to a good Chinese restaurant reveals today.

In the seventh century the technique of producing raw sugar from sugar cane came from India, and by the end of the Tang dynasty white refined sugar was also available. Another imported sweetener was 'thorn honey', derived from a leafless desert plant common in Central Asia. On the other hand, Chinese cooks continued to develop their own methods, one of which was the preservation of food by pickling, fermentation, drying and smoking. We know that pickled meat and fish were prized by the imperial palace, in particular a 'meat pickle' of deer, rabbit or goat. It is also believed that the making of *doufu*, soya bean curd, was mastered during the ninth century. Foreign food, clothes, music and dances were *de rigueur* at aristocratic banquets. Indeed, the liberal attitude of the Tang Chinese towards things foreign, combined with the skills of native cooks, ensured the richness and variety of modern Chinese cuisine. The import of Buddhist texts from India and Central Asia went side by side with the arrival of equally new culinary ideas.

After a brief period of disunity, possibly connected with the invention of gunpowder, China came under the rule of Song emperors (960–1279). Despite continued troubles with nomadic peoples on the northern frontier, which ended in the destruction of the capital, Kaifeng, in 1126 and the loss of the northern provinces, this period saw an unprecedented abundance of food brought about by a twin revolution in agriculture and commerce. It was an age of great cities, even after the removal of the imperial palace to southern Hangzhou. Their growing populations were largely sustained by a shift to rice cultivation, which was helped by double cropping, using a highly drought-resistant strain introduced from Champa, modern Cambodia. At the same time the commercialization of agriculture made produce more easily available, and previously rare ingredients became common in Song markets. Production kept pace with the increase in population, to the amazement of both contemporaries and modern historians; the Song Chinese were undoubtedly the best fed people then alive. By 1270 the number of people living in Hangzhou had passed the million mark, and to feed them some 200 tonnes of rice was needed daily. Amid this prosperity the cooks working in the cities had scope for experimentation; they were able to cater for an official class as well as the wealthy merchants, and they took full advantage of their interest in good food. Above all else, there was an empirical approach towards cooking and eating, and an acceptance of innovation; from these, present-day Chinese cuisine was born.

Song cities were filled with eating places, eating out being considered the essence of city life. Restaurants offered the best provincial dishes, including unusual ingredients like shark's fin, besides entertaining their patrons with other pleasures. The better restaurants served the rich bureaucrats with menus containing up to 200 dishes, and there were 'wine restaurants' which also provided alcohol and women as part of their fare. One of the latter establishments boasted 'couches' in 110 private rooms. The Song restaurant was a place of sensual indulgence, and the pinnacle of luxury was found in the floating restaurants on the West Lake, a beautiful expanse of water immediately beyond the city walls of Hangzhou. There private parties could hire splendid boats with expert chefs, or be entertained on one of the vessels belonging to rich individuals. The catering service furnished all necessities, even to the extent of advice on matters of etiquette. In humbler establishments the usual pattern was specialization in a particular kind of cooking: noodles, cakes, snacks, local dishes, and Buddhist 'temple food' for vegetarians.

Additionally, a wide range of cooked food was prepared in workshops for street vendors, and in a Song 'night market' one could eat right through to dawn when the tea-seller took over for breakfast.

After 1126 the Song diet was that of the Yangtze delta. Rich and poor shared the same cooking methods and basic cuisine, as it is today. The difference between their eating habits lay in the degree of variety and richness each could afford. The daily pattern of eating was the same as now: three meals were supplemented by snacks, except that the Song Chinese ate fruit before, during and after a meal. In parallel with all this hedonism there were at work the religious influences of Buddhism and Taoism. Buddhist feasts and customs were observed, with their taboo on the consumption of meat, and especially beef. Taoist intellectuals added their support for rustic simplicity too. They argued against over-consumption and said that it was unnatural to eat out-of-season food. Natural, home-grown produce was best in their eyes, a point of view which did much to strengthen the old relationship between diet and medicine. Interest in cookery was profound. The poet Su Tungpo (1036–1101) is credited with the invention of several dishes, and his poems contain many references to drinking and eating. Su Tungpo's official career lapsed badly, forcing him to remain in exile for a number of years.

Part of a tomb mural showing cooks in the Yuan dynasty (1279–1368)

Following the fall of the Song dynasty, China endured the harshness of the Mongols (1279–1368). These fierce horsemen devastated the northern provinces, laid waste vast areas, and oppressed the peasantry. Marco Polo marvelled at the magnificent court of Kublai Khan; but the conquerors had little permanent effect on Chinese culture, while on the Chinese diet they had none. The eating habits of the steppe – whole boiled lambs carved with daggers, heavy drinking of fermented mare's milk, *koumiss* – did not generally appeal, while the exclusion of Chinese scholars from official appointments until the final years meant that the Mongols themselves were not influenced by China. An unintended consequence of Mongol rule was the publication in 1330 of *Principles of Correct Diet* by Hu Sihui, a scholar with time on his hands. He claimed that all food was medicine and, if eaten in the correct manner and under the right circumstances, it had curative properties. His emphasis on nutritional therapy, with drugs as a last resort, has remained a basic Chinese idea ever since.

The Ming dynasty enjoyed over 200 years of peace and order, from 1368 to 1644. The national recovery was started by the founder emperor, Chu Yuanchang, of peasant stock. His humble background may partly account for the attention paid to rural conditions. Water conservation schemes improved the farmer's lot, and later allowed the introduction of new crops from America – maize, peanuts, tobacco, and sweet potatoes, which had great impact on Chinese diet thereafter. But the first Ming Emperor was also concerned to re-establish the imperial kitchens, since traditionally food had always been a part of ceremonies and rituals. He even formed two sets of kitchen staff: one to serve the living and one the dead. Insulated ships packed with ice blocks from the mountains were used to transport perishables from the southern provinces for state sacrifices. They came up the Grand Canal to Beijing, the capital from the early fifteenth century onwards.

At all levels of society, however, the Ming Chinese were discerning about the quality of food and demanded the best. It became the practice to catalogue the best dishes of a locality, with information for connoisseurs on where and when to obtain them. Culinary skills were held to be desirable and honourable, something both men and women should be pleased to possess. The rise of the cook socially is hardly surprising in China and probably began with the amateur efforts of scholars during the Mongol period.

Rice was of course the standard staple, and pork the basic meat. Beef remained under Buddhist disapproval, while mutton was too malodorous as well as a meat firmly associated with the nomads. Although meals could be quite plain for the poor, the rich were able to enjoy the best ingredients from all parts of the empire.

Increased travel did much to encourage provincial cookery in the major cities. Officials on inspection tours, students sitting the imperial examinations, traders selling and buying goods, and tourists seeing the sights created a demand which was met by the development of 'clan hostels', *huiguan*. Beijing itself absorbed the cookery of the provinces, since high officials were recruited by means of examinations held initially in every provincial capital. Tourism was also widespread. Travellers spent vast sums visiting scenic spots and famous places mentioned in guidebooks, which were written for the first time, and found their way into 'wine restaurants'. Restaurants catered for home parties and 'take-away' foods.

Meanwhile, scholars were at work recording culinary methods, writing about foods in plays, novels and poems and most important of all, they were discussing food as medicine. In the very first year of the Ming dynasty the throne was presented with a work entitled *Essential Knowledge for Eating and Drinking*. Its author was honoured, not least because of his age: over 100 years old, Qia-Ming had outlived Mongol rule. By far the greatest study on diet and health was written by Lee Shizhen (1518–93), a renowned doctor. It took him twenty-seven years to write this survey of 1,800 foods, plants and minerals. What distinguishes its approach from the 800 earlier works he consulted is a very modern analysis of medicinal properties. In fact the book, *Pencao Kangmu*, is still used by doctors today.

The last imperial dynasty before the founding of the Republic in 1912 was the Qing, which the Manchus set up in 1644 after their invasion of China. Although the Manchus were outsiders, they came to admire Chinese traditions so much that eventually they lost their own language. Nevertheless, they felt obliged to maintain their position by means of a stringent censorship, so that, as under the Mongols, Chinese scholars found it advisable to stick to safe subjects such as food. Even the famous novels of the period were crammed with details of good living, as an aspect of cultured life. References are made in the *The Dreams of the Red Chambers* to rare foods such as 'preserved goose feet', and 'cypress-smoked Siamese suckling pig' and to foods as remedies for individuals. In a novel of sensuality entitled *A Floating Life*, food is a part of sensual indulgence. In *The Scholars* people are seen as what they eat. At least half a dozen writers expressed their views on food strongly. Some writers stressed that gourmet eating and drinking consisted of a combination of frugality and refinement. It was customary to serve the formalized Manchu and Chinese dinner parties with sixteen dishes, eight platters, four desserts, and so on.

An important work called *Sui-Yuan Shitan* ('Sui-Yuan menus'), was published in 1792 by Yuan Mei, a renowned writer and poet, who not only enjoyed fifty years of literary fame but also enjoyed and knew about food. His work covered fourteen aspects of food, with 326 regional recipes, and was written not only for the cook but also for the reader as a sensitive eater. One aspect was that of *xuzhi*, or warnings and guidance, in which the natural properties of food, scrubbing and rinsing, the art of flavouring, accompaniment to food, ingredients, control of heat, one-ingredient dishes, colour and fragrance, variety, utensils, serving and rescue, and other matters were discussed at length. Many of these warnings are still relevant to cooking in general and Chinese cooking in particular today.

Yuan Mei emphasized the importance of first-grade ingredients and insisted on the search for the best. He maintains that only 60 per cent of the credit for a successful meal should go to the cook, and the other 40 per cent should go to the buyer of the ingredients. Preparation, he says, is crucial, and he insists on cleanliness and meticulous care. For successful stir-frying he specified that the amount should not be more than 280 g (10 oz) for meat, or 230 g (8 oz) for fish or chicken. This is the origin of the present-day Chinese small wok, stir-fried dishes. Roundly condemned is what Yuan Mei calls an 'eye feast': extravagant displays of food, some of which may well be uneatable, as opposed to a 'mouth feast'. Only good-quality ingredients cooked and immediately served, course by course, offer a first-class meal; there should never be precooked or warmed-up food. One taboo, according to Yuan Mei, is on cooking several things in a single cauldron, such as boiling pork, chicken, duck and goose together. He compares this to educating different talents at once, when each really needs separate tuition. 'If the chicken, pig, goose and duck had souls,' he claims, 'they would lodge a complaint in the underworld.' Finally, he advises that carefully prepared and cooked foods should not be gobbled down.

In spite of the opening up of China to foreign powers during the nineteenth century, there was virtually no influence on Chinese eating habits as happened in the Han and Tang periods. There was no meeting of culinary minds between China and the West. The only impact on diet was opium, which the British dumped in enormous quantities in Guangzhou (Canton). Opium spread to restaurants, where it was served with meals, especially in 'wine restaurants'. Poorer people found solace in humbler eating houses, and the very poor made do with boiled left-overs from restaurants, *zacui* – anglicized as 'chop-suey'. Until quite recently this was the diet of beggars and rickshaw pullers.

The twentieth-century culinary scene may be divided into two periods, that of the Republic (1912–49) and the People's Republic (1949 onwards). During the former the diet remained much the same as in the nineteenth century, though the population began seriously to overburden traditional agriculture. Shortages of basic foodstuffs were frequent events, and these developed into famines in north China, where the climate was drier. Political and economic uncertainties aggravated this breakdown, since the chief cause of malnutrition before 1949 was uneven distribution of staples rather than overall scarcity. The rich ate milled grains with meat and the poor whole cereals with vegetables, salted fish, and occasional meat on feast days.

The People's Republic has improved the standard of eating through better distribution and increased output. Irrigation schemes permit the growing of rice and wheat in marginal areas such as Manchuria, so that sorghum (*kaoliang*), millet and sweet potatoes are now less dominant. The ordinary meal remains traditionally low in meat and relies on grains and vegetables. In the northern provinces steamed wheat bread, grain porridge and noodles are eaten with few fresh vegetables owing to the long, severe winter. But in the rice-eating regions, south of the Yangtze river, rice is eaten with a great variety of vegetables, pork, fish and seafood. Soya beans, prepared in various ways and combined with other legumes and vegetables, are eaten all over China. Soya bean curd is rationed together with rice, wheat flour and meat.

Today tourist restaurants offer visitors the sophisticated pre-1949 cuisine, unlike the simpler fare in the restaurants for the mass of the people. Restaurants in north China have a slightly different arrangement to those in the south, in that the kitchens are usually sited near the entrance so that customers entering can observe the chefs at work. They often possess private rooms, but not for the purposes for which they were originally used under the Song emperors. All restaurants have large halls on the ground floor and segregation is based on numbers, not class. If a number of workmen turn up in a group, they may be assigned a private room. In recent years there has been a strong revival of interest in traditional cookery as well as a curiosity about foreign foods, including ice cream, hamburgers, hot-dogs and croissants. No doubt Chinese ingenuity will shortly produce a hybrid croissant sprinkled with sesame seeds or filled with red bean paste, if this has not already happened.

However, the twentieth century has also witnessed the culmination of the spread of Chinese cookery abroad. Even before the Ming period Chinese emigrants had taken their cuisine to South-East Asia, where today a sizeable overseas Chinese population lives. In the longhouses of Borneo the native peoples can be found enjoying bean-curd sticks, 'wood ears', winter mushrooms, lily buds and vermicelli during festivals. Interesting hybrid dishes have also been developed by the *nonyas* or *babas*, as the Malays call Chinese women and men born and brought up in Malaysia and Singapore. Their Chinese cuisine took on the local flavour, with more spices such as lemon grass, galangal and lots of chillis, and with plenty of coconut milk and the use of a local shrimp paste, *blachan*, which make their food so delicious. The Southern Chinese took their cuisine, especially the Cantonese version, to North America too via Hawaii and San Francisco. There they introduced the familiar chop-suey, fried rice, crispy noodles and sweet and sour pork. Until the 1970s these dishes were often thought to be the Chinese cuisine, but the opening of better restaurants in many Western countries has broken through the sweet and sour barrier. Beijing duck and mandarin pancakes are well known, though perhaps the most significant change has been the availability of Chinese vegetables and preserved ingredients in supermarkets, which makes Chinese cookery possible for all.

Food
and
Health

Of all the peoples in the world the Chinese are the most preoccupied with eating. They spend a greater proportion of their personal income on food than any other people, except perhaps the Italians. This joy in eating has been prompted by the constant threat of famine, which hung over China until quite recently. Throughout the country's long history, the peasants have sought knowledge of all the edible plants in the countryside so that they could be used as famine foods, and this country lore remains a living culture handed down from generation to generation. The desire for longevity is another ancient impulse behind the Chinese concern for a healthy diet. During the Han empire (202 BC–AD 220) there was a firm belief that longevity and even material immortality could be attained. Not only were members of the aristocracy buried in specially made jade suits along with elaborately prepared dishes of food for some kind of earthly afterlife but, even more, their cooks and physicians took an interest in the value to the living of certain ingredients and preparations. Cooking and health have never been divided in Chinese tradition. Food is not simply a means to satisfy hunger; it is always looked upon as an aid to good health and a preventive medicine.

Specifically, the Chinese see a healthy diet as the correct balancing of the *yin* and *yang* of food. All ingredients are classified according to their *yin* and *yang* nature. *Yin* is cold, *yang* is hot, and between the two categories fall those that are cool and warming. Some foods are in themselves a balance of *yin* and *yang*, and these are the best. Chinese medicine holds that for a person to be healthy the body's own *yin-yang* balance must be maintained. Consumption of a disproportionate amount of *yin* food would tip the balance towards the *yin* and in consequence bring about illness. If this happens the individual can recover through consuming *yang* and avoiding *yin* food. So fundamental is this notion of balance in Chinese culture that a traditional doctor will invariably ask about a patient's diet before attempting diagnosis.

Examples of 'hot' food are oily or deep-fried dishes, fatty meat, chicken and peanuts. 'Cold' foods include water chestnuts, crabs, gourds and winter melons. A Chinese housewife would thus cook winter melon soup as a remedy for sore throats in the family. Its *yin* nature would help to balance the *yang* (heat) in the sufferers.

Apart from the cold-hot equilibrium, the Chinese believe that each individual at various stages of life has a unique requirement in terms of diet. Even before birth dietary considerations come to the fore. The food taken during pregnancy is intended to aid the development of the unborn child, which incidentally is regarded as being one year on delivery. According to a Chinese proverb, 'A pregnant woman is a ball of fire and shuns 'hot' food; a post-natal mother is a basin of ice and shuns cold food.' So in pregnancy a Chinese woman abstains from alcohol, strong tea, coffee, greasy or deep-fried food, and highly spiced or fermented seafood such as shrimp paste. After birth the child's diet is regulated through breast feeding, sometimes for as long as three years. The lactating mother follows a strict diet, and eats foods which help the milk flow and avoids 'windy' ones. Traditionally, the mother and baby remain indoors for the first forty days following childbirth. The mother is served with specially prepared dishes, some of which may be prescribed. The commonest of these is chicken cooked in wine with herbs and ginger. Usually the mother-in-law does the cooking, since her daughter-in-law is seen as the vital means of continuing the family for another generation. In the ancient ideal of four generations under one roof two chief concerns of the Chinese are evident: longevity and procreation, both of which are dependent on good nutrition.

No matter how well educated, the Chinese woman accepts the enforced rest period as a biological necessity. Her relations seek to protect her with *yang* food from ailments attendant upon childbirth, such as the 'winds' which bring aches and pains in the head and body in later years. The special diet is designed to pep up the blood, 'chase the wind', stimulate circulation, clear up extravasated blood, move the bowels and establish general good health. Another classic dish at this time is pig's trotters cooked in black rice vinegar. To celebrate the birth this dish, known as 'a gift of illustrious posterity from heaven' would also be sent to relations, friends and neighbours with eggs added. Black rice vinegar from Guangdong is often labelled as 'Many Descendants Vinegar'.

Equal care is taken over the diet of the elderly members of the family. They do not eat the same dishes as the young and robust, but enjoy rice porridge enriched with meat and medicinal herbs suited to their condition. They take less greasy, less rich, less 'windy' food. In China, at a big celebration, often special banquet tables are laid out with menus for the elderly.

Perennial shortages of foodstuffs have forced the Chinese into a habit of frugality, and overindulgence in food and drink is a sin. An old saying captures these sentiments: 'A great eater is a small gambler.' Frugality has had a beneficial influence on eating habits, by ensuring that even in times of plenty there is moderation.

In a similar way medical knowledge has encouraged the development of a sensible cuisine. Since it is thought that beauty is not skin deep, but begins with inner health, the Chinese have foods to feed every part of the body: the hair, the teeth, the eyes, the skin, and so forth. Certain herbs are known to darken the hair, to strengthen the muscles and bones, even to slow down the process of ageing. In daily life this awareness is deeply rooted in the home; the housewife cooks according to the physical state of the family and the weather conditions. If the weather is dry and hot she prepares a cooling soup and omits *yang* dishes. If someone is not sleeping well or is constipated, an appropriate dish appears on the table. The Chinese normally cook ingredients in season, as they believe that these are in harmony with prevailing conditions only when they are available. As a result of this attitude a constellation of vegetables, fruits, nuts and herbs is used. Below are some examples of the common foods that have become medicines and some medicines that have become common food, and of the part they play in the Chinese diet.

Abalone: this shell fish has always been regarded as a highly nutritious food. It is a tonic for nourishing the *yin* and for the blood. It calms the liver, clears the '*yin* fire' and rids toxic humidity from the body. For someone whose liver is in poor condition and who is constantly plagued by headaches, giddiness and lack of sleep the abalone is boiled with lean pork and eaten as a soup. The same soup is a food supplement to the treatment of TB, but in both cases only the soup is drunk. Generally if anyone has a poor digestion, the meat is not eaten. In fishing villages in South China the fisherwomen cook abalone in their shells with pig's bladder as a remedy for women's ailments. (For culinary uses, see pages 52 and 71.)

Angled luffa: this gourd is a vegetable that is balanced in nature. It has long been a folk remedy for the lack of milk in a healthy mother; 450 g (1 lb) of angled luffa is boiled with 30 g (2 oz) of dry-fried black soya beans, sometimes with a fish head or tail. The matured and dried angled luffa is a folk remedy for non-rheumatic aching bones and muscles, particularly in the elderly. The hard skins and seeds are removed and 30–60 g (1–2 oz) of the dried fibre is boiled plain or with pork in plenty of water for three hours and eaten as a soup. (See also page 72.)

Aubergine (eggplant): cold in nature, it is a preventive of diabetes and high blood pressure, and is used as a food supplement to the medical treatment of these ailments. (See also page 73.)

Bamboo shoots: these help intestinal muscular movements and disperse grease from the intestines, among their other nutritious properties. (For normal culinary use, see page 66.)

Bear's paws: one of the highly prized treasures of banqueting dishes (which are normally liver and kidneys, as well as 'phoenix marrow', panther's womb, carp's tail, camel's hump, ape's lips and cicada) the bear's paws are eaten as a remedy for rheumatism, for wind and cold in the body and as a general tonic for a weak constitution. The paws are covered with clay and baked for several hours until the fur and skin fall off; then the gelatinous part is sliced, sandwiched with sliced ham and fresh winter mushrooms and steamed. This is one of the rare foods.

Bird's nest: this is the solidified rock-hard saliva of cave-dwelling, fish-eating swifts. The saliva is regurgitated during the process of digestion and the jelly-like saliva dries in the nest, which is made of down (not twigs) in the crevices of the cave. The dried saliva or bird's nest takes the shape of arcs and contains down which is thoroughly removed before cooking. Different species of swift share the same cave and produce the different grades of bird's nest on sale. One species produces inedible bird's nests, because they build the nests with moss. The bird's nest has long been used as a medicine, but is seldom included in a prescription; usually, if need be, the doctor would recommend it in a patient's diet to supplement medical treatment. It is a tonic food suitable even for the very weak and is therefore popular for young children and the elderly. But it has to be taken regularly on a long term basis to be effective. Steamed with rock sugar (a specially processed cane sugar in large crystalline lumps) and eaten as a dessert, or with lean pork as a savoury soup, it is always on the banquet menu; it is one of the treasures in the food hierarchy. (See also page 53.)

Bitter gourd: good for the skin and for strengthening the body's resistance, it is eaten regularly to whet the appetite and aid digestion. Modern analysis reveals that among other things a given weight of bitter gourd contains as much Vitamin C as seven times that weight of tomatoes or 17 times the amount of apples. The ancients believed that it 'clears the heat, combats tiredness, clears the mind and brightens the eyesight'. It has long been a remedy for summer ills such as heat, thirst, diarrhoea and sore eyes. In China it is also used as a food supplement to the treatment of diabetes. It is a *yin* vegetable, very 'cold' in nature and anyone with a 'cold stomach' or weak constitution should not eat too much; nor is it good for an asthma sufferer. It is a great cooler when boiled with meat as a soup, and ginger is always added to counteract the 'coldness'.

Boxthorn leaves: these are eaten regularly for the prevention and cure of skin itches and rashes. They are also good for a condition of dehydration in the body through too much sweating and exposure to heat, which is followed by constipation and difficulty in urinating, resulting in aching joints all over the body. These leaves are also good for the eyesight.

15

Normally they are taken in soup only. The classic combination is lean pork with liver added for good eyesight.

Buddha's hands: a type of citron divided into fingerlike segments, this is a tonic food of a warm nature, suitable for someone with a 'cold stomach' (who cannot take any *yin* food) or with a weak constitution. It is beneficial to the liver, stomach and the lungs, and its main medicinal efficacy is for indigestion, coughs and phlegm. For indigestion it is boiled plain or with pork as a soup. For coughs and phlegm it is steamed with rock sugar for 30 minutes and eaten as a snack once a day until symptoms are cleared. Treated with other herbal medicines and wind dried, it is used as a remedy for asthma. In some villages in Guangdong in South China the fruit is eaten regularly steamed with pork. (See also page 74.)

Celery: the nature of celery is cooling. It lowers blood pressure and has a calming effect on the body. It is also good for the stomach, is diuretic and beneficial to high blood pressure sufferers or those who suffer headaches and pressure in the head caused by a heated liver.

Chinese caterpillar fungus: the botanical name of this fungus is *Cordyceps sinensis*; its Chinese name is *dong-chongcao*, meaning 'winter insects and summer grass', because it begins life as a parasite in the body of a caterpillar, consuming its host, and then grows into a grass in summer. It is used in medicines, and has also become a tonic food. Warm in nature, when steamed or boiled with meat it is a supplement to medical treatment or a tonic for those in poor health. Among its many virtues, it calms the nerves and induces sleep. It is a popular strengthener for male virility; about 10 g (⅖ oz) is steamed with a very old male duck (best about 10 years or over). For those with poor digestion the duck is skinned and any fat removed before steaming for several hours as a soup. The pedantic would insist on a very old *male* duck with *pure white* feathers only. But there are many Chinese recipes that combine the ordinary duck with this fungus for gastronomic pleasure (it has a lovely flavour) as well as medicinal value. When steamed with a chicken it is a remedy for deteriorating memory and eyesight. But for anyone with a liver condition lean pork is used instead. (See also page 68.)

Chinese 'celery' cabbage: this vegetable counteracts the acidity in meat, and is always eaten with meat. (See also page 75.)

Chinese chives: a tonic food for the liver and kidneys, it is a strengthener for male virility, and a remedy for weak, aching knees and back and for incontinence, to mention but a few. Warm in nature, it is not suitable for anyone with a heated constitution. (See also page 76.)

Chinese wolfberries: these are the ripe seeds of the boxthorn bush (*lyciem chinense*) and are called *gouguzi* in Mandarin. In the shops in Britain they are labelled as 'red medler berries', though they have nothing to do with the medlar, European or oriental. They are the size of cooked long-grain rice and lacquer red in colour. They have been used as a tonic food and medicine for millenia in China. The ancients believed that they strengthen the bones and tendons, sharpen the eyesight, calm the nerves, reduce excess heat in the body, nourish the lungs, kidneys and liver and are essential to the vital force of energy. A panacea for delaying the ageing process, they also have the Chinese name *Chiehlautze* or 'drive-away-old-age berries'. An elderly sage of the Ming dynasty (1368–1644) imparted the secret knowledge of these berries to a young man, saying that if eaten regularly over a long period they would lengthen one's lifespan, strengthen one's limbs, darken greying hair, grow new teeth and increase male virility: one would be more or less reborn. Of course, the old sage was referring to the berries' effect on the liver and kidneys. Modern analysis has found evidence to support the ancient claims, and also that they lower the blood sugar and are used as a food remedy for diabetes in the aged in China today. A common tonic food in the Chinese diet, they are boiled with meat in soups together with knotty yam or some other ingredients. For backaches, joint aches, giddiness and poor eyesight in the elderly, red medler berries and rice porridge are taken as a remedy. (For their culinary use, see page 69.)

Dried lily flowers: known as 'golden needles', *jinzhen* or *jinzhencai* in Chinese, and also with the medical name 'sorrow-be-gone', for the eating of this lily flower makes one happy. It is a folk remedy for nose-bleed, which is cured by taking a soup made from the lily for a fortnight. The soup is also taken regularly for poor liver condition and by those who have suffered hepatitis. (See also page 67.)

Dried longans: these fruits are highly valued both as a medicine and as a food (see also page 67.) Longans are eaten as a tonic for the blood, for nourishing the nerves, and for repairing deteriorating memory and general run-down condition. They are particularly valuable to a woman in the post-natal period. For the elderly person who feels weak and tired but does not sleep well, longan and rice porridge is a food remedy; it may be taken as breakfast or supper all the year round. Longan wine combats anaemia and premature greying.

Figs: eaten regularly to ensure the working of the bowels, and to prevent bloodshot eyes, bad breath and piles. When boiled with lean pork (only Chinese white figs should be used here) and eaten as a soup they are beneficial to those with poor liver condition. This fruit may be taken as a sweet after a meal. Eating three or four figs by themselves every day on a long-term basis is deemed to improve poor digestive condition. (See also page 67.)

Green ginger: in Chinese cuisine this is like the lemon in eastern Mediterranean cooking or the tomato in Italian cooking. The spice is used all the year round and in almost all foods and some medicines. Slightly warm in nature, it is a great 'wind chaser', anti-toxic, counteracts excessive humidity, is a mild stimulant and a sudorific if eaten raw. It stimulates the digestive system and increases appetite, and is a panacea for a lot of ills such as colds, wind, headaches, coughs and 'cold stomach'. A hot drink made with green ginger peeled, bruised and boiled with brown sugar is a traditional remedy for colds and flu. (For culinary use, see page 63.)

Hairweed: fine, hair-like, pitch black when dried and dark greenish brown when wet. Called *facai* in Chinese, it is an alga like seaweed but is harvested on land in the Gobi desert area and in the semi-desert areas in Xinjiang, Ningxia, Gansu, Qinghai in north-western China, and in Inner Mongolia, the western part of which is called 'hairweed land'. The Chinese deem it 'the treasure of the Gobi', a highly prized food, for it is diuretic, anti-toxic, clears phlegm, cures coughs and nourishes the body. Eaten regularly it is a preventive food for high blood pressure and malnutrition. Nutritional and medicinal values apart, it is an auspicious food eaten at the New Year's Eve dinner, as the homonym for the word *facai* means 'prosperous'. (See also page 54.)

Knotty yam: a herbal medicine that has become a common tonic food in the Chinese diet, it is regarded as highly nutritious as it not only strengthens the body generally but is also beneficial for anyone with a weak constitution, poor digestion, prone to frequent diarrhoea or weakened by involuntary emission. The knotty yam is also given to children who sleep badly, with poor appetite and poor bowel movements. This root is regularly eaten as a soup for the family. A classic combination is with lotus seeds, lily bulbs, fox nuts, jade bamboo, bitter almonds and dried longan, simmered with pork for one to two hours. (For culinary use, see page 69.)

Maltose: this name is not used in the correct chemical sense to denote a type of sugar, but for a sweet malt extract made from sprouted wheat or barley, or from maize or sweet potatoes. Sticky and brown, it is less sweet than ordinary sugar. It is considered nutritious and easy to digest; it does not aggravate the lining of the stomach, and it nourishes the intestines. Maltose is always given to convalescents, the elderly and the young as a tonic food; and is also used as a binding ingredient in Chinese pills. (See also page 60.)

Persimmons: fresh persimmons are cold in nature. This fruit helps to lower blood pressure and is a remedy for heated blood, itchy skin and constipation. But fresh persimmons are not suitable for people with a 'cool' or weak constitution, with low blood pressure or poor digestion, or just recuperating from malaria. Dried persimmons are a popular tonic food in the Chinese larder. These are *not* cooling in nature, and are suitable for a 'cold stomach' or a weak constitution. They may be soaked in boiling water, steamed or boiled with mixed dried fruits or rice, and eaten as a sweet. (See also page 69.)

Pig's bladder: a folk remedy for the control of the bladder particularly during pregnancy. A thoroughly cleaned pig's bladder is boiled with no more than ten ginko nuts for an adult or five for a child (more than that is poisonous), with some dried bean curd sticks and a few Chinese water chestnuts. If the woman is not in perfect health the ginko nuts are omitted. The pig's bladder is a safeguard against occupational hazards for those whose work involves a lot of contact with water. In China the people who cultivate young fish wade in cold water winter and summer, and therefore very often end up with incontinance, hernia and diseases associated with the urinal tract in old age. The traditional Chinese preventive remedy is to partake regularly of pig's bladder steamed with dried hops.

Pig's trotters: a popular item in the special diet of a woman after childbirth, the pig's trotter cooked in black rice vinegar and ginger is a preventive food for wind pains in the body and 'head winds' in later years, and as a tonic for the blood. It also helps general recuperation and increases milk flow for the lactating mother. The high gelatine content of the trotters is broken down by the black vinegar and the gelatine is more easily digestible and absorbed by the body. Some women believe that the black vinegar assists their organs to return to shape after childbirth. The ginger root chases the winds and humidity from the body – of particular value in Guangdong province in the south where the moist climate leads to excessive humidity.

Red or black 'dates': not the same kind of fruit as the dates of the Middle East. The red dates are green jujubes dried in the sun until they turn a dark red, wrinkled and with a lacquered appearance. The same fruits boiled, wind dried and then heat dried until they turn black and wrinkled are the black dates. Both are used in prescriptions and as a tonic food. They are highly valued as a general tonic and for the anaemic, for women in childbirth or at the change of life, and for the generally weak and the insomniac. Ordinarily they are braised or steamed with pork in soup and eaten regularly as a tonic food in the diet. This fruit has a balanced nature.

Sea cucumbers: not a vegetable but an animal (also known as sea slug, bêche de mer or trepang), these are regarded as a highly nutritious seafood, and contain among other things many minerals and gelatine. In particular they are highly prized as a food supplement to the treatment of the hardening of arteries, for TB, for debilitated nerves and to improve male virility. Balanced in nature, sea cucumber is a popular preventive food in the Chinese diet, suitable for everyone all the year round, and is one of the treasures in the Chinese food hierarchy. (See also page 53.)

Sesame: both sesame seeds and sesame oil are eaten regularly in the Chinese diet. Apart from flavouring food they are regarded as an aid to the smooth working of the digestive tract. They prevent constipation and provide an alternative to laxatives. Sesame oil is sprinkled on almost every soup and dish, mixed in with minced meat and fish, particularly lean dry meat. Sesame seeds are also made into porridge or 'glue' and sesame cakes. They are always roasted and crushed before use so that the body is better able to digest and absorb the otherwise tough-skinned seeds. The black variety in particular has strong double skins. For women after childbirth pork and chicken are cooked entirely in sesame oil for the prevention of constipation. Eating of the sesame oil also enriches the hair. Modern research has shown it to be high in polyunsaturates. (See also page 67.)

Silver wood ears: also known as 'jelly fungus', this tree fungus is highly prized by the Chinese for its medicinal efficacy. It is deemed to be beneficial to the lungs, the kidneys, the spleen, the stomach and the large intestines. For centuries it has been used as a tonic food for the blood; for strengthening the digestive system and lungs; for coughs; as a tonic for the brain and the heart and for rejuvenating the skin. Before silver wood ears were cultivated, the wild strain was food for the Emperor and the wealthy only. There is an anecdote regarding its efficacy on the Emperor Ming Shih-Tsung (1507–1566), an autocratic ruler swayed by a succession of worthless favourites. His reign was troubled by external threats and internal uprisings. Much time and resources were spent in search of an elixir – the secret of longevity. The imperial pharmacists were commanded to prepare the magic drug, composed of processed minerals. After taking the potion the Emperor became restless and hot-tempered, and developed insomnia. On the recommendation of an herbalist he ate steamed silver wood ear soup as a remedy. His composure was restored and the insomnia was cured. Since then Chinese have been eating silver wood ears.

Spring onion: this has anti-toxic, antiseptic and sudorific qualities, and aids digestion. In Chinese cooking it is used in almost every dish, every day, together with green ginger. It is also used in conjunction with herbal medicine and in folk remedies for cold, influenza and many other ills. The spring onion's property of promoting perspiration helps to clear the body of impurities, and 'chases the wind'.

Stag's reproductive organs: the polite name in Chinese for this tonic food is

20

lu-chong. They are the stag's penis and testicles from which the fat and meat have been removed; what is left is wind dried. Obtainable from the Chinese pharmacist, in the East they are usually imported from Australia, New Zealand and Europe, but some are from China herself. They are highly valued for their efficacy for male virility and for female infertility and frigidity: 60 g (2 oz) of this dried organ are steamed with various medicinal herbs, ginger and a chicken as a remedy. But the Chinese never eat this tonic food without first consulting their doctors. It is generally avoided by those who cannot take any strong tonic; those who have a fever or a cold; and those with high blood pressure or a poor digestive system.

White rice porridge: after big feasts or rich fried and greasy foods, particularly in the Spring Festival, when the digestive system suffers and the appetite is jaded, the Chinese resort to white rice porridge for a few days to remove the obstruction. The proportion of rice to water is 1 to 20. Sometimes a piece of dried tangerine peel is added. For the young and robust the rice porridge is ladled boiling hot on to some finely shredded raw lettuce. After a couple of days of this diet, the appetite returns and all symptoms of ill health disappear.

Winter melon: this gourd is cold in nature. It is diuretic, good for coughs and phlegm, and beneficial to the large and small intestines. The ancients said of this vegetable, 'For those who wish to grow fat, do not eat; those who wish to slim eat regularly.' This is a popular cooling vegetable taken in a soup in the hot summer months, and is also used for lowering fevers. (See also page 86.)

Winter mushrooms: in China around 300 species of edible mushrooms exist. Of these the winter mushroom, *dongku*, also known as 'fragrant mushroom', *xiangku*, is crowned as the queen, highly prized for its nutritional and medicinal values. Amongst other nutrients and vitamins it is rich in the B group, in particular B_{12}, the level of which is higher than meat. Not only is it eaten as a preventive food for pernicious anaemia and a tonic food for the nervous system, but also for lowering blood pressure and strengthening the body's immunity against viruses, epidemic diseases and cancer. When eaten with meat it balances the meal. It is also one of the staple foods in Chinese vegetarian diet. (See also page 68.)

Wood ears: these ear-shaped tree fungi are regularly eaten in the Chinese diet for the cooling of the liver, bloodshot eyes and the general health of the eyes. They also clean the digestive tracts and the lungs. The ones with a white back are mainly used as a medicine when cooked with wine. (For some of their culinary uses see pages 67 and 227.)

Tea
and
Wine

Tea

Although we always associate the drinking of tea with Chinese food, in China the domestication of the native tea plant was quite a late event. Whereas alcoholic drinks are known to have been prepared as early as the third millenium BC, tea only became important during the Tang empire, which lasted from AD 618 to 906. Nonetheless, tea is now a key item in the Chinese diet, with a surprising number of uses. Apart from that of a simple beverage, it is regarded as a folk remedy for certain ailments; it is considered an aid to better health, especially for digestion and the disposal of unwanted fats; it serves as a colouring and a flavouring, as well as a smoking ingredient for meat and fish; and its tender young leaves are eaten as a vegetable in the tea-producing areas of south-western China.

The Chinese today drink mainly hot water or plain, unsweetened tea. The low amount of sugar in their diet has ensured that diabetes is almost unknown in the country. But now China, which gave tea to the West, has received in return the doubtful gift of sweetened soft drinks. Consumption of these is constantly increasing, and it is feared that diabetes will become a common disease.

The history of tea is fascinating. The legendary Emperor Shen Nung is said to have discovered tea, when he taught the Chinese the art of agriculture and discovered the medicinal properties of plants. Endowed with a transparent stomach, Shen Nung was able to observe the effects on his body of all that he ate and drank, and found that tea thoroughly cleaned out his intestines. Realizing that tea had medicinal qualities, he named it *cha*, meaning 'to investigate', a homonym of the word in Mandarin. However, on the occasion when he was investigating an unusual grass called *tuanchang-cao*, 'intestine-breaking grass', he had no tea with him and perished. Thus tea began its career as a medicine.

Historians believe that tea became a beverage during the 'Spring and Autumn' period (770–481 BC). But the conquest of what is now the province of Sichuan by the state of Qin in 316 BC seems to have been decisive in bringing about its general acceptance. Sichuan was the tea-growing area and under the Qin emperors and their Han successors, conditions assisted the spread of the tea-drinking habits of Sichuan nobility throughout China. Yet there is a possibility that tea drinking amongst the minority mountain people of Yunnan in south-west China existed as early as 1000 BC. During the Han empire (202 BC–AD 220) the cultivation, production and drinking of tea became widespread in the north of China as well as along the Yangtze river valley.

With the rise of the Buddhist faith after the fall of the Han dynasty, there developed an enormous demand for tea by its adherents. Meditation was found to be easier as tea kept the monks awake and their brains clear; so monasteries planted vast tea estates. A great number of famous names in tea still come from areas around these monasteries, such as Yunwu, Longjing, Maofoong and Pu-erh. Tea became a popular beverage and the attention paid to it by scholars and poets ensured that a cult arose. Works on tea appeared and literary gatherings were conducted around the teapot. Even the nobles of Tibet succumbed to the fashion, especially after the Tang Emperor Tai Tsung sent his daughter, Princess Wunchen, to become one of the two queens of the Tibetan king. Big religious tea parties became a regular feature of the Lamaist monasteries. The nomadic lands beyond the Great Wall soon followed suit, abandoning their favoured milk and yoghurt. In China itself tea houses mushroomed in villages, towns and cities.

About 140 BC tea seeds were carried from China to India. But not until AD 805 did they reach Japan, as a result of Buddhist monks visiting Chinese monasteries. By the seventeenth century the tea habit had reached South-East Asia, East Africa, Russia, Holland, France and England. In 1637 the English first imported tea direct from Fujien, South China, and re-exported it to the American colonies. The English word 'tea' does, in fact, come from *te* in the Fujien dialect. Possibly Catherine of Braganza, wife of Charles II, made tea drinking fashionable when she adopted it in 1662. Soon consumption overtook that of port and sherry, making the English the greatest tea-drinking nation outside China.

While the Chinese never went to the ritual extreme of the Japanese tea ceremony, they came to look upon the drinking of tea together as an essential part of social life. Tea parties were held indoors and outdoors, usually at places where the water was thought to be excellent for brewing. At these gatherings poetry was recited or inspired, and famous teas were tasted and praised. In Buddhist monasteries tea parties with the reading of Buddhist scripts were regular activities. In Hangzhou, temporarily the imperial capital in the twelfth century, we are told that tea houses entertained their customers with music, paintings and flower arrangements. Thereafter the tea house remained a meeting place for all classes, though some obviously specialized to satisfy local demand. By the Qing dynasty (1644–1912) tea houses began to offer snacks such as pumpkin seeds, *shaobing* (hot pasties), spring rolls and cakes. But in Canton, tea houses began as a cheap eating place for working men. Their cuisine was the forerunner of the Cantonese *tim sum* found today in many overseas Chinese restaurants; it consisted of such things as *siumai*, meat dumplings; *hakaw*, prawn dumplings; and *pau*, steamed buns. The drinking of tea and eating of *tim sum* is part of the Cantonese lifestyle today, as visitors to Hong Kong or Singapore know.

Tea-sellers at a tea tasting competition, Yuan dynasty (1279–1368)

Chinese custom requires that tea is always served on the arrival of visitors. And tea is drunk at the beginning of a banquet, when it cleans the palate and whets the appetite. It has been the practice for centuries that tea is sent to absent friends and relatives, as a reminder of affection and of past gatherings. In China now the custom of sending tea is maintained in the tea-growing provinces. As a symbol, tea represents fidelity and everlasting love. This came about because the tea bush can only be propagated by seed germination, never by transplanting saplings. Hence the tea bush is said to possess a constant, reliable nature. Gifts of tea are exchanged when an engagement occurs, and the strength of the pledge is recorded in the saying, 'One girl does not drink tea from two families.'

From ancient times the Chinese have held that the medicinal properties of tea aid digestion, clear phlegm, disperse fat, sharpen concentration, improve eyesight, calm nerves and nourish the brain. Young tea leaves are still considered to be diuretic, anti-toxic and anti-bacterial. A standard treatment for diarrhoea is strong tea. The Pu-erh tea, grown in Yunnan province, is used for slimming purposes as well as for lowering blood pressure. It is thought to be beneficial for the arteries. Another tea for slimmers is Wuloong, which is always served after a rich meal. At a banquet tea may also be taken between courses.

Even more dramatic is the protection tea is supposed to provide against radioactivity. According to research in China and Japan, people who drink tea regularly and over a long period of time are less susceptible to the harmful effects of radio-activity. For this reason in China tea is now compulsory for workers likely to be exposed to nuclear hazards.

A special medicinal preparation, *hongcha jun* ('red tea fungus') may contain nutrients for the renewal and stimulation of the body's cells. The tea is made by growing a yeast culture in a red tea sweetened with sugar. At present it is used as a cure for constipation, but observation suggests that its consumption could strengthen the liver and kidneys, raise the body's resistance to toxins, lower blood pressure, and reduce cholesterol in the bloodstream. Its powers against cancer are the subject of investigation, but for centuries 'red tea fungus' has been considered in folk medicine as a method of prolonging one's lifespan, the eternal preoccupation of the Chinese. Originally prepared in the north-eastern province of Shandong, it spread to Arabia in the nineteenth century and was later adopted by the Japanese, who still consume large quantities.

From these few medicinal examples it can be readily understood why the Chinese approach tea drinking with great care. They never drink too much strong tea. Damage to the stomach, the intestines, even the nervous system, is said to result from such overindulgence. Additionally, people who are highly strung or have weak hearts tend to keep their daily tea drinking to a minimum.

Six main types of Chinese tea exist: red, black, green, Wuloong, flower and brick.

Red tea is fermented. In the form of leaves and bags, it is made in the cup; otherwise broken leaves or powdered tea are brewed in a teapot so that it may be strained. It is mainly taken plain in China except in Canton where milk and sugar are added for nourishment.

Green tea is more popular in China and there are at least thirty-four named brands. Its delightful green colour often ensures that brewing is done in toughened glass, though so-called 'gunpowder' tea requires a porcelain teapot if the delicate flavour of the leaf is to be fully appreciated. Lower-grade green teas are usually made in a teapot too, but only to allow for straining. Dried without fermention, green tea has a distinct and fine taste, much favoured by scholars and poets in the past and those whose jobs demand much detailed attention today. In Zhejiang province, the Longjing, a green tea, is popular. In Hunan province, where green tea with a smoky flavour is preferred, the leaves are chewed while the tea is being drunk.

Wuloong tea is semi-fermented, having the strength of red tea and the flavour of green tea. It was the first tea taken to the West and for a while all Chinese tea was known as Wuloong. It is mainly produced in Fujian, Guangdong and Formosa. In Fujian and Guangdong they are very particular about the quality of Wuloong and the spring or stream water used. In Fujian the brewing of Wuloong has become something of a ritual. The kettle there holds a mere 100 ml (4 fl oz) of water and the fuel is charcoal, dried sugar-cane pulp or olive stones. The minute teapot is scalded with boiling water and the Wuloong tea, taking up about three-fifths of the capacity of the teapot, is put in; then boiling water is added and it is covered. The whole is then bathed in boiling water. It is allowed to stand for 2 to 3 minutes. One pot makes about four cups each containing a single mouthful. The proper manner to drink is to lift the cup up to the nose, move it slowly away, then back again several times, before approaching the mouth in order to fully savour the aroma as well as the taste. There is no haste when enjoying a cup of tea, an ancient art associated with Wuloong tea that has survived to this day.

Flower-scented teas are fine green teas mixed with choice dried fragrant flowers, such as those of jasmine, zhulan (choleranthus or scented capers), orchids, pomelo (a citrus tree whose large fruit is also known as shaddock), cassia (sweet-scented osmanthus), and rose. The majority of flower-scented teas are based on jasmine, however. Flower teas are usually made in a white porcelain cup, with a cover, so that the tint of the tea is more visible and the fragrance is kept in. A pinch of the flower tea is put in and boiling water is poured in; then the brew is covered and steeped from 4 to 5 minutes. For more people it may be made in a pot. In Chinese villages every morning a large pot of flower tea is made and drunk throughout the day.

Brick tea comprises a mixture of broken teas pressed into a block which may be the shape of a round cake, or like a bowl, brick or ball. It is popular among the nomadic people of China and Tibet for its portability. In Tibet a kind of creamy tea is preferred. The brick tea is crushed, brewed, strained and poured into a mixing vessel to which some butter and salt are added. It is blended until it is milky and served from a teapot. Creamy tea is drunk at breakfast: after several cups, halfway through the last cup some black rye flour is mixed into the tea and finished off as a porridge. Tea at lunch time is generally mixed with wheat flour, butter and sugar into a paste and eaten hot. In Inner Mongolia, in the cities and farming areas the teapot method is used. In the nomadic parts an everyday savoury tea is made in an iron pot. A milk tea is served on special occasions. The brick tea is crushed, boiled, strained and poured into a large pot to which cow's milk is added. It is boiled and poured into a teapot and salt is added to make a savoury milk tea. Sometimes toasted rice is added. This tea is drunk thrice daily: the morning tea as a breakfast and the evening tea as a beverage. The Uygur (Uighur) people in the Xinjiang Uygur Autonomous Region brew the brick tea in the same manner as their Mongolian counterparts except that they chew the tea leaves as a vegetable, which compensates for the lack of fruits and vegetables in their diet.

Some special teas: today tea as a beverage is well-known but the following are very ancient methods of tea brewing existing in Yunnan, Guangsi, Hunan and Zhejiang today:

Toasted tea or 'crackling tea' is drunk by the minority groups in the north-east and north-west of Yunnan. This tea is made by toasting a handful of green tea leaves in an earthenware pot, which is turned over a fire until they become golden, fragrant and crackling; then hot water is poured over and it is brewed briefly. When a froth appears the tea is served in cups. The first round is rather strong, so the cup is only half filled and then topped up with water. A pot of toasted tea serves three to four rounds. The toasting gives the green tea a burnt fragrance and a delicious flavour; the liquor has a clear amber colour. One gets addicted to this tea, and the older people could not live without it first thing in the morning.

Braised tea is brewed by the minority groups in the Yunnan border areas. It is similar to toasted tea except that fresh tender shoots of five to six tea leaves are used. This tea is lacking in flavour and slightly bitter with a raw, green fragrance.

Oil-fried tea is eaten in the villages along the border areas of Yunnan, Kuizhou, Hunan and Guangsi. The tea leaves are boiled, mixed with a soft-boiled rice, then dried and used as a basic ingredient for the preparation of this tea. Other ingredients such as peanuts, soya beans, sesame seeds, maize, glutinous rice crisps, dried young bamboo shoots, dried bracken sproutings, squash and so on are fried in hot oil and put in individual bowls. The dried tea leaves and rice mixture is also stir fried in oil and boiling water poured over, sometimes flavoured with salt, ginger and spring onion. When boiled, the tea is ladled onto the mixture in each bowl. The better-off host always includes peanuts and soya beans in this tea. The tea leaves are saved, pounded and used again and again till only the ribs remain. This tea is eaten thrice daily. Without this tea the older people suffer aches and pains. Some babies start their first solid food on this tea. In some areas this tea is eaten as a meal in itself.

Bamboo-tube tea: The minority groups in the south of Yunnan take this tea as a vegetable. Fresh tea leaves are boiled till wilted and then rubbed and compacted into a bamboo tube, sealed with pomegranate or bamboo leaves and left upside down to drain for two days, after which the tube is sealed with clay. The fermentation takes two to three months when the tea leaves turn yellow. The bamboo tube is split open and the compressed and fermented tea leaves are dried and marinated in sesame oil in a china jar. This preserved tea is used in cooking with leeks or other vegetables.

Preserved tea: Along the border areas of Yunnan a preserved tea is also made. The word 'preserved' for Chinese foods generally implies the use of salt, but here no salt is added. Freshly picked tea leaves are immediately put into an urn. The leaves are pressed down with a heavy weight as the urn is filled. When full it is covered and left undisturbed for several months. When the leaves are taken out they should be moist, for which reason the tea is prepared in the rainy season. This tea is mixed with spices and masticated.

Longjing tea with prawns: This is a speciality from Hangzhou. New Longjing tea is cooked with fresh prawns, egg whites and rice wine. Here tea is used as a flavouring.

Wine

Jiu or wine covers the whole spectrum of alcoholic drinks, including distilled spirits. From Shang days (c 1500 BC), there survive both written accounts of wine drinking and the utensils in which drinks were prepared. The Shang aristocrats used millet wine in the rituals of ancestor worship, as indeed fermented beverages have been included in such ceremonies down to our own times. By the Tang period (AD 618–906) rice formed the chief ingredient in wine making in southern China, though millet and wheat held their ground in the northern provinces. Grape wine was imported from Central Asia for some time before Chinese troops conquered Turfan in 640, after which a choice purple grape called 'Mare's teat' was successfully transplanted in the imperial gardens and knowledge of wine cultivation spread to the countryside. Importation of grape wine ceased after the Arab conquest in the eighth century of what is today Afghanistan, but the Chinese were able to make up for this loss by home production, since by then important vineyards had been established in

Jiangsu, in eastern central China. Another famous grape wine centre was Liangzhou, an oasis town near the Great Wall in the north-west. The 'Cleopatra of China', Yangkuifei, the favourite concubine of the Tang Emperor Ming Huang, is said to have drunk Liangzhou grape wine from a jewelled cup. Reputed to have been the most beautiful inmate of the imperial harem, she is the only fat lady among China's historical beauties. No trouble or expense was spared to satisfy her desires, gastronomic or otherwise, even tropical fruit such as litchis were rushed a thousand miles

Yangkuifei drinking wine: a scroll depicting the famous gourmet and unusually plump concubine of the Tang Emperor Ming Huang

to the old capital by 'pony express' from Guangdong in the south. Under Yangkuifei's intoxicating spell, Ming Huang neglected the affairs of state and civil war rent the empire; she died at the hands of mutinous troops in 756. However, the grape wine never really caught on, although some grape wines are produced in the north today. Rice wine or millet wine has always been preferred.

Tang poems often celebrate spring wine, *chunjiu*, which became mature and palatable about late January or early February, when the first blossoms appeared on the cherry and pear trees. Spring wine from western Sichuan was deemed to be the best. Since it was then customary not to strain wine, brown husks floated on the surface of the wine cup; they were called *fuyi*, 'floating ants'. Sometimes peppercorns, saffron, or honey were used for flavouring, but wine was also made from chrysanthemum flowers, pomegranate, pears, and ginger. Water from limestone caves was always preferred for wine-making as the alkaline content counteracted the acidity in wine. In the warmer south of China beverages were brewed from coconut and palm flowers.

In the Tang period, one of the peaks of Chinese culture, the drinking of alcohol was so well established that official bacchanalia were proclaimed by the throne and everyone joined in. In these state-sponsored festivities there were magnificent processions of floats with historical and mythological themes, while the spectators consumed government wine. The revels, lasting between three to five days, usually celebrated an imperial birth, a victory or some other important event.

A brief interlude of barbarian rule in northern China after the end of the Tang dynasty introduced *koumiss*, fermented mare's milk, a strong drink of the steppe people living beyond the Great Wall. During the Song period (960–1279), *koumiss* was consumed in the imperial palace, especially at banquets, and served in restaurants. The Mongol conquerors of China, who next ruled as the Yuan dynasty for eighty-nine years, naturally insisted that *koumiss* become the official drink at state ceremonies. One of their drinking feasts lasted for three uninterrupted days, during which the participants all changed into clothes of a certain colour for each of the days; and these were known as 'one-colour' banquets. Distilled beverages were also available, the first technical manual on distillation having appeared in 1117. Drunkenness was an abiding problem of the Mongols and bedevilled the successors of Kublai Khan until the last one fled to the ancestral steppes in 1368.

By Qing times (1644–1912) the current attitude to intoxicating drinks had crystallized. Wine and food were seen as symbols of good living and refinement by the scholarly and well-to-do classes. However, heavy drinking was frowned upon and restricted to brothels and low-life resorts, an event which explains the association of vice with heavy drinking in the Chinese mind today.

Probably for this reason, wine does not now figure in family meals. The Chinese reserve alcohol for banquets, feast days and special occasions when even children around the age of ten are allowed a sip. Moreover, they never drink on an empty stomach, and something is invariably eaten as an accompaniment, from the vast repertoire of snacks served with drinks. As the Chinese proverb has it, 'Drink in the morning, drunk until dusk.' In the northern provinces, particularly in the winter months, wine is warmed before serving. There is a charming story referring to this practice. A bibber, dreaming that he was warming some excellent wine, woke up. He said regretfully, 'I should have drunk it cold.'

The Chinese are not very particular about alcohol, for even at banquets only one kind of wine is served to guests, and today the Tsingtao beer is often offered as a second choice. But the quality of Chinese lager is excellent. There are two kinds, Great Wall and Tsingtao. The latter is an historical accident, a legacy of the German occupation of part of Shandong province in the late nineteenth century. It tastes very similar to Löwenbrau.

The Chinese never drink cocktails or mixed drinks, believing these to be too intoxicating and unhealthy. As the banquet commences the host fills everyone's wine cup and replenishes each one as new courses are served, unless a guest persistently declines further drink. The host has to be sure that politeness is not the cause of any reluctance by asking the guest three times. Men are expected to imbibe moderately and women to show hardly any desire for alcohol at all. As almost every Chinese readily flushes after a tipple, it is believed that a person who reddens is grateful and unlikely to prove treacherous. The preference for drinking in company on happy occasions probably accounts for the absence of alcoholism in China. The solitary drinker is unknown.

Of the value of wine the famous Ming doctor and herbalist, Lee Shizhen (1518–1593) wrote:

A beautiful gift from heaven; taken moderately it tones up the blood and stimulates circulation; strengthens the nerves and fortifies one against the cold; brings joy and disperses melancholy. Taken in large quantity it damages the nerves and wastes away the blood; wears out the stomach; destroys the inner essence; induces phlegm and inspires fire in the body.

The white wine, *baijiu*, available in Chinese supermarkets in the West, has evolved over the last eight hundred years. In China it is the most popular drink. Based on some kind of grain, there are numerous grades and flavours, though the alcoholic content tends to be around 17 per cent, or 30 degrees proof. There are also grain spirits: one is distilled from glutinous millet and sometimes termed *sanshao*, 'thrice fired'. Corrupted in European tongues as 'shamshoo', it is the closest equivalent the

Chinese have to brandy. *Kaoliangjiu*, a spirit made from sorghum (*kaoliang*), is reminiscent of vodka and gin in colour and clarity but much stronger; when flavoured with rose petals it is called *meikuilu*, 'rose dew'. Cooks use both to flavour dishes and preserve food. The southern Chinese have their own vodka-like spirit which is exceedingly strong as it is often 'fired' twelve times over. It is mainly used for steeping medicinal herbs.

A wine waitress warming wine, Henan.
Northern Song dynasty (906–1126)

The commonest household wine is *Shaoxingjiu* from Shaoxing in Zhejiang province. Used at the table and in the kitchen, this amber-coloured wine is made from glutinous rice. Less well esteemed is *huangjiu*, or yellow wine, also from Shaoxing. It is cheaper, being based on glutinous millet. *Maotai*, a famous wine from Kuizhou, is typical of one of the five main categories of *baijiu* classified according to their bouquet.

The best European vintages to accompany Chinese food are dry white ones such as Graves, Chablis or Touraine from France and Soave or Verdicchio from Italy. Red wines may be drunk with red-cooked dishes in rich gravy, but on the whole they spoil the taste of most Chinese food.

Alcohol is also put to medicinal use and, consumed moderately, it has long been regarded as an essential remedy. Home-made medicinal wines are prepared by steeping herbs in wine and spirits. There are in existence more than a hundred kinds of professionally steeped medicinal wines for every ailment related to every part of the body. There are preparations for lengthening one's lifespan; some for strengthening the kidneys and increasing male virility; stimulating the brain; nourishing the nervous system; others for dealing with neuralgia, wind, rheumatism and arthritis; and of course those concerned with regenerating the body generally. Special medicinal wines exist for women after childbirth, and some families would prepare their own traditional recipes for such occasions.

It goes without saying that the Chinese approach medicinal wines with great care. The dosage is carefully controlled. Normally no more than 10 ml (2 teaspoonfuls) is consumed at a time. The wine must be taken for no more than three months at the most, sometimes one month, after which there is a rest period. Nobody takes medicinal wines during an illness such as a cold, flu, or fever. Heart sufferers should not take it. Nor should pregnant women or anyone undergoing treatment for cancer. Anyone with a *yin* or weak constitution, with thick tongue or dry mouth, avoids it.

Recipes for Medicinal Wines

The following are some medicinal preparations that may be made at home, using either distilled white wine, *shaojiu*, or rice wine. Please remember how small a Chinese wine cup or glass is (3 fluid ounces, if filled to the brim). As home-made medicinal wine is less potent more than 10 ml may be drunk at a time.

Fig wine
450 g (1 lb) dried figs
1.4 l (2½ pt) rice wine or *shaojiu*
110 g (4 oz) white sugar
3 lemons

1. Do not wash the figs.
2. Thinly peel the lemons so that no pith is left on the rinds. Shred the rinds. Tie them in a piece of muslin.
3. Put the dried figs, wine, sugar and bag of lemon rind in a suitable-sized wide-mouthed jar. Cover, seal and store in a cool, dry and dark place.
4. After a month discard the rind bag. Re-seal and store the wine for another 6 months, then discard the figs. Store the wine for another year before use.

The Chinese always used figs as a folk remedy for constipation and exhaustion, for lowering high blood pressure, to counteract anaemia and to nourish the stomach and intestines. One or two glasses daily.

Chrysanthemum wine
110 g (4 oz) dried chrysanthemum flowers
1.1–1.4 l (2–2½ pt) rice wine or *shaojiu*
170 g (6 oz) white sugar

1. Remove the stems from the flower heads.
2. Put all the ingredients in a suitable-sized wide-mouthed jar. Cover, seal and store undisturbed in a cool, dry, dark place.
3. After a year remove the flowers and discard them. Store for another year, then strain and use.

Traditionally chrysanthemum wine is associated with longevity; it is now drunk as a preventive for high cholesterol levels. It also clears the head and stimulates the nervous system. However, it should be avoided by anyone with high blood pressure. One or two glasses are drunk as an aperitif before dinner. Fresh chrysanthemum flowers of *sinensis* origin and only white or yellow ones may be used, in which case the amount is increased to 1 kg (2 lb). Use only the petals.

Dried persimmon wine
12 dried persimmons
1.4 l (2½ pt) rice wine or *shaojiu*
110 g (4 oz) white sugar (optional)

1. Do not wash the persimmons; they are covered in a layer of natural fruit sugar. Quarter them.
2. Put all the ingredients in a suitable-sized wide-mouthed jar. Cover, seal and store in a cool, dry, dark place undisturbed.
3. After 6 months or a year, strain into new bottles and use.

The Chinese drink this wine for the strengthening of male virility, to combat exhaustion and as a preventive for cold and flu. It is also an appetizer. If the sugar is omitted increase the amount of persimmons, a sweet fruit. Only one or two small glasses are drunk daily.

Red date (jujube) wine
450 g (1 lb) dried red dates
1.4 l (2½ pt) rice wine or *shaojiu*
110 g (4 oz) honey

1. Wipe the fruit clean with a dry tea towel. Discard any bad ones.
2. Put all the ingredients into a suitable-sized wide-mouthed jar. Cover, seal and store in a dry, cool, dark place undisturbed.
3. After 6 months to a year it is ready to drink. There is no need to remove the dates.

A delightful wine, it is used as a remedy for cough and the onset of a cold or flu. One or two little glasses are drunk at bed time.

Chinese wolfberry wine
230 g (8 oz) dried Chinese wolfberry
1.4 l (2½ pt) rice wine or *shaojiu*
230 g (8 oz) honey

1. There is no need to rinse the berries.
2. Put all the ingredients into a suitable-sized wide-mouthed jar. Cover, seal and store in a cool, dry, dark place.
3. After a year, strain the berries and reserve them. They may be used again with the same amount of wine and honey for another year.
4. Transfer the wine into clean bottles and it is ready for drinking.

Chinese wolfberries are, to the Chinese, a panacea for all ills. This wine strengthens male virility and the stomach. It is a folk remedy for diabetes and kidney trouble and is also good for the liver. A little glass is drunk daily.

Chinese Cooking and Eating

Traditionally, Chinese cuisine is divided into four main regions: the southern, Guangdong and Fujian; the south-western, Sichuan, Yunnan and Hunan; the central and eastern, Anhui, Jiangsu, and Zhejiang, including Shanghai; and the north, Beijing and Shandong, Henan, Hebei, Shanxi, Shaanxi, and Inner Mongolia. But they all share a number of basic features.

As with all good cuisine, Chinese cooking depends on first-class ingredients. No Chinese housewife would buy a tired-looking fish, day-old meat or vegetables not picked on the same day, since freshness and quality are the basic requirements for a tasty and nutritious dish. Chinese cuisine is a feast of the senses, an aesthetic experience: the colour, the fragrance, the flavour and the texture appeal to the various senses. In a dish there is always a contrast of colour and texture, just as in a menu the dishes contrast with one another: some dishes may be rich and smooth, some crisp and succulent, some pure and clear in taste, some spicy and hot. There is no main dish, as there is in Western cookery. Chinese eating is a delightful experience of enjoying a selection of tastes and textures.

A formal dinner usually comprises a selection of cold platter dishes; *re-cao*, hot stir-fried, deep-fried and other fast-cooking dishes; *tacai*, whole pieces of meat or whole birds usually simmered, braised, steamed, roasted or deep-fried; and a couple of sweet meat dishes – meat cooked with sweet ingredients and sugar or caramel, or frosted. Finally there is the *tien-sin*, cakes and pastries, followed by dried and fresh fruits. Rice or grains are sometimes served before the dessert. Soup normally comes in the middle of the dinner. The cold platter dishes are about 15 per cent of the dinner, the hot fried dishes about 20 to 25 per cent, the whole pieces and sweet meat about 40 to 45 per cent. Dishes are chosen to whet appetite and to avoid monotony. When entertaining, the hostess is more concerned with the quantity, quality and variety of food presented than the silver or the tablecloth.

Chinese cuisine employs a maximum of preparation and a minimum of cooking, because everything is cut up and marinated or par-cooked; the final putting together takes only a few minutes. A family meal may be cooked in around half an hour, apart from the long, slow-simmered dishes; but with these too, the work is done in advance. The menu for the day is decided by what is freshest and best at the market.

Chinese culinary art is a blending of flavourings and combining of ingredients. More often the ingredients are not cooked alone: the combination may bring out the best of each ingredient or emphasize some flavour, texture, colour or richness; the result is an infinite variety of tastes. In Chinese eating no condiments are needed at the table, as food is always seasoned in the kitchen. Seasoning is most effective when the food is still being cooked, since the heat sets off a chemical reaction and enables the flavour to penetrate the food better. The only exception is plain cooked meat which is always served with dips, spiced salts, and sauces. All foods are cut into bite-size pieces in the kitchen before serving, not least because knives are regarded as inauspicious at a Chinese dinner table.

The south

Regional cooking has evolved from the varied terrain, climate and natural resources of a big country. The southern region covering Guangdong, Fujian, Hainan island and Formosa, has a subtropical climate with an abundance of vegetables and exotic fruits, a double crop of rice and a great variety of fish and seafood from the coast. In consequence the cooking is rich and full of variety.

Historical influences have also played a part in the shaping of regional cookery. The waves of migrants who came south during turbulent times brought with them their own cuisine, which after a while was perfected into a local hybrid. Cantonese cooking, for example, though noted for its stir-fried dishes, is very varied through having assimilated things from the northern provinces in the seventeenth century. After the fall of the Ming dynasty in 1644 the invading Manchus took over control, with the result that many patriotic officials left government service and went south to Guangzhou (Canton), the capital of Guangdong province. Here the mandarins had their chefs cook northern dishes, and over a period of time their style of eating evolved into today's Cantonese style, especially in its red-cooked dishes, roast duck and barbecued pork.

Cantonese cooking is noted for its use of salted black beans as a flavouring in stir-fried dishes. It also has excellent ways with fish and seafood, either fresh or dried, very often mixing seafood with meat in the same dish. Steaming is another strong point among the Cantonese. They like fish steamed with ginger, spring onions, salted black beans and chilli peppers, or pork steamed with preserved vegetables or salted eggs. Exotic tropical fruits such as litchi, longan, pineapple and papaya are cooked or served with meat too.

The *kejia* or Hakkas, in Guangdong province have a clean, healthy and clear style of cooking; they do not use strong flavourings or oil. *Kejia* means 'guest families', for these people were migrants from the troubled north – guests who never went back. Soya bean curd and other soya products are their staples. One particular clan, the Dapo, are best at vegetables such as aubergines, bitter gourds, chilli peppers, fuzzy melons, stuffed with minced fish or minced pork flavoured with salted fish. Their speciality is *jongtaufu*, bean curd stuffed with minced pork. The Chaozhou or Teochiu people in the same province are well-known for their steamed goose dishes and a beef fire pot.

Fujian, a south-eastern coastal province, favours pork, duck and duck's eggs, with a lot of fish and seafood, a speciality being oyster omelette or pancake. Lard is the favourite cooking fat used here, which makes Fujian food slightly on the greasy side. Many Fujian rice cakes and pastries have spread to South-East Asia, where large numbers of the Fujian emigrants have settled.

Fuzhou county loves 'soupy' meals. Every dish is swimming in water, mainly with crustaceans as ingredients. Very often a Fuzhou banquet could have as many as seven soups out of ten courses.

The south-west

Sichuan, Hunan and Yunnan cooking belongs to the south-western region, which has the most diverse flora of any region outside the tropics. One old Chinese description of this region is 'one mountain with four seasons and within ten miles a different sky'. It enjoys temperate, subtropical and tropical climates. The warmth and moisture have allowed the region to adapt plants from every major region on earth. It is rich in flowers, fungi, medicinal herbs, walnuts, chestnuts, pine nuts, wild game, birds and freshwater fish. The Chinese call this region 'the botanical kingdom' and 'the animal kingdom'. South-western food is rather fiery and spicy. Sichuan peppercorns (*fagara*), chilli, garlic, nuts and poultry predominate in Sichuan and Hunan cooking.

The local specialities of Hunan province are preserved meats of all kinds, smoked, steeped and roasted. One favourite Hunan winter dish is steamed mixed smoked pork, duck and chicken. Another local flavour is the fire pot, but with a difference: the country folk place the pot on an earthen stove and the cooking and eating are conducted round it. As in Sichuan, chilli peppers and Sichuan peppercorns are the main flavourings. Two Hunan specialities are hot and sour soup, and spicy crisp duck deep-fried in tea oil.

Sichuan cooking is well known for its chilli and Sichuan peppercorn flavours. Famous dishes include tea-smoked duck, tangerine peel stir-fried chicken, and many hot and spicy quick-fried chicken and meat dishes. Less well known but equally traditional are nightstock flowers stir-fried with chicken, chicken slivers cooked with jasmine blossoms and tea, jasmine in abalone soup, and a sweet made from jujube paste rolled in lotus-flower petals.

There is a fanciful legend about how chilli peppers came to grow in Sichuan. During the Song dynasty (c 960–1279), when the illustrious poet and literary figure Su Tungpo was lecturing in the city of Loshan in Sichuan, its literary institute was situated on a mountain which had a secret subterranean passage linked to the abode of the mythological Dragon King of the Eastern Sea. Hence the latter sent his son to study under Su Tungpo. The prince successfully completed a three-year course, to the delight of the Dragon King who invited the poet to a sumptuous banquet in his palace. Of all the lavish food offered Su Tungpo found most interesting a bright red, fragrant and hot vegetable, called 'hot chilli peppers'. Before he left, Su Tungpo asked for some seeds and a piece of land on which to grow the plants. The Dragon King granted both, but it was agreed that the land would be returned on the stroke of the 'fifth gong', which was struck at dawn. But Su Tungpo arranged with the towncryer of Loshan to refrain from beating the fifth gong, and by this device the chilli peppers have been successfully kept on earth. (In fact chilli peppers are of American origin, and first reached China in the sixteenth century, together with other New World vegetables.)

Sharing a border with Sichuan, Yunnan boasts cooking with a strong Sichuan influence, hot and spicy, but with fewer pungent flavours than Sichuan cooking. Pork is consumed in every form here; lard is the favourite cooking fat, and Yunnan ham and 'head cheese' (preserved pig's head) are the famous specialities. A less famous speciality is Yunnan qikuo, made in a clay casserole with a steam vent. In this dish medicinal ingredients such as Chinese caterpillar fungus, Chinese wolfberries (red medler berries), and angelica roots are used, so that it is eaten mainly as a tonic food. Yunnan roast duck is borrowed from Beijing but with a difference, as only a very young plump duckling of about forty days old, weighing around 1 kg (2 lb), is roasted on a pine-needle fire. Historical events have clearly left their mark on the cuisine here: dairy products such as yoghurt, fried milk cheese, and milk are consumed by the Yunnan Muslims who trace their origin to the troops brought into the province by Kublai Khan in the thirteenth century. This milk cheese may be braised, steamed, pan fried or deep fried. The region teems with wildlife, and elephant's trunk, bear's paw and deer's tail are high-class banquet dishes. Bamboo rats are steamed with ham, mushrooms and bamboo shoots; also a species of silkworm-like maggots which live in the roots of bamboo stumps are deep fried and served sprinkled with salt flavoured with Sichuan peppercorn. Wild ducks, pheasants, rabbits and frogs are among the animals consumed. In the spring wild flowers are eaten as vegetables. Chilli peppers are eaten in this humid region to counteract humidity.

Central and eastern

This region covers Jiangsu, Zhejiang, Anhui south of the Yangtze river, and includes Shanghai-style cooking. A rice-eating area with many vegetables, pork, poultry and plenty of fish from rivers, lakes, and the sea, it has a long tradition of good cooking and high life: Hangzhou was the capital in the late Song period (1127–1279), when the culinary arts were at their peak. Chefs from all over the country gathered to work in the cities here.

Hangzhou became such an attractive tourist centre that it was a magnet for sightseers and gourmets. The cookery of the younger Shanghai is rather eclectic. It relies on slow-braised, raw stir-fried and deep-fried and steamed dishes with a profusion of cold platters. There is also considerable Western influence in Shanghai food, as evident in the use of breadcrumbs in coating deep-fried food, and the use of tomato ketchup and milk in some dishes. Some other well-known dishes of the region are 'lion's head' with crab meat from Jiangsu, West Lake carp in vinegar, prawns in Longjing tea from Zhejiang, and the exotic 'clay chicken' from Hangzhou. Famous ingredients include the dark and delicious Zhenjiang vinegar, the amber-coloured Shaoxing wine, and the pink, sweet and succulent Jinhua ham.

The north

Northern regional cooking includes that of Beijing and Shandong as well as the northern provinces of Henan, Hebei, Shanxi, Shaanxi and Inner Mongolia. Beijing cooking is so eclectic that, according to some experts, there is no such thing as Beijing cooking. It is a conglomeration of specialities from all over the north of the country. Historically, Beijing has been an important city for a long time, being the capital and cultural centre. Chefs from every corner of the country came to seek their fortunes and brought with them their local flavours which turned into a Beijing hybrid. Here also the Manchus, Mongolians and Chinese mingled. This is reflected in dishes such as the Mongolian fire pot; the Mongolian grill, eaten standing up with one foot on the bench; the 'all-lamb banquet' of the Muslims; and many other lamb and beef dishes. Of all these outside influences, however, by far the strongest is from Shandong, through long contact in trade. The use of garlic, leeks, spring onions and chives in

Shandong cooking, particularly raw leeks and preserved chives, is apparent in Beijing cuisine. Shandong cooking has, during a long period in Beijing, undergone a change in its flavourings: for instance, in Shandong the sweet salted soya bean paste is employed for a quick-fried chicken dish, but in Beijing a plain salted one is preferred; in the Beijing pan-braised *doufu* (bean curd) there is no stuffing nor soya sauce, but the Shandong one has a prawn stuffing and soya sauce. The famous Beijing Duck alone of course may claim a true Beijing tradition along with the Mandarin pancake usually served with it. But *shaobing*, a sesame bread bun, has a Middle Eastern origin. Shandong chefs take great pride in employing strong clear stock or milk stock as a flavouring rather than monosodium glutamate. Although the coastal cities such as Qingdao, Weihai and Yantai are famous for their seafood, Shandong is also the land of apples, pears, lotus roots and Chinese celery cabbage.

Wild game and birds are highly prized by the Chinese and they are eaten everywhere. The game eaten varies from region to region: in Guangzhou (Canton) snakes and frogs are highly regarded for their medicinal values; in Beijing and the north they eat camel's hump; in the south-west bear's paw, elephant's trunk and deer. Pheasants, quails, rabbits and wild ducks are eaten all over China. The Chinese believe that wild animals have the healthiest flesh, as they eat natural food and have had to survive in harsher conditions than the domesticated animals. Wild game tends to be found in important banquets, and is also sometimes eaten as tonic food.

Another aspect of the Chinese diet is vegetarian cookery. As early as Han times (206 BC–AD 220), there was discussion about the ill effects of rich food. One writer devoted a whole chapter to the question of rich food being poisonous and the cause of illness. The first record we have on vegetarian eating dates from Chou times (1027–256 BC). Wang Mang, who seized the throne in AD 9, is recorded as having eaten vegetarian food in penance when there was a severe drought. In Qin times (221–206 BC), the nobles used to eat only vegetarian food on certain days in memory of the tragic death of two former kings, and this ritual became a custom even for the common people. Vegetarian food was also eaten by the bereaved. On the death of parents, it was customary to wear white unadorned silk and shun meat. Even now, vegetarian days are sometimes observed in remembrance of an ancestor.

The religious beliefs of Taoism and Buddhism also reinforced the habit of vegetarian eating. A Taoist seeks peace, harmony, and happiness through leading a tranquil life with simple food and meditation. A Buddhist disapproves of any killing and therefore favours vegetarianism. Because of its Indian origin, Buddhism forbade the consumption of beef. The Chinese themselves regarded oxen as the friends and assistants to men in tilling the soil, so that it was almost sacreligious to eat their meat as well. Veal is virtually unknown in the Chinese diet. Today, the first and fifteenth days of each lunar month are still observed as vegetarian days by most Chinese families; these fasts derive from Buddhism, which teaches that on at least two days in the month animals should not be killed. In particular, the first day of the Chinese New Year is kept as a vegetarian day.

In some parts of China vegetarian eating is observed for health reasons: the sixth month of the lunar calendar is known as *luyeshu*, '*vegetarian June*' (actually it corresponds more closely to our July). This is because during high summer, meat deteriorates faster and is often the cause of illnesses. Moreover, it is also deemed to be too hot for the body to deal with the climate and the heating effect of the meat simultaneously.

During the imperial period, some vegetarian days were ritual days for offerings to the powers of heaven, earth and the ancestors, and these were rigidly observed from the Emperor downwards. Moreover, it was the custom for the Emperor to fast or eat vegetarian meals before an important event, or a state banquet.

Thus three main styles of vegetarian cooking emerged: palace, monastery, and folk. While the imperial kitchen had a vegetarian department, the monasteries prepared vegetarian foods for monks and nuns as well as for visitors. It was an ancient custom when travelling in China to take rest and refreshment at a Buddhist or Taoist monastery. This custom was reinforced when an edict of the Tang Emperor, Te Tsung, in the seventh century, declared that the conditions in monasteries be made fit for secular visitors, as it was the aim of both Taoist and Buddhist religion to look after the welfare of all living beings. Some famous vegetarian foods are found in the monasteries of Guangzhou (Canton) and in Xiamen (Amoy) in Fujian province, as well as in Hangzhou, Anhui and Shanghai. Some mountain resorts are also well known for their vegetarian foods. The ordinary people have their own style of vegetarian cooking and some exquisite vegetarian restaurants are found in Tianjin, Shanghai, Beijing and Guangzhou, where vegetarian culinary art is carried to a very high standard: vegetarian foods are even made to look and taste like meat and poultry.

It is hardly surprising that vegetarian cooking has such a long tradition in China, when the diet includes so many grains and vegetables. Vegetarian eating is in no way a deprivation when there are such ingredients as dried soya products, fresh bean curd, and salted, dried or preserved vegetables.

Chinese eating is also punctuated by a cycle of festivals throughout the year, starting with the feast of the 'kitchen god', on the twenty-fourth day of the twelfth lunar month. A sumptuous meal is offered to the deity so that when he makes his annual report to higher authorities on the household's culinary activities that night, the family will have a favourable mention. This old custom is still kept very much alive by the Chinese

New Year celebration: lantern lights and feasting on the last (fifteenth) evening of the Spring festival. Part of a Ming dynasty picture (1368–1644). The banner says 'Bumper harvests of the five grains'.

of South-East Asia, particularly Malaysia and Singapore. Then comes the New Year's Eve feast, around the end of January or early February, a family reunion dinner. This is closely followed by the New Year celebration, which lasts for fifteen days. Rice cakes, yeasted rice cup cakes, rice dumplings in syrup and various meat foods are consumed during this festival, which ends with a big feast on the last day. After the New Year there is a gap till the Qingming ('pure and bright') festival in the third month of the lunar calendar, when the graves of the ancestors are swept. On the fifth day of the fifth lunar month is the 'Feast of the Patriotic Poet', Qu-yuan, who was also a minister, drowned about 287 BC. It became customary for the people to row out into the river and offer rice dumplings to appease his soul annually. Today, dragon boat racing takes place and people eat sweet or savoury triangular rice dumplings containing delicious filling and wrapped in bamboo leaves. The feast of the fifteenth day of the seventh lunar month offers food to lost souls, since on that day the underworld briefly lets out its inmates. This custom is still rigidly observed by the overseas Chinese. On the fifteenth day of the eighth lunar month comes the August Moon festival, a harvest festival. On this day there is feasting and the eating of a special 'moon cake', a pastry filled with red bean paste, lotus paste or various combinations of fruits and nuts. According to one legend, this originated towards the end of Mongol rule, when the moon cake was designed to carry a secret message urging the slaughter of the Tartar officials who were billeted in Chinese households. The ninth of the ninth lunar month is Chongyang, the feast of *tengkao*, 'mounting the height'; metaphorically this refers to a promotion and was therefore very popular with officials in imperial China. On this day people head for a mountain or high ground; eat a special cake, a symbol of attaining success; drink chrysanthemum wine in order to attain longevity; and fly a kite. This festival originated in Manchuria where everyone on that day picnicked on the mountainside and had a nap in the wild. The cycle of feasts draws to a close with the feast of the Winter Solstice, the turning point of the season in China, around 22 December. In ancient days a ritual welcoming the arrival of the sun was held led by the Emperor himself; this was as important as the New Year. Now the day is celebrated with a feast including rice dumplings in syrup, and the children are told that they are now a year older, as the New Year is just around the corner.

Festive eating provides the chance to replenish the body with protein and nutrients from foods which may be too expensive or too complicated to prepare for everyday meals, such as shark's fin and bird's nest; and of course it is cheaper to eat in a group and more fun. Not only is eating a shared pleasure, but it is also a shared activity in which close relatives and friends help to make dumplings and noodles, as well as cook the various dishes together. Every Chinese knows how to cook.

Chinese eating is also a social language. The kind of food given at a dinner or banquet indicates the importance of an event or a guest, or the degree of appreciation or gratitude on the part of the host. A story from Fujian succinctly illustrates the point. A father and mother were very dissatisfied with the work of their son's tutor. When the time had come to give an annual dinner, as was the custom, the father engaged him in lengthy discussion while the mother did nothing but carry on seasoning hot oil with garlic and pouring hot water into it, producing no more than the smell and noise of cooking dish after dish. Unlike Su Tungpo, the teacher did not actually get any food at all. Of course the story is exaggerated; but for the Chinese, food is a powerful social language.

The life of a Chinese family centres on the meal times, just as ancestor worship revolves around rituals in which food is shared with the honoured dead. Harmony, happiness and calm at table are the Chinese ideal. Demeanour should be pleasant, never angry or noisy, as the 'table god' who watches over the dinner might be displeased and withdraw his blessing from the household. One virtue at dinner is slowness. As one old Chinese saying puts it, 'Work should be hastened but not the dinner.' A dinner must be carefully chewed and savoured, never gobbled. If one has no time to eat, one has no time to live. 'The beggar is an emperor when he eats.'

At table the rice bowl should be lifted. It is extremely bad manners to pick up rice with chopsticks without lifting up the bowl: this would be interpreted as an insult or a challenge to fight. Also if the rice bowl is not lifted, one's head tends to go down, and this is bad as the Chinese believe that one should eat one's meal with the head raised, unashamed. One should not go for the same dish twice in succession, which means that every dish must be tried, irrespective of what is offered. One should never pile food in one's bowl for fear that it may run out soon. Nor should one help oneself while the mouth is full. One Fujian rhyme goes like this: 'One piece chewing in the mouth, one piece waiting in the bowl, another piece halfway' – describing very bad table manners. Out of respect, the children do not start eating until at least one of their parents has picked up chopsticks. Even children of quite tender age are taught this rule. Similarly, at the banquet table the more junior in age or rank invariably waits for the more senior one or the host to start eating.

Another virtue is not to eat too much. A great eater is regarded as greedy. Normally a manual worker would be expected to eat three bowls of rice, a moderately active person two bowls; whilst a sedentary worker or scholar has one bowl, a little more or less. Another virtue is the consumption of little salt, though again a workman may be expected to eat more salty food than a sedentary worker.

As a guest one has to be urged to eat. Normally the Chinese have a snack before attending a dinner or banquet, so that they are able to enjoy the food slowly and have civilized conversation. The host would do the same and would offer the best part of every dish to guests, whether the drumsticks of a chicken or duck, the head or belly of a fish, as the best part of a fish is from the head to the belly. The guest would politely decline and the host would insist, and offer again, at least three times. The same applies to drinks. A guest always keeps his glass half full, since an empty glass would be considered uncouth. Rice seldom appears at a special meal or banquet, although towards the end sometimes a fried rice or noodle dish may be offered to clean the palate before the sweet.

At a celebration or farewell dinner one should never turn over the fish when one side is eaten, a superstition dating from a time when most travelling was done on waterways. One should never pick at food, but go straight at it and pick up one piece without touching the rest. Likewise, chopsticks should never touch the lips nor should they be licked clean. Soup must always be drunk with a spoon, as only medicine is taken from a bowl.

A special dinner normally includes a sweet, which does not often appear in a Chinese daily meal. A guest cannot refuse this last sweet dish, since it is more ceremonial than gastronomic, symbolizing a sweet ending of the relationship between the partakers. One is not expected to eat all of it, and it is perfectly all right to leave the rest after a mouthful.

At a birthday dinner there is always served towards the end a 'long life' noodle dish. On serving or eating, it must not be cut or snapped, but just pulled and pulled. This noodle is symbolic, very much like life itself, long, entangled and complicated; quite a struggle to eat, but a pleasure.

Ingredients

Cooking Oils and Fats

Oils from animal and vegetable sources are used. The Chinese criterion for a cooking fat or oil is its freshness and clarity. Cooking oil should have no rancid taste or carry the odour of other food; indeed, stale oil is considered to be highly toxic. Any oil that produces black smoke on heating is also thought to be harmful to health. Since vegetable oil was once entirely cold pressed, the Chinese name for any vegetable oil remains *senyou*, 'raw oil'. Nowadays, most of these are chemically extracted. To disperse whatever residue of chemical there is left in the oil it is always preheated before food is put in, or before tossing food in it. Vegetable oils in use are mainly from peanuts, cotton seeds, sesame seeds, rape seeds and soya.

Sesame oil: this is highly prized as a delicious and a nutritious oil. Its Chinese name is *hsiangyou*, 'fragrant oil'. It is pressed from roasted white sesame seeds, and the best is cold pressed, though today some of it is chemically produced. Sesame oil is high in polyunsaturates. The Chinese variety has a milder and more delicate flavour than the Greek one, which must not be substituted for it; though Greek *tahini* may be used for the Chinese sesame paste, as here there is hardly any difference. Sesame oil is used to flavour both sweet and savoury food, and is added just before serving so that the fragrance is not lost. But in many areas in China – Hebei, Anhui, Shandong and Sichuan – very often sesame oil is used in deep frying and cooking some special dishes. In the southern provinces dry meats are also cooked in sesame oil, such as rabbit, chicken and lean pork.

Rape-seed oil: this is considered a sweet, palatable, and wholesome oil. It is used in Yunnan, Anhui, Zhejiang and Jiangsu provinces. The rape plant is a member of the *Brassica* genus, which includes cabbage. The oil is highly polyunsaturated with plenty of linoleic acid, which is a dietary requirement.

Cotton-seed oil: although still used in some areas, this has been found to cause male infertility.

Peanut oil: a popular oil for deep frying and used all over China, this is considered a good rich oil, particularly suited to the cooking of vegetables.

Tea oil: this is obtained from the seeds of a species of tea (*Camellia sinensis*). Quite delicious, it is used in tea-producing areas such as Hunan and Sichuan.

Lard: home-rendered pork fat, flavoured with garlic and salt, is a far cry from commonplace supermarket lard. Although it is used all over China, only certain dishes are cooked in it. It is the favourite cooking fat in Fujian province and in south-west Yunnan on the plateau.

Rendered chicken fat: sometimes home-rendered chicken fat is used in cooking or flavouring dishes where a velvety texture and rich taste is required.

Rendered duck fat: home-rendered duck fat is also used in cooking or flavouring dishes, particularly green leafy vegetables.

Butter: this is favoured by the Chinese Muslims and the nomadic tribes of the north and west in Mongolia, Xingjiang, Tibet and Yunnan.

Rice

Rice is eaten mainly by people living south of the Yangtze river; in the north some rice is eaten, but much less than wheat, millet, sorghum and sweet potatoes. In the Chinese language to have one's dinner is to eat *fan*, literally 'cooked grain'. For a southerner *fan* means cooked rice, while to a northerner it may be steamed buns, noodles, rice, millet porridge or other things. A Chinese meal is made up of *fan* and *cai*, which is mainly vegetables and some meat and fish. The *fan* is the bulk of the meal, and it is the function of the *cai* to send the *fan* down. So it is good manners and healthy to eat rice with little *cai*, particularly the meat part. A small child learns this concept as soon as he or she sits at table. The *fan* is to line the stomach and absorb the grease and rich sauces of the *cai*. The *fan* is to keep one satisfied. The importance of *fan* is reflected in the language: to look for a job is 'to look for *fan*'. The 'rice bowl' is one's source of income. If 'the rice bowl is dancing', one's job is at stake. In rural areas today, as always, the daily meals are mainly of rice with fresh greens, pickled mustard plants, sweet potatoes, bean curd and dried salted fish as *cai*, flavoured with soya sauce, salted soya beans, fish sauces, chilli pepper and pepper and vinegar. This is a healthy diet as the fish sauces, salted fish and soya products balance the cereal with the protein and provide necessary minerals.

Long-grain rice: there are numerous local varieties of rice, some of which are more glutinous or more fragrant than others. The Chinese prefer a tasty rice of a long-grain but often sticky type. Tastier rice needs less *cai*. In urban areas white polished rice is preferred. Its relative lack of nutrients is made up by the other ingredients of the complex dishes. In rural areas the people used to buy unpolished rice and mill it by hand themselves to a semi-polished state, which is delicious and still quite high in nutrients. But today, owing to mechanization, white rice has become readily available everywhere. Whole brown rice, completely unmilled, is not eaten at all in China, or anywhere in Asia, except as a food remedy for beriberi. It is considered to be indigestible.

Aromatic rice: this is a long-grain non-glutinous rice with a beautiful fragrance and taste.

Glutinous rice: mainly used for ceremonial foods, for making cakes and puddings, for stuffing poultry and for fermenting into wine. When cooked it changes from opaque to transparent and glistening, the grains cling together, and the flavour is fragrant, sweet and delicious. Glutinous rice contains no actual gluten (a substance found mainly in wheat); the stickiness comes from dextrin, starch and a small amount of maltose sugar. This rice is normally eaten only on feast days and at special ceremonies. It is regarded as unhealthy to eat it too often, and it is one of the first things taken off the diet of a sick person or child. The ancients believed that it made the system sluggish and, in the long term, would weaken the limbs.

Purple or black rice: purple or black in colour, with some varieties more glutinous than others. When cooked it is a dark burgundy and fragrant. It is occasionally eaten instead of white rice, but more often as a sweet snack.

Flour

Wheat flour: Comparable with those of Canada and the USA, the flour from the hard wheat of northern China is used for noodles and pastry. Northern noodles are typically pale in colour, with a firm texture when cooked. The softer flour from the south, however, produces a poor, greyish noodle, lacking in texture. This is probably why in the south, 'lye water' (in this case potassium carbonate solution) is always added in the making of noodles and pastry to give a more attractive yellowish colour and a reasonably *al dente* texture when cooked. Lye water also stops fermentation in the warm and humid southern provinces.

Dried wheat gluten: This is extracted from wheat flour by washing it in water and then drying in the sun. It is sparingly used to strengthen the flour where a strong flour is required in a recipe. Wheat gluten is also an important source of extra protein in the Chinese vegetarian diet. Home-made wheat gluten is used without drying out.

Farmers milling grain, Ming dynasty (1368–1644)

Wheat starch: what is left after the gluten has been removed from wheat flour; it is used for dumplings or cake.

Rice flour: This is flour from ordinary long-grain rice. The rice is soaked in water, then ground with water, pressed dry and sun-dried. Rice flour so prepared in a wet mill is regarded as superior to ordinary ground rice.

Glutinous rice flour: This is ground in the same manner as the previous type of rice flour, and is mainly used in cakes and puddings for ceremonial purposes.

Fish Sauces and Pastes

Fish sauces and pastes are important sources of protein and nutrients in the Chinese diet. By their agency plain vegetables and soya products are transformed into delicious and nourishing foods. The normal fish sauces and pastes in the Chinese kitchen are:

Oyster sauce: a thick brown sauce made from oysters boiled in soya sauce and salt, and thickened with wheat flour. As a seasoning it enhances the flavour of food and gives a smooth, rich velvety touch. But it is rather salty. If stored in a cool, dry place, it will keep indefinitely.

Shrimp paste: a pinkish, thick sauce made from shrimps fermented in brine and wine. Again it is rather salty, and is used sparingly and in cooking only.

Shrimp sauce: made by salting and concentrating whole shrimps. An amber-coloured clear liquid, rather salty, it gives food a shrimp flavour. It is used in cooking only.

Fish gravy: made by salting and concentrating whole small fish, it is light amber-coloured and rather salty. It is used both for seasoning food and in cooking.

Sweet and Pungent Sauces

These are some sweet, sour and pungent sauces which provide gastronomic enjoyment as well as a source of vitamins and nutrients:

Chilli sauce: made from ground fresh chillis and vinegar, sugar and sometimes plums, it is used in cooking or as a dip. One sort is finely ground without seeds, the other coarsely ground with seeds.

Hoisin sauce: made from salted soya bean paste with spices, vinegar and sugar, it has a rich, sweet, salty and mildly spicy taste. It is delicious as a dip or as a base for a marinade.

Plum sauce: made from plums, apricots, vinegar, salt and sugar, it is used as a dip for deep-fried food or roasted meat, or in a marinade for meat, or in a sweet and sour sauce.

Sacha-jiang (Barbecue sauce): originally from Chaozhou county of Guangdong province, where it remains a popular sauce for the fire pot, this barbecue sauce is made from peanut oil, peanuts, spices and dried shrimps. It may be used as a dip or a marinade for meat.

Soya Sauces, Salted Soya Beans and Pastes

Soya sauce provides protein and nutrients as well as flavouring. The nutrient value of the soya bean is heightened by the fermentation process which renders them easily digestible. Soya sauce is made from fermented soya beans with a little wheat flour, salt and sometimes sugar (caramel). It gives Chinese food its unique taste. The best sauce is made by a natural fermentation and ageing process. There are three main grades of soya sauce:

Heavy soya sauce: more or less a paste, it is hardly salty, more starchy and sweet owing to the high content of wheat flour and molasses. This is used mainly to colour red-cooked dishes, without oversalting them. Food sticks and burns rather quickly if too much is used.

Dark soya sauce: this has caramel added and is used for cooking and

50

sometimes as a dip at table. A good quality one has a full-bodied and delicious taste and is not too salty.

Light soya sauce: also called white soya sauce. The colour of a light tea and light in consistency, it does not contain wheat flour. It has a delicious flavour and is used for white meat and soup and as a dip at table.

Other soya products include:

Salted soya beans: fermented with salt, brown in colour, and used as a flavouring in cooking.

Salted soya bean paste: the same fermented beans ground up. This may be prepared at home.

Hot salted soya bean paste: this is the above paste with chilli powder and sugar added, and may also be mixed at home.

Sichuan chilli paste: a very hot Sichuan speciality made from ground dried chilli peppers with their seeds, and salted soya bean paste. It is used for cooking.

Sweet salted soya bean paste: this is the salted bean paste with sugar and some sesame oil. It is used in cooking or as a dip at table, and may be prepared at home.

Salted black soya beans: these are fermented with salt and seasoned with soya sauce; a favourite seasoning for fish, meat and bitter gourd dishes.

Dried salted black soya beans: fermented black soya beans, salted and dried. Possessing a rather stronger, pungent flavour, they are usually rinsed and soaked before use.

Red fermented bean curd: these brick-red cubes are made from pressed bean curd fermented in wine and spices. They enhance meat, fish and vegetable dishes. Their pungent flavour gives dishes an 'aged' taste. They may also be eaten as a side dish. Sealed and stored in a cool dry place, they will keep for as long as a year.

White fermented bean curd: this is similar to the above except that the cubes are buff-coloured and have a smoky taste, being mainly eaten as a side-dish. Some has chilli added.

Chilli oil: a condiment rather than a cooking oil, it is a chilli-flavoured oil used in sauces for cold platter food and in hot soups. It may be prepared at home.

Sesame paste: made from ground roasted sesame seeds, it is mainly used in sauces for cold platter food. *Tahini* may be used instead.

Dried Seafood

Dried seafood plays a very important part in the Chinese diet. It not only supplements fresh fish, meat and poultry, but also has a role as a flavouring and a nutritious food. It is a source of iodine and minerals, particularly for those who live in the mountains and rural areas. North China, except along the coast, relies heavily on dried and salted seafood. As with soya products, salted fish is rich in protein and nutrients.

Products made from fish include:

Dried anchovies: these are sun dried without salting. The heads have to be removed, the fish split open and the backbones removed before use. The heads tied in a piece of muslin are often used to enrich the stock pot.

Dried bream: the sea bream is dried without any salt. Its only use is as a flavouring.

Dried fish maws: these are gelatinous meat of the lips from large fish. They have to be soaked till well swollen before use in boiled, braised or steamed dishes.

Dried fried fish air bladder: looks like deep-fried pork rind in large, crisp pieces of a light honey colour. Again soaking is essential. Not fishy in taste, it may be braised, steamed or boiled.

Dried silver fish: these are little fish about 2.5 to 10 cm (1 to 4 in) long, sun dried without salting. They have to be soaked in hot water to soften before use. They may be stir fried or added to an omelette.

Salted fish: there are many varieties, large and small, each with different texture and taste. Some are preserved in oil. They may be steamed plain or with pork, pan fried or boiled with meat as a flavouring. They must be washed well before cooking. A small amount goes a long way.

Shark's fin: the cartilage of the shark's fin is considered a great delicacy and most nutritious. Whole unprocessed shark's fins are raw and sun dried. They take days of soaking and cleaning before they are ready for use. Nowadays, processed shark's fins are readily available, though they still need boiling before use. The cartilage comes in a needle shape; the longer and fatter needles are better.

Products made from other sea creatures include:

Abalone: this is available dried; silver-grey in colour and of a flat oval shape, it has to be soaked and gently simmered before cooking. But it is very tasty and highly nutritious. Tinned abalone is easily available in Chinese supermarkets. Since it is already cooked, little preparation is necessary, and of course the juice can be used in cooking too. Fresh frozen abalone is also available here at a price. (See also page 14.)

Bird's nest: A byproduct of the sea, bird's nest is the hardened saliva of a swift that feeds on fish. There are three grades: red, the best; white, second; and grey-black, third and cheapest. The grading only refers to the amount of down embedded rather than the difference in the actual quality. The nest must be soaked and the down picked out before use. (Also a medicinal food; see page 15.)

Dried cuttlefish and squid: both are sun dried without cooking or salting. They are soaked in water and then used mainly in stir-fried dishes.

Dried mussels: these are sun dried without cooking or salting. They are rock hard and must be soaked before steaming, or braising with meat.

Dried oysters: similar to dried mussels in appearance, they are raw oysters sun-dried without salting and they need to be soaked before use. Their rich smoky taste is quite remarkable.

Dried sea cucumbers: also known as sea slugs. Considered a great delicacy, they are black and rock-hard when purchased. There are many varieties from the size of carrots to that of little courgettes. They swell to about eight times their original volume when soaked in water. Once softened, they are wonderfully delicate and gelatinous. (See also page 19.)

Dried sea scallops: these are coral-coloured cylinders about 2 cm ($\frac{3}{4}$ in) across and slightly less in height. When soaked they may be broken into fine shreds which are used to flavour food. The beautiful colour has a decorative value.

Dried mini shrimps: are very fine, soft, minute (about 2.5 cm or 1 in or less from head to tail), sun-dried and unsalted planton-like shrimps. They are transparent and pink when fresh (not available here) and delicious, but turn creamy and opaque when sun-dried or cooked. They must be picked through, soaked briefly and rinsed thoroughly before use as a flavouring, or in omelettes or stir-fried plain.

Dried shrimps: these are shelled, boiled and sun-dried. They are rock hard and must be picked and soaked before use.

Salted jellyfish: a thin, leathery, round disc about 25 mm (10 in) in diameter, preserved in brine, it must be soaked, shredded, and rinsed thoroughly before use in cold salad platters. It has a crunchy texture.

Products made from algae include:

Agar-agar: this is transparent, very light for its bulk. It is flavourless and is used like gelatine in savoury and sweet dishes. It must be soaked and boiled to dissolve before use.

Dried hairweed: although this grows wild on land, it is included here because it is actually an alga like seaweed. Black and fine like oriental hair when dried, and dark greenish brown and crunchy in texture when soaked in water, it is an ingredient in soup, braised or steamed dishes.

Dried seaweed: there are several varieties. One is kelp, with wide, dark green blades. This must be soaked before use; pieces swell enormously. Good for soups, it is sometimes used in sweet dishes too. Another variety is called purple laver or *tzecai* ('purple vegetable') in Chinese. Its Japanese name is *nori*. This comes in wafer-thin sheets, rather like the rice-paper but dark in colour. They should be moistened before use as wrappers or put straight into soups.

Preserved Vegetables, Fruits, Rice and Eggs

The climatic variety of China has ensured that there is an impressive range of traditionally preserved vegetables. Over two hundred supplement the Chinese diet, especially in the northern provinces where for six months of the year nothing grows. The range of climate is from the tropical and subtropical in Hainan and Guangdong, through the temperate conditions prevailing in Yangtze valley and Sichuan, and the continental ones near the Great Wall, to the cold desert of Tibet and the hot desert in western Xinjiang. Because of the immense distances involved in transporting foodstuffs, vegetables grown in the warm south can only act as a limited extra source of supply. As a result, a wide range of vegetables is sun dried, or steamed and sun dried, or salted, or pickled during the growing season by every Chinese household in the north. Such methods of preservation are also conducted on a commercial basis. From Chou times (1027–256 BC) the Chinese have eaten preserved vegetables. *A Manual for the Common People*, written in the seventh century AD, even includes detailed instructions on the proper ways in which to preserve individual vegetables.

Vegetables are preserved in salt, in fermented soya beans, in shrimp sauce, in sugar, in vinegar or in wine; so that they may taste salty, sour, sweet or hot. It is a fine way of storing otherwise highly perishable food, for preserved vegetables are not only most appetizing but also nourishing; although in the preserving process some vitamins are lost, they gain minerals from the sauces in which they are kept. They play an especially important role in the diet of country folk, whose cuisine is simpler than that of town dwellers. Salted vegetables make meat go further. They are traditionally considered to be alkaline in nature, and to balance the acid in meat, thereby contributing to a healthy diet. Health considerations apart, each preserved vegetable has such a distinct taste and flavour that it totally transforms a given meat into a unique dish.

Chinese mixed pickle: delicious, crunchy, sweet, sour and piquant, this mixed vegetable pickle has a colourful appearance with carrots, green peppers, cucumbers, ginger, mustard stalks, hot red chilli peppers, white radishes and other tasty ingredients. It is eaten with cold meat, preserved eggs, or fried food, and is used in the cooking of sweet and sour dishes.

Pickled leeks: although labelled 'pickled leeks', these are actually the bulbs of a bulbous spring onion with leaves like those of European chives. They are rather sweet and tasty when fresh, in which state they are eaten stir fried. When pickled, they are eaten plain or with cold meat.

Pickled young ginger: very tender young ginger stems are pickled in sugar, vinegar and salt. They are eaten with preserved eggs, with cold platter meat dishes, or steamed with fish.

Preserved chinese 'celery' cabbage: this is known as *dongcai*. It is made in Tianjin, in the northern province of Hebei. The cabbage is chopped fine like confetti, and preserved in salt and garlic. It is packed in a dark brown terracotta jar. Before sprinkling on soups or noodle dishes, or steaming with minced meat, rinsing is advisable.

Preserved cucumbers: cucumbers are preserved at various stages of maturity from baby size up, though the commonest ones are the fully grown. Cut in 8 cm (3 in) lengths and preserved in soya sauce, they are mainly eaten as a side dish or with rice porridge, or cooked with meat or fish. Sweet preserved baby cucumbers are prepared in Guangdong. These delicious little vegetables are called *chakua*, 'tea cucumbers'. Their sweetness adds an interesting taste to rice porridge.

'Red-in-the-snow': literal translation of *xuelihong*, a name given to the vegetable because it has red leaves and grows in winter. It is a type of mustard, rather like turnip tops apart from the colour. Fresh red-in-the-snow is bitter and hot. It is preserved in the provinces of Zhejiang and Jiangsu. Stir-fried or braised with meat it is delicious, but very salty. There is also a fermented version (*meikancai*), which is salted and sun-dried. The long preserving process gives it a strong fragrance. It must be soaked and rinsed thoroughly to remove any grit, after which it is no longer salty. It may be stir fried, steamed, braised or boiled with meat.

Salted radish: the large white radish, also known as 'mouli' is sliced lengthwise, sun dried and salted. One of the cheapest vegetables, it is popular all over China. Some are salted with hot chilli pepper, spices and sugar and are eaten without further cooking. The plain salted type is used as a flavouring in fish soup or stir fried with meat, or in omelettes, or eaten raw. It keeps indefinitely. Smaller radishes are also salted; they have a flavour that is slightly sweet as well as salty, with a firm and crunchy texture. They can be eaten raw, but rinsing is essential. Often shredded and stir fried with meat, salted small radish also adds taste to an omelette or soup. It keeps indefinitely.

Sichuan preserved vegetable: called *zhacai* in Chinese, this is the knobbly stem of a vegetable dried and salted with plenty of chilli powder and spices. Rinse before use to remove excess chilli powder which covers it. It may be stir fried, steamed or boiled with meat.

Sour and salted mustard greens: this is the bitter mustard plant parboiled whole and preserved in brine, or even wine. The fermentation process gives it a tangy and piquant fragrance. Used in soup, and in braised, stir-fried or steamed dishes, they can be cooked purely as a vegetable. Once opened they should be kept in the refrigerator.

Turnips: Yunnan pickled turnip is a famous product of that province. The sliced turnip is preserved in salt, soya sauce, maltose and brown sugar for 70 to 80 days, then sun dried, which turns it dark brown. It may be stir fried with meat or steamed with minced pork. Preserved turnip bundles, known as *chungkai*, are a popular vegetable from Guangdong. The whole turnip including its head is preserved in salt. It is then sliced vertically and bundled and tied into little parcels of about 5×2.5×2.5 cm (2×1×1 in). They are covered with salt crystals. They are boiled in soup, or steamed with minced pork or stir fried with meat. Rather salty; a little goes a long way.

Salted or pickled plums: the Chinese term for these is *suanmei*. They may be dry salted, when they are tiny and crinkled, with a rather salty, sour flavour. They are sucked as a sweet, or used as a flavouring for cooking after they have been soaked. Whole fresh plums are also pickled in brine. Brownish in colour and soft, they are used sparingly as a flavouring for fish and meat dishes.

Fermented rice: glutinous rice is allowed to ferment alcoholically, giving it fragrance. It is used for flavouring fish and meat dishes, or preserving food. It may be made at home.

Salted duck's eggs: these are preserved in salt and covered in a layer of sooty-looking burnt earth. The yolk hardens into a firm bright orange ball, whilst the white turns watery. They can only be eaten well cooked; they require about ten minutes boiling, after the removal of the earth. When cooked the yolk is golden and shiny with oil and has an exciting sandy texture, delicious but not salty. The white is salty, so dishes flavoured with salted eggs do not need salt.

Fermented eggs: these are often called 'hundred-year-old eggs', though they are usually only a few months old. Generally chicken eggs are used. They are coated with a clay-like mixture of lime, ashes and salt. The white turns a sparkling dark amber colour and is rubbery in texture, which explains the Chinese name *pitan*, 'leather egg'. The yolk is the colour of boiled spinach, and tastes cheesy. These eggs are eaten uncooked with pickled young ginger or mixed pickles. Nowadays some are preserved differently without the clay covering, and these must be boiled for 10 minutes before eating.

Legumes

Legumes form an important element in the largely vegetarian Chinese diet. Indeed, the Chinese derive a high proportion of protein from cereals, legumes and legume products. The cultivation of legumes as a rotation crop also enriches the soil, since leguminous plants have root nodules containing bacteria which fix nitrogen in the soil. This natural process enhances the protein contents in legumes and makes them highly nutritious. The legumes most commonly eaten in China are peas, mung beans, red aduki beans, broad beans, black soya beans, soya beans and peanuts.

Broad beans: whole, they are eaten as a vegetable. Ground into flour, they are used for noodles, cakes and thickening. Sprouted they are eaten as a vegetable. In Yunnan broad beans form the most important food crop after rice.

Mung beans: these are eaten in a savoury soup or as a sweet snack. They are made into a sweet paste for cakes, dumplings and puddings. Sprouted, they are eaten as a vegetable. Ground into flour, they are made into cakes, puddings, vermicelli and mung bean skins.

Peanuts: they are eaten as a vegetable in soup, braised meat dishes, and other vegetables, or as a snack. They are also made into confectionery.

Peas: fresh or dried ones are used as a vegetable or made into a purée for a dessert. They are also ground into flour and made into noodles, cakes and dumplings, particularly in north-east China.

Red aduki beans: they are eaten as a savoury soup or as a sweet snack. The sweetened purée is used in the making of cakes and puddings.

Soya beans: black soya beans are eaten mainly as a savoury soup. For other soya bean products, see the next section, and also the earlier section on soya sauces, salted soya beans, and pastes (page 50).

Soya Products other than Sauces and Pastes

The Chinese never eat unprocessed soya beans, boiled or roasted (except for the black type – see above), for cooked whole soya beans are very indigestible and heating them does not make the nutrients significantly easier to assimilate. Soya flour from roasted beans is tasteless, and the nutrients are equally unavailable. Yet soya beans contain more protein than any other animal or plant. A given weight of soya beans contains twice the amount of protein in that weight of beef steak, besides which soya beans are rich in Vitamin A and B complex vitamins including thiamin and riboflavin, contain valuable amounts of calcium, iron and other minerals, and are low in cholesterol. Their calorie value is low in relation to these amounts of nutrients. However, these important nutrients are not available to the human body without being hydrolyzed – that is, they must be broken down into a digestible form by the action of water and heat, or other agents. The Chinese have developed a whole range of hydrolyzed and sometimes dried soya products whose protein is acceptable to the human body in a form digestible and enjoyable, and nutritionally comparable to that of meat. Sprouting and fermentation render the beans easily digestible, and also increase their available nutrients many times.

Doufu: commonly known as bean curd, this is made from soaked soya beans reduced to a liquid then curdled to a solid, creamy-coloured, protein-rich product with burnt gypsum. *Doufu* has a high water content, a smooth texture and a delicious taste. It may be steamed, boiled, braised and used in combination with other ingredients in innumerable recipes.

White firm bean curd: called in Chinese *paidoukan*, it is a versatile, firm bean curd that may be sliced or shredded and used as a meat substitute when stir fried with vegetables, or it may be flavoured with meat or seafood.

Yellow bean curd: this type, known as *huangdonkan*, is similar to the white firm one but is coloured with tea, spiced and steamed. It has a tight, smooth texture, is delicious in taste, and used in the same way as the white kind.

Deep-fried doufu: the term for this is *youdoufu*. It is plain, firm *doufu* cut into cubes and deep fried till a golden crust is formed on the outside. It is used in stuffed *doufu* dishes.

Soya-bean milk: called *doujiang*, it is made from soya beans soaked overnight and ground with 20 times their volume of water. It is strained through a muslin bag and boiled till the raw taste is gone, for about five minutes, then sweetened, and drunk hot or cold. The milk can be curdled to make *doufuhua*, which has the consistency of a milk junket. This is eaten hot with preserved vegetables or other savoury ingredients sprinkled on top, or as a hot sweet with caramel syrup.

Fresh bean-curd skin: a resilient thin skin, the thickness of a Greek or Turkish filo pastry, and known as *doupi*. It is made by gently boiling soya-bean milk in a wide container so that a thin skin is formed at the top. This is lifted off and placed on a perforated tray made from thin bamboo slats to dry, when it stiffens. Layer after layer is lifted till the liquid is exhausted. A common use is as a wrapping for meat rolls.

Dried bean-curd skin: dried, crisp bean-curd skins all folded up in a packet. It is called *paiyeh* ('hundred leaves') for the number of folds. It has to be softened in warm water briefly and patted dry before use as a wrapping or in other ways.

Dried bean-curd stick: known as *fuchu*, and made from rolled-up and dried bean-curd skin. It is soaked in boiling water to soften, rinsed and cut into 5–8 cm (2–3 in) lengths before cooking. A good meat extender or substitute, it is suitable for boiling and braising.

Sweet bean-curd skin: a dark-coloured sweet-tasting bean-curd skin, called *tienchu*, which is a byproduct of the making of the other types of bean curd skin; it is the thick layer left at the bottom of the pot. It is sold in an oblong packet of about 10×5 cm (4×2 in), and must be soaked before cooking. It is popular in vegetarian cooking, as it gives a richer, sweet taste than plain bean-curd skin.

Soya-bean meal: the residue after soya-bean milk has been extracted, soya bean meal, *douzha*, is often cooked with spicy seasoning as a vegetable. It is also used as an animal feed.

Soya-bean sprouts: known as *douyah*. Soya-bean sprouts are tougher than mung-bean sprouts and are usually cooked for about 20 minutes. They may be stir fried or boiled.

Fermented bean curd and other soya products are described in the section on soya sauces, salted soya beans and pastes (page 50).

Seasonings

Traditional Chinese cuisine recognizes five basic tastes: sweet, sour, bitter, hot and salty. The seasoning used to impart these tastes are described here. (Spices and herbs are described in the next section.)

Sugar: the Chinese are not a sweet-toothed people, and in general prefer a savoury snack. Many of their confections are in fact preserved fruits, such as olives, plums, apricots, and haws. The average annual sugar consumption per head before 1949 is said to have been 2.7 kg (6 lb), and to this day the nation has a relatively low incidence of diabetes. Although both cane and beet sugar are refined, cane sugar predominates. Apart from the usual brown and white sugars, rock sugar, maltose and honey are used.

Rock sugar: this is processed cane sugar in amber-coloured or white crystal lumps. It is less sweet than ordinary sugar and imparts a fragrant flavour to food cooked in it. Chiefly an ingredient in the cooking of tonic food, it must be crushed before use.

Maltose: the term used for a sticky malt extract made from sprouted wheat or barley, and nowadays also obtained from maize and sweet potatoes. Long known to the Chinese, maltose is not intensely sweet and has a beautiful taste, so that it is often eaten plain like a lollipop. It is used a great deal in the manufacture of confectionery, cakes and biscuits, not least because it gives the finished products better colour, taste and fragrance. Another use is in the roasing of meat, as for Beijing duck and suckling pig.

Honey: not greatly used in cooking sweet dishes, it features more as a food remedy and as a pill binder.

Vinegar: Chinese vinegars are made from sorghum, long-grain rice or glutinous rice. There are three kinds: white, red and black. The colour ranges from pale golden through deep red and purple to completely black.

White wine vinegar: mainly made from rice wine, and pale golden in colour. It is a valuable aid in both cooking and preserving.

Red (or Zhejiang) vinegar: reddish black, or the colour of burgundy, it has a low acid content. The best kind comes from Zhejiang. It is a popular dip for boiled or steamed crab.

Black vinegar: has a low acid content, and is used in braised meat dishes, or as a dip. Several varieties come from Guangdong.

Zhenjiang vinegar (labelled as Chinkiang vinegar): a well known dark, thick vinegar from Jiangsu province with low acid content and a lovely fragrance. It is used in the cooking of meat, and as a dip at table, but is most delicious when added to shark's-fin soup.

Salt: four kinds of salt are used in China: sea salt, rock salt, well salt and lake salt. Coarse sea salt is used in the preserving of fish and vegetables.

Monosodium glutamate: this additive (EEC reference number E621) is a white substance, almost tasteless and odourless in itself, but which enhances the taste of food. It is found in Chinese restaurant food in particular, to such an extent that a well known allergic reaction to MSG is actually called 'Chinese Restaurant Syndrome'. Though MSG is used a great deal in Chinese restaurant kitchens, this is not the case in every Chinese household. Some people believe that it is quite harmless, but others consider it is bad for health. Whereas one family might add MSG to some dishes, another would shun it altogether. This apparently Chinese ingredient only arrived in China during the First World War; it was imported from Japan, where in 1908 a professor at Tokyo University had isolated the substance from seaweed. After 1914 Japanese MSG flooded the cities of China and carried all before it, till an enterprising Chinese scientist in Shanghai bought a tin and analysed its contents. Thereupon he established a cottage industry for MSG, which was welcomed by Chinese patriots who were then worried about Japanese military ambitions. From this Chinese MSG production expanded, and a franchise was obtained to sell in the West. At first MSG was derived from seaweed, wheat gluten or soya beans. From the 1960s onwards the chief source has been maize starch, as it is thought to be too wasteful to use wheat. Production is now worldwide. MSG is potent. It can have its effect even when diluted in 300 times its volume of water. For this reason, one should never increase the amount of MSG in proportion to the size of the dish. Another point to bear in mind is that MSG is not added to food before cooking, since a high temperature is liable to render it toxic. And it should never be added to egg, chicken and fish dishes – as these produce MSG on their own when cooked. In the recipes given in this book, MSG is not included because in Chinese culinary art it is no more than an extra, optional item. Food cooked from genuine and fresh ingredients ought to be tasty without any additives.

Starch: this plays an important part in Chinese cuisine. It thickens the liquid in food, and binds meat or seafood together as in fillings and meat balls. The starch employed varies from area to area. The common ones are mung-bean flour, Chinese water-chestnut flour, lotus-root flour, broad-bean flour and arrowroot. Cornflour or potato starch may be used instead. Tapioca starch is used in cakes and pastas only.

Wine: Chinese wines are fully described on pages 28–35. For the rice wine used in cooking, you can substitute pale, dry sherry.

Spices and Herbs

Chinese cuisine has been described as a manoeuvring of a number of basic ingredients with a few spices. But the Chinese awareness of the medicinal properties of spices ensures that they are used sparingly, so that they give a subtle flavour. The spices and similar flavourings most frequently used are as follows:

Cardamoms: the pale green pods contain little brown-black seeds. Aromatic and warming, they are used in some regions in the spice bag for the steeping liquor which is used in the preparation of some dishes. A larger type, ovoid cardamom, is brown and as large as an olive, with grooves on the skin. This is an ingredient for the spice bag in some areas.

Cassia bark: dark, thick and known as Chinese cinnamon, this originally came from Burma around 2500 BC. Cassia bark is very pungent and better suited to the spicing of meat than the delicate cinnamon stick, which is more suited to sweet dishes. (See also Dried cassia flowers, below.)

Celery: the smaller, green and bitter variety is favoured by the Chinese as a flavouring.

Cloves: originally from South-East Asia, though Zanzibar is the main world supplier now, cloves have been enjoyed by Chinese for more than 2,000 years. They are used whole, or ground in combination with other spices.

Coriander: also known as Chinese parsley, it is used all over China as a garnish and seasoning. The plants are harvested very young, about 8 to 10 cm (3 to 4 in) tall, so that the fragrance is not too strong.

Dangkui: Chinese angelica root is a medicinal herb with a pungent flavour, slightly bitter, and often used in flavouring food. It is also deemed to be good for the circulation and is mainly eaten in the winter months; but it should be avoided by people inclined to headaches.

Dried cassia flowers and rose petals: used separately in the flavouring of various sweet confections and the preserving of some vegetables.

Dried hot chilli peppers: dark red, they are fiery hot and must be soaked before use. They are favourites in Sichuan, Hunan and Yunnan cooking. The seeds may be removed to reduce the hotness.

Dried tangerine peel: very dark brown, it is used as a flavouring for both sweet and savoury dishes. It is also available in powder form.

Fennel seeds: fine rice-sized seeds, whose flavour is similar to that of star anise, but less sweet. Their main use is as a spice in steeping liquor.

Five-spice powder: this ready-made seasoning powder contains star anise, cloves, cassia bark, fennel and Sichuan peppercorns and it is suitable for both meat and fish dishes.

Galangal: also known as galangal ginger or lesser galangal, this fibrous bulbous root has a creamy-coloured, red-tinged skin and a pale creamy inside. Native to south China, it has been used there in cooking since antiquity. Still a popular spice in southern Chinese and South-East Asian Chinese cooking, it is used in duck, goose, pork and beef dishes, and in the Hainan chicken speciality.

Garlic: a fundamental spice of Chinese cookery, especially for seasoning oil. In some recipes meat is braised with whole cloves. Minced raw garlic is always eaten with shellfish as an antiseptic.

Ginger: a gnarled-looking root, it has been used for millenia in China both in food and as medicine. It is an indispensable ingredient in Chinese cooking, where its main function is to neutralize the odour of meat and fish.

Liquorice root: this is dried and sliced, and pale yellowish in colour. It has a sweet taste when chewed. It is used in red-cooked meat dishes and in preserving fruits.

Mint leaves: leaves of the horse mint are used in Guangdong with duck and goose dishes in a sweet and sour mint sauce. In the north they are deep fried and sugared, and eaten as a dessert.

Mixed spices for the steeping pot or luliao: these include cassia bark, star anise seeds, cloves, fennel, liquorice root, dried tangerine peel, and Sichuan peppercorns. They may be bought in a packet or made up at home and tied in a muslin bag.

Shallot: the red variety is popular with the Chinese particularly in Fujian and Guangdong.

Sichuan peppercorns: also known as *fagara*, these resemble black peppercorns, but are reddish brown in colour and have a seed inside. In fact they come from a quite different plant. Mildly hot with a pleasant aroma, they are used in red-cooked dishes, pickles and salt dips, especially in Sichuan, Hunan and Yunnan cooking.

Spring onion: like ginger, it is indispensable in Chinese cookery. Spring onions season oil, add flavour, and garnish cooked food.

Star anise seed: from an evergreen native to China, the seed is dark brown with eight pointed petals. It is called *pachiaw* in Chinese. Its flavour is like anise seed, though much more bitter and pungent. This is a favourite spice for red-cooked dishes.

White peppercorns: Commonly used in Fujian and Guangdong as a flavouring in cooking, but not as a table seasoning.

Colourings

A red powdered colouring made from a vegetable base is used in ceremonial foods. The following colourings are used in everyday cooking:

Tea: for shades of brown and yellow.

Soya sauce: for brown.

Caramel: for red and dark rich dishes.

Red rice: *hongqu*, a dried red fermented rice used for red and pink.

Tomatoes: for red in pasta and sauces.

Pocai: or spinach, for green in pasta and cakes.

Preserved Meats

There are many local varieties in China, each having its own special flavour.

Pressed ducks: known as *lahya* or 'waxed ducks' in Chinese, because of their appearance, they are precooked, boned, pressed, wind dried, and then soaked in peanut oil. To eat: rinse, dice and steam for 30 to 35 minutes, or till tender. Pressed ducks are eaten with plain rice, and sometimes with fresh duck meat so as to give a contrast of taste and texture. They may be steamed with fresh pork, or sausages and preserved pork, or mixed with pork or beef and steamed, as a flavouring. The best known kind is Nanking duck, though those on sale here have most probably come from Guangzhou (Canton).

Chinese pork sausages: called *lahchang* or 'waxed sausages', they are reddish with white marbling, waxy looking and thin, about 15 to 18 cm (6 to 7 in) and tied in pairs. Sweet and savoury, rather like some kinds of Italian salami, they are made from lean meat and fat seasoned and wind dried. They must be cooked before eating. They are best sliced and steamed, or they can be stir fried with rice, chicken, or other meat or vegetables as a flavouring.

Duck-liver sausages: similar to the pork sausages in appearance except that the red part is darker; the flavour is less sweet. They are eaten in the same way.

Preserved pork: known as *lahyu*, 'waxed pork', this comes in waxy-looking sides of meat, which must be cooked before eating. It is rinsed, sliced and steamed with fresh pork for contrast or with any combination of the other preserved meats, so that there is an interesting selection of taste and texture.

Chinese ham: cured and smoked pork. It is moderately used as a flavouring for soup and other dishes. Two well known varieties from China are Jinhua and Yunnan ham. For cooking purposes a suitable substitute is smoked back bacon, which has a similar taste and colour.

Fresh and Dried Noodles and Vermicelli

Noodles and vermicelli may be turned into a quick meal or snack. They are easy to prepare and versatile, so that they can be made into a delectable dish in combination with whatever happens to be in the larder or refrigerator. There are many varieties and qualities of Chinese noodles.

Wheat noodles: Generally called *mien*, meaning 'wheat vermicelli', these come in ribbons of various widths and as thin vermicelli. They may be fresh or dried, and made with or without eggs. Some have had lye water added, as a yellow colour shows (see Flour on page 48). The fresh ones take little time to cook to an *al dente* texture, but the dried ones must be boiled briefly to soften them before adding to other ingredients.

Wheat threads: known as *miensien*, these are fine, pale cream-coloured and slightly salted, and sold in skeins. They are so thin that they need hardly any cooking at all, and can be popped into a boiling soup for just a few seconds. A most popular noodle in Fujian province.

Rice noodles: these may be fresh or dried, and come in widths from 1.3 to 1.7 cm (½ to ⅔ in). Dried ones are boiled briefly to soften them before they are used in soup or stir fried.

Rice sticks: dry rice vermicelli in two thicknesses. They must be boiled briefly to soften before use in soup or stir fried.

Mung-bean vermicelli: known as *fensi*, these are white and transparent, very fine and strong, and they can only be cut with a sharp pair of scissors when raw. They must be soaked in boiling water before use, and as they swell a great deal in soup they must be served immediately. They may also be stir fried.

Mung-bean sheets: called *fenpi*; semi-transparent white discs of about 18 to 20 cm (7 to 8 in) diameter. They are boiled briefly and cut up before use.

Soya-bean noodles: made with soya and a little wheat flour. Pale yellow in colour, the thickness of a wire coat hanger, they are popular in vegetarian dishes. They must also be boiled briefly.

Crispy noodles: deep-fried noodles which originated in Guangzhou (Canton) and are now very popular in North America. In the West 'chow mein' or fried noodles are associated with this type of noodle, but authentic *chaomian* are soft fried in oil. Crispy noodles are usually prepared at home, but commercial versions are available.

Wan ton skins: used for making a filled pasta like rather large ravioli. The skins are made with wheat flour, salt, water and lye water. They are paper-thin squares, sold fresh only.

Dried Vegetables, Nuts and Seeds, Fruits, Flowers and Fungi

These are harvested and sun dried in the summer. They keep almost indefinitely.

Vegetables include:

Bamboo shoots: these are sliced, blanched and sun dried. They must be soaked before cooking, and are used mainly in boiled and braised dishes. (For their medicinal value see page 14.)

Chinese cole: this is dried without salting. The leaves look dark brown and the stems pale golden and stringy. After soaking, they are usually braised or boiled with meat; a high-fibre food.

Gourds: leathery, beige-coloured, thin strips of sun-dried gourds are used mainly as a soup ingredient. Soak before cooking.

Lotus roots: sliced and sun dried, these are rock hard. They are always boiled to make a soup. (For fresh lotus roots, see page 82.)

Among the nuts and seeds are:

Almonds: sweet almonds are blanched and split and are used in sweet and savoury dishes, cakes, biscuits and puddings, and as garnishes for meat and seafood. Bitter almonds are used sparingly in sweet dishes, cakes, puddings, drinks and in soups for a delicious flavour.

Cashew nuts: Ivory-coloured, kidney-shaped, they are stir fried with meat or used as a garnish, besides being eaten as a snack.

Chestnuts: similar to the Western dried chestnuts. They must be parboiled and any red skin removed before cooking. They give a rich, sweet, smoky taste to red-cooked meat dishes.

Ginkgo nuts: from the ginkgo or maidenhair tree, an ancient survival in China and Japan. They have a tough, beige shell and ivory-coloured, firm meat. They must be shelled and blanched before cooking in soup, meat, vegetarian and sweet dishes. But no more than ten should be eaten for an adult or five for a child, since a large number could cause poisoning.

Lotus seeds: these are about 1.3 cm (½ in) long, oval-shaped and ivory-coloured. They are soaked and boiled in soups and sweets, and made into a sweetened paste as a filling for cake and pudding.

Pine nuts: used in both savoury and sweet dishes.

Sesame seeds: white sesame seeds, fine and ivory-coloured, are used in both savoury and sweet dishes. They are rinsed, dry fried till fragrant and used either crushed or whole. There are also black sesame seeds, which are rarely used in savoury dishes, but mainly in sweets, cakes, biscuits and other confections. (Sesame seeds also have a medicinal use; see page 20.)

Walnuts: the same as English walnuts. They feature both in meat dishes and in confectionery.

Fruits which are dried include:

Figs: shaped like little onions, about 2.5 to 4 cm (1 to 1½ in) long, Chinese figs are creamy in colour and covered in natural fruit sugar. They are eaten as a confection or boiled in soup. The ordinary brown figs are also eaten but not cooked. (For their medicinal use, see page 17.)

Red or black 'dates': these are dried jujube. Red dates or *hongzao* are jujube which have turned red after being sun-dried. They have shrivelled skins. When soaked and stoned, they are boiled in soup, braised with meat and steamed in puddings and cakes. A sweetened purée made from them is used in both sweet and savoury dishes. Black dates or *heizao* are fresh jujube steamed before being sun-dried. The Chinese treat them in much the same way as the red dates. However, they are not used in sweets or cakes.

Longans: they are stoned before drying, and take on a dark brown colour. They must be rinsed before cooking in soups, drinks and desserts. They are used in small amounts. (Also a medicinal food; see page 17.)

The flowers most commonly dried are:

Lily flowers: these come from the day lily. When dried they are leathery-looking, about 10 cm (4 in) long and needle-shaped; hence their Chinese name of *jinzhen* or *jinzhencai*, 'golden needles'. After soaking, they are excellent for soups and braised or stir-fried dishes. They have a distinctive fragrance and a mildly sour taste. (Also used medicinally; see page 17.)

The principle dried fungi are:

Silver wood ears: also known as 'jelly fungus', these are a cock's comb-like fungus, pale honey-coloured and very light when dried. They grow on old pine-tree trunks in cool places. Today they are also commercially cultivated, but in China the wild ones are highly prized. When soaked they turn white and increase twenty-five times in volume. They have a crunchy texture but if gently cooked for a long time they become gelatinous; they are good in both sweet and savoury dishes. (For their medicinal use, see page 20.)

Winter mushrooms: these are dark brown, leathery-looking mushrooms with a strong fragrance. They must be soaked before use in soups, stir-fried, steamed, or braised dishes. (Also a medicinal food; see page 21.)

Wood ears: ear-shaped fungus that grows on old tree trunks. When dried they are black and charred-looking with irregular shapes, but when soaked they swell to six times their size, about 8 to 10 cm (3 to 4 in) wide. They must be soaked and rinsed well before use in soup, or stir fried. (Used medicinally; see page 21.)

Some Dried Packet Soup Mixtures

Packaged soup mixtures are sold, consisting of sun-dried fruits, nuts, seeds, vegetables and sometimes medicinal herbs. They should be rinsed, then boiled with meat. Here they are listed under the usual names by which they are sold.

Dried watercress: this is steamed and dried watercress. It is simmered in plenty of water with meat as a soup, about 2 to 3 hours. It swells a great deal and only a little is needed. A high-fibre food.

Lohankuo and dehydrated cole soup mix: this contains *lohankuo* (a medicinal fruit related to the mangosteen), honey date or zizyphus (related to jujube), Chinese cole, bitter almonds, red date (jujube) and carrot. This is boiled with meat as a soup.

'Nourishing and cooling soup': *ching po leung* in Cantonese. This one has as ingredients lily bulbs, pearl barley seeds, lotus seeds, jade bamboo (polygonatum), fox nuts, dried longan and dioscorea. It can also be boiled as a sweet.

'Nutritious soup mixture': this contains Chinese cole, mushrooms, potato and carrot. It is boiled with meat as a soup or braised.

'Soup mixture': this contains purely medicinal herbs. It is rather warming and is eaten only if one is not heated. It is usually steamed with meat in water for use as a tonic food eaten mainly in winter.

Some Special Ingredients

Chinese caterpillar fungus: this looks like a yellow coloured matchstick with a spent end. It is a medicinal herb that has become a tonic food, and is used sparingly for steaming with meat. (See also page 16.)

Chinese wolfberries (Red medler berries): the shape and size of grains of rice, lacquer red in colour. They occur in soups, often with other medicinal herbs (for their medicinal use, see page 16). They are boiled or steamed with meat as tonic food. In Hunan they are also used in desserts.

Crystallized melon: an ingredient for sweet meat dishes, cakes and dessert, and also eaten on its own as a sweet. It is in the form of transparent white lumps or sliced finger-sized covered in crystallized sugar. Best stored in the freezer if bought frozen; otherwise in an air-tight jar.

Dangkui: a kind of angelica root, somewhat different from the western one. It is sold very thinly sliced in a Chinese drugstore, since it is used in medicinal prescriptions. In the kitchen it is a flavouring for fish soup, or boiled with meat as a tonic food. It has a strong, pleasant fragrance and a slightly bitter taste.

Dried lily bulbs: called *paihe* in Chinese, these are the bulbs of the madonna lily. When dried they are shaped like petals, hard and ivory-coloured. They are boiled in soups and used in savoury and sweet dishes, and also medicinally.

Dried red fermented rice: known as *hongqu*, this is a kind of long-grain rice fermented and dried so that it turns a powdery lacquer-red. It is so light that the best quality should float on water. It is used as a flavouring, a colouring (see page 64) and a tonic food.

Dried persimmons: are round, flattened, leathery-looking, dark reddish brown fruit covered in a white layer of natural fruit sugar. They should be soaked, boiled or steamed before eating. They are an ingredient in steamed puddings. (For their medicinal use, see page 18.)

Knotty yam: this is called *waisun* in Chinese. It is a medicinal root (see page 18), white and smooth, fine and firm. When sold in sliced and dried form, it looks rather like a flattened piece of chalk. It is boiled in soup or ground into flour for cakes.

Lye water: this is a solution of 42 per cent potassium carbonate in 58 per cent water. It is used in some noodles, pastries and cakes, and sometimes for softening dried ingredients.

Wine yeast: for home-made Chinese fermented rice wine, this comes in the shape of a ping-pong ball, round and smooth but slightly smaller, white and rather light. It should be crushed before use.

Fresh Fish and Seafood

Both freshwater and sea fish are eaten by the Chinese. Because they like them to be really fresh, they favour freshwater fish for the reason that they can be kept alive until the very last moment. Carp and eels can thus be seen swimming about in special tanks in Chinese restaurants. But sea fish are valued for their minerals. The important thing about cooking a fish is that it should never be greasy or soggy. Always described as 'clear steamed', 'clear simmered', or 'crisp deep-fried', fish dishes are neither overcooked, which would render them dry and tasteless, nor under-cooked lest they should give off a fishy odour or have a flabby texture. Large fish are usually cut up, but smaller fish weighing up to 1 kg (2 lb) are always cooked whole, not only for aesthetic reasons but for conserving the juice within the fish. According to Chinese belief, the head of a fish is the most nutritious part, which explains the availability of large fish heads for making soup in Chinese supermarkets. Ginger is considered in-dispensable in the cooking of fish, as it neutralizes the fishy smell. Rather than eat fish that is not fresh, the Chinese resort to a variety of fish preserved in salt. However, in Britain one can buy many kinds of fresh fish: grey mullet, red mullet, whiting, haddock, cod, halibut and turbot are excellent for Chinese cookery, as long as they are really fresh. White fish are good for fish balls. Any frozen fish should be thoroughly defrosted and towelled dry before cooking. Fish that has been frozen for a long period of time is inevitably tough, dry and tasteless. The following are some fish in the regular Chinese diet available here:

Pomfret: may be steamed, pan fried, or deep fried. Steaming makes the flesh less rich.

Grouper: may be deep fried, steamed or stir fried. Heads from larger ones are boiled to make soup.

Red snapper: may be steamed, deep fried, pan fried or pan braised with a sauce.

Sea bass: is a firm favourite with the Chinese, but it may be replaced with carp or grass carp, or grey mullet. It is normally steamed and finished with a seasoned hot oil.

Carp and grass carp: are traditionally steamed like the sea bass, but they may also be red – cooked or pan fried.

Apart from fresh fish, a wide variety of fresh seafood is eaten in the Chinese diet, particularly in the south in Fujian, Guangdong and along the coast of Shandong in the north. Abalone, crabs, prawns, lobsters, oysters, clams, cockles, shrimps, snails, squids and cuttlefish are all popular. Frozen seafood must be thoroughly defrosted before cooking. All seafood is cooked very briefly, as prolonged heating causes toughness and makes it indigestible.

Abalone: fresh ones are exceedingly expensive. They may be sliced and stir fried, or cooked in soup very briefly. In China they are sold in their shells. For dried abalone, see page 52; for medicinal use, see page 14.

Clams: scrubbed clean and prised open or steamed open (about 5 minutes) to extract the meat for cooking in a curried sauce, or coated and deep fried with a sweet and pungent sauce. They are sometimes served in half-shells with garlic sauce.

Cockles: scrubbed clean and cooked either by pouring boiling water over them if small, or by dipping them in boiling water for half a minute or so if large. They are eaten with vinegar, garlic, chilli and minced ginger and soya sauce. The shelled meat may be stir fried with bean sprouts, or noodles or rice.

Crabs: bought live, they are scrubbed and then stabbed through the mouth before boiling or steaming. When they turn bright red they are cooked. Steamed crab meat is used in cooking as fillings or flavouring. It is chopped up raw and steamed or stir-fried. To shell a cooked crab, remove the tail or apron, and pull the upper and lower shells apart. Discard the soft spongy parts. Crack the pincers, remove the meat and discard the cartilage.

In some parts of China around the eight or ninth month of the lunar calendar (September–October) some especially big fat crabs are bought and kept in a terracotta urn with mud, broken stalks of an aubergine plant and some sesame seeds. The urn is sealed with a bamboo cover and secured, creating a small habitat for hibernation. These crabs are eaten around January and February for the New Year festival. They are called 'fairy crabs' or *shenxianxie*.

Lobsters: are seldom cooked at home, being more a restaurant food. In China they are mainly eaten along the coastal areas in Fujian and Guangdong. They are bought live. Steamed whole, lobster is eaten with minced ginger and black vinegar. Lobsters are mainly used as a cold platter at banquet.

Mussels: only eaten dried; see page 53.

Prawns: Shelled and minced prawn meat is used as a filling or mixed with other meat or fish, to enrich the flavour of a dish. Often unshelled prawns are stir fried, deep fried or pan fried to retain their maximum flavour and tenderness. Medium and small prawns are more tender and finer in texture, and are preferred.

Scallops: fresh scallops are cut into round slices and stir fried. For deep frying they are halved or quartered. For dried scallops, see page 53.

Sea cucumbers: only eaten dried; see page 53.

Sea snails: Both round and spiral sea snails are blanched in boiling water and served with vinegar, garlic, ginger, chilli and salt or soya sauce. The tails of the spiral snails have to be chipped off before cooking, or the meat will not slip out.

Squid and cuttlefish: fresh ones are usually stir fried or deep fried. For dried ones, see page 53.

Meats

Pork is the favourite meat eaten in China except among the Muslims, who eat lamb and some beef. Poultry is the second favoured meat, of which duck is the most popular followed by chicken, pigeon and goose. Turkey is very rarely eaten. Nowadays, beef is eaten slightly more than before; but veal is virtually unknown. Wild game is considered healthy and is eaten occasionally at banquets or as a tonic food.

Fresh Vegetables

The Chinese diet is mainly vegetarian; that is to say, in a meal vegetables by far outweigh meat or fish. In rural areas meat is not eaten every day, but is a luxury reserved for the feast days. Instead salted fish and salted eggs are used to complement the vegetables, which are made tasty by flavouring sauces. If meat is taken at all, it is usually as a flavouring.

Today there are around 116 kinds of vegetables cultivated in China, of which only about 57 are native plants. Foreign vegetables began arriving in China during the Han period (202 BC–AD 220), mostly coming from Central Asia along the Silk Road. Some other vegetables came from India and South-East Asia via Yunnan and Guangsi in the south-west. Later under the Ming and Qing dynasties (1368–1912), more foreign vegetables reached China by sea. Through both natural and artificial selection, all these vegetables went through changes.

The following are some of the vegetables available here in the Chinese markets. By nature, Chinese vegetables are very tender and need very little cooking, about 2 minutes stir frying on high heat being enough.

Angled luffa: this gourd is a cheap and common vegetable in China. Though said to be a native of India, it has been in China a very long time. Dark green with ridges, it is about 5 to 8 cm (2 to 3 in) in diameter in the fattest part and about 30 to 45 cm (12–18 in) long. To cook, shave off the ridges with a peeler and then peel off the rest of the rather leathery skin as you would with a cucumber. If the gourd is young and tender (when the ridges are close together, and the gourd is slender), leave the skin on, so that it looks stripy where the ridges have been removed. There is no need to remove the seeds, which are tender. The flesh is pale green, very tender and spongy. Cut into wedges, it may be stir fried plain, or with eggs, or shrimps, or crab meat and eggs; or boiled in soup with meat, eggs or prawns. It needs very little cooking and is deliciously sweet. In China another variety, also edible when young but very fibrous when mature, is grown to provide the 'loofahs' exported to the West. The dried spongy inside is used not only in the bath, but also as a pot scourer and to make the soles of slippers. Either kind of luffa is high in dietary fibre. The Chinese name is *sigua*, 'fibrous gourd'. (For medicinal use, see page 14.)

Aubergine: a native of India and Burma, this plant has been cultivated in China since the Tang era (AD 618–906). Those normally seen in the West are ovoid in shape and dark purple in colour. The Chinese aubergines are usually long and slender, the colour ranging from dark purple to pale purple, and from white to pale green. Some are small and round like eggs, pale green-white in colour. Aubergines are one of the vegetables best loved by the Chinese. The dark ones are generally peeled before cooking. But the Chinese never seem to need to sprinkle salt on their aubergines to remove the juice before cooking. They are plain boiled, stir fried, baked, deep fried, braised, stuffed and braised, or steamed. And they may be flavoured with a sweet and sour sauce, with salted soya beans; with fermented rice, with garlic, mint, mustard or salted eggs. They are cooked with minced meat or crab meat, and in numerous other ways. They are even preserved. The only way they are never cooked is in a soup. Choose waxy, unblemished ones with the cup-shaped leaf at the stem end intact. (For medicinal use, see page 14.)

Bitter gourd: a native of Vietnam, it arrived in China at the beginning of the Ming dynasty (1368–1644). It is now grown mostly in the warmer parts of China: Guangdong, Fujian and Formosa in the south, Guangsi and Yunnan in the South-West; and in South-East Asia. Also known as 'balsam pear' in English, it has a warty, pale green skin, with hard golden seeds covered in a bright red velvety skin. Some are fatter than a cucumber and as long, but the ones sold here are usually stumpy. The thinner, greener immature ones are more bitter and are boiled with meat to make soup. Boiling reduces the bitterness, but the soup remains slightly and attractively bitter, with a pleasantly sweet aftertaste. To cook, slice lengthwise and deseed, then cut diagonally into thin slices. To reduce the bitterness, rub on a little salt and leave to stand for about 10 minutes, then rinse well before cooking. Another method is to blanch it in boiling water and refresh in cold water. For soup, the vegetable is usually cut into oblong pieces and cooked without pre-salting or blanching. Rounds about 2 cm ($\frac{3}{4}$ in) thick are deseeded, filled with minced meat or fish, and braised. The Chinese never sugar this vegetable as the bitterness is enjoyed. The favourite combination for stir frying is with sliced beef, or boiled fatty pork, or fresh crab, flavoured with salted black soya beans, ginger and red chillies; or it can be stir fried with eggs. Canned bitter gourd is available and convenient, though some of its taste is lost.

Boxthorn leaves: this vegetable belongs to a large family which includes the tomato, potato, aubergine and even tobacco. It is grown in the USA to make hedgerows, and in Britain is simply dismissed as a weed. But the Chinese, especially in Guangdong, thrive on this plant. It is a delicious vegetable with a rod-like, straight, stout stem, sometimes with thorns, and small, oval, dark green leaves. The leaves are boiled in soup; the classic recipe is to boil them with pork or pork and liver. They take about 3 minutes to cook. The leaves are also stir fried in northern China. (Also used medicinally; see page 15.)

Buddha's hands: A variety of bitter citron, these gourds look like two hands clasped together with the fingers folded. One can clearly see the knuckles. Hence the Chinese names: *hezhangua* or 'folded hands gourd', and *fusaugua* or 'Buddha's hands gourd'. The citron sold in this country is apple green in colour and pear-shaped. It has a large centre seed which is removed before chopping. The flesh is firm and white and may be eaten raw or pickled in salt, sugar and vinegar; or stir fried, boiled in soup, or steamed with pork, peel and all. The variety grown in China has a strong fragrance, is darker in colour, and is very bitter and not edible raw. (For medicinal use, see page 16.)

Celery: Chinese celery is stronger and more aromatic in flavour than that in the West. In China various colours are available: pale green, dark green, yellow, white and purple; but the majority is green. The best green celery comes from the Guangdong and Hubei area, with fat stalks and a crunchy texture. The best white celery comes from the Beijing area, and is tender and crisp. Celery is sliced into matchstick-sized slivers and stir fried with meat; celery and beef is a favourite combination. A little shredded celery is always added where an aromatic flavour and a crunchy texture are desired, as in the stir frying of cuttlefish or squid. When cooked with other food, the celery is always stir fried first for a minute or two to bring out its taste and flavour. The Chinese also eat the leaves, which are cooked with the sliced stalks; nothing is wasted. Sometimes the green aromatic leaves are shredded finely and sprinkled on food, or mixed with minced meat or fish as a flavouring. In China celery is also preserved in salt, in shrimp sauce or in other flavourings. The English celery takes beautifully to Chinese cooking: it is less strong in taste and flavour, but crisp. When cut to matchstick size, it may be substituted for mung-bean sprouts or Chinese 'celery' cabbage for texture, though not for taste. One fine way of eating English celery as a vegetable is to stir fry it plain or flavoured with shredded crispy bacon. Also available is a kind of pale yellow celery, in limp-looking bunches. It is very tender, aromatic and delicious, and is grown in a hothouse, out of sunlight (as are the famous Chinese yellow chives). It shrinks when cooked: a big bunch cooks down to a small dish, so it is used mainly as a flavouring vegetable for beef and other meat.

Chinese 'celery' cabbage: so called only because it has an upright shape like a bunch of celery, and also known as 'Chinese leaves', this cabbage is a native Chinese plant. Although it is grown extensively in the north, it flourishes all over China. Around 2,000 local varieties are grown, and differences in soil and weather conditions also combine to produce interesting differences in taste. Some are sweeter than others, some store better, some are suited to preserving, some have more moisture. In north-east China this cabbage is stored in large quantities by every household during the winter. It has a tall, cylindrical head. One variety available here is about 30 to 45 cm (12 to 18 in) tall; another is shorter and fatter and about 30 cm (12 in) tall, with a pale yellowish colour. Some British types of 'Chinese leaves' have green leaves, which are very often waterlogged. With this kind, after stir frying it is important to drain away the water. This cabbage is known as 'Shandong cabbage', 'Tiantsin cabbage' and 'Beijing cabbage', and many other names. The vegetable keeps well in the refrigerator for many weeks, or it can be hung in a cool, dry place. It tastes sweeter if the excess moisture is allowed to escape when it looks limp. It may be eaten raw, especially the heart, as is done in northern China; or it can be blanched and tossed in seasoned oil, or in fish sauces; or stir fried with meat, seafood, soaked dried shrimps, or with other vegetables such as mushrooms, bamboo shoots, or mange-tout. If boiled thoroughly, it makes a delicious soup with meat, and it also goes well with fish balls or seafood. In a famous Sichuan dish called 'hot-water cabbage', the cabbage heart is steamed in a strong clear stock. A well-known Shanghai dish is 'lion's head', in which large fried meat balls of a flattened shape are braised on a bed of this cabbage. Shredded Chinese cabbage is a good substitute for bean sprouts, either in a salad or in stir-fried dishes. 'Beijing pickled cabbage' is made with sliced cabbage, carrots, pears and apples and seasoned with salt, spring onion, garlic and chilli powder, covered in cooled boiled beef stock or water; it is weighted with a stone and kept in a warm place for two to four days. Another pickle from the north is *lahbaicai* or 'hot cabbage'. The sliced cabbage is salted, flavoured, and marinated with sesame oil that has been heated with spring onion, ginger, sugar, vinegar and a little water and cooled. Before serving, some freshly shredded ginger, spring onion, and chillis are sprinkled on and the pickling liquor poured over. This cabbage has been a subject of much pickling and preserving in China. (For its medicinal properties, see page 16.)

Chinese chives: a plant native to China, it is used both as a herb and a vegetable, and has been known from very ancient times. In an agricultural treatise of the sixth century AD there is a recipe for cooking scrambled eggs with chives. In northern China the arrival of its sweet and fragrant shoots in early spring is much appreciated after a long winter of preserved and dried vegetables. Poets have long noted the event as a sign of seasonal change. At the time the *Manual for the Common People* was being written in the seventh century, it became fashionable in the imperial palace for ministers and high officials to partake of spring chives in specially prepared rolls called *chunbing*, 'spring pasties'. Although available from spring to autumn, chives are neglected during the hot summer months, probably because of their strong flavour in the heat, and the profusion of other vegetables. Spring and autumn are the favourite seasons, but in subtropical areas the vegetable is available throughout the year. Known as 'the lazy man's vegetable', because no replanting is required, Chinese chives are dark green in colour, and have strong flat blades rather than the tubular kind of the European variety. The flowers are white with a hint of pale purple, unlike the pink balls of European chives. The fragrance is strong, the taste sweet and the texture chewy. The vegetable is cooked very quickly, about 1 minute's stir frying on high heat in hot oil. Overcooking would ruin its bright green colour, fragrance and sweet taste. Both the white part and the green blades are chopped into 2.5 cm (1 in) lengths. It may be stir fried with shredded meat or bean curds, or cooked with eggs in an omelette or scrambled; or with shrimps or shellfish, or on its own. It is used as a herb flavouring a meat filling in a dumpling, roll or pasty. If used in soup it is first stir fried briefly in hot oil and then added to a soup such as a *doufu* (bean curd) soup for contrasting colour just before serving. Sometimes it is eaten raw, when it is chopped fine and sprinkled on a dish as a flavouring. Another way is to blanch it in boiling water very briefly and toss in hot oil. In the northwestern regions of China such as Inner Mongolia and Qinghai provinces, where chives grow wild, they are preserved in salt and used as a flavouring for lamb and other meats. Incidentally, this vegetable together with garlic, onion and leeks are forbidden food to the Buddhist priesthood. They are considered a meat food. Chives are high in fibre. Chive flowers are also eaten; they are the tender buds of the plant before it blooms. Each succulent green stem has a conical, pale green-white bud at the tip. They are eaten in the same way as ordinary chives. The tougher end is broken off before chopping. In northern China chive flowers preserved in salt are always served with lamb fire pot or with plain boiled pork. (See also Chinese yellow chives, below.)

Chinese cole: this is also called 'Chinese white cabbage', and is another form of rape. It looks rather like Swiss chard, except that the white stem is rounded and crisp instead of flat and limp. Chinese cole is called *qingcai* in Mandarin, or *bokchoi* in Cantonese, the latter being most useful as Chinese greengrocers in Britain mostly understand it. This vegetable has been eaten in China since antiquity, and is still in everyday use. The white stalks are succulent and the leaves are tender, their taste quite delicious. The Chinese love this vegetable stir fried plain in seasoned hot oil; it cooks in about 2 minutes. It may also be stir fried with meat, prawns, or noodles or vermicelli. If used in soup, there are two ways: one is to pop it in a meat or mixed meat soup 2 minutes before serving, so that it is tender and a jade green; the other is to boil the whole leaves till very tender with pork or chicken and red dates. In China this vegetable is blanched and sun dried for winter use. The dried cole can be boiled in soup or braised with meat.

Chinese kale: Another member of the cabbage family, though with a difference. It is quite similar in taste to English Brussels tops (not Brussels sprouts), but it has white flowers instead of dark purple, and a white haze on its leaves. The stalks, which are rather stout, are peeled and sliced before cooking, and in fact they are considered more tasty and succulent than the leaves themselves. It tastes best stir fried in hot oil plain or with beef, prawns, pork or chicken.

Chinese radish: Also known as 'mouli' in English, the white radish is cylindrical in shape, as large and long as a cucumber; some may be larger. The skin is thin and shiny and the flesh is white, firm and solid. It tastes and smells like the round red salad radish, and is crisp and juicy. When choosing this radish, pick one that is heavy for its size; if not, the flesh will be pulpy and dry. It may be eaten raw or cooked. If eaten raw, the Chinese way is usually to sprinkle it with a little salt first, leave for a while, then rinse out and use it in a pickled salad or as a part of a cold platter. Sometimes, after soaking in brine, it is peeled and cut into paper-thin slices and used to roll up sticks of cooked ham, chicken, carrot, and cucumber which have been marinated in vinegar, sugar and salt, and serve it as an appetizer. This is particularly popular on the island of Formosa. It may be sliced or shredded and stir fried with meat, clams, or cockles. Or it may be diced in wedges and braised or boiled with stewing beef or pork with a piece of bruised ginger and sometimes with a few soaked dried shrimps to enrich the flavour. Shanghai boasts a dish in which finely shredded white radish is simmered with pan-fried small whole fish till the soup is milky white. Sichuan province in the south-west has a 'mock bird's nest soup', using white radish thinly sliced and finely shredded on one edge rather like the teeth of a comb; when cooked the slices look beguilingly like real bird's nest. This is the Chinese solution to the problem of a vegetarian bird's nest soup: the look and texture are excellent though not the taste – but the price is much lower. From Guangdong comes a savoury radish and rice pudding with minced roast pork, sausages and pounded dried shrimps. The tops are also eaten as a leaf vegetable. The white radish is one of the most preserved vegetables in China. Salted plain and dried, it is a popular vegetable for stir frying, boiling or braising with meat; even when preserved it retains its crisp texture. One kind preserved in soya bean paste and ginger is crisp, dark, and salty and sweet in taste. Another hot, sweet, sour and salty, has hot red chilli, ginger, leek and vinegar added. These preserved radishes are appetizing as a side dish or as a flavouring vegetable for meat and fish dishes.

Chinese spinach: The Chinese name is *xiancai*. It is not the same as Western spinach, and neither tastes nor looks much like it. It has a slender, pencil-like stalk from the tip of which sprouts a cluster of broad, oval leaves; one variety has red centres and another is completely green. The plants are sold with their roots, as they are pulled out at seedling stage; otherwise they would grow coxcomb-like seed heads. To cook: break off the leaves and break the stalks into 2.5–5 cm (1–2 in) lengths, peeling off the thin film of fibre at the same time. The tougher end should be discarded. This vegetable is stir fried starting with a cold wok and cold oil, not preheated. When it is put in, the heat can be raised and the spinach stir fried. This way it remains a beautiful green and tastes better. Sometimes shelled prawns or soaked dried shrimps are added. Or the vegetable can simply be put into boiling stock to make soup. Some classic examples are Chinese spinach with *doufu* soup, Chinese spinach with egg fuyung soup, and Chinese spinach and shredded meat soup.

Chinese yellow chives: these are Chinese chives (see above) grown in darkness. They have a colour, fragrance and taste which qualify them for a high place in the Chinese cuisine. In some market stores in southern China they are tied with red cotton threads and displayed in a prominent position; they fetch a higher price than other greens. Normally these yellow chives are reserved for banquets and feast days. They are used only as a complementary vegetable to seafood and meat. A well known Sichuan dish is yellow chives and pheasant rolls; from Shanghai come yellow chives stir-fried eel and yellow chives stir-fried eggs; and from Shandong farther to the north come yellow chives stir-fried razor clams and yellow chives stir-fried oysters. The chives must be stir fried briefly in hot oil before mixing with the separately cooked meat or seafood, as overcooking would ruin the texture and taste. Stir fried plain in oil, they appear as a lining vegetable at the base of a cold platter, or mixed with shredded salted jelly fish, or soaked and pounded dried shrimps, or cooled boiled rice noodles. This vegetable enhances the taste of poultry, fish, pork, beef, prawns and crab. In the north-western region of China they are chopped and sprinkled on to soups, soup noodles or noodles as a flavouring, and scattered on cold dishes. In the Zhejiang area they are indispensable flavouring for meat filling in dumplings and rolls, and they also appear in the spring rolls of Guangdong and Fujian provinces. However, yellow chives have suffered a chequered career, for in the Song time (960–1279), it was declared in the *Pen-Cao-Yen-I* ('Discourses upon Pharmaceutical Natural History') that yellow chives had not been grown in natural conditions and were therefore harmful to man, as they would obstruct the flow of the *qi*, or vital energy, in the body. Under the Ming emperors (1368–1644), yellow chives were produced in heated underground chambers at noble homes in the winter. The illustrious contemporary doctor and herbalist, Lee Shizhen, remarked that yellow chives were food for the rich only. Later the Ming Emperor prohibited the consumption of any hothouse food, the imperial edict proclaiming that 'anything out of season should not be eaten, it is harmful to health', and that almost 2,000 years before Confucius had said, 'What is not in season, do not eat.' All this brought about a 'yellow chives scare' – which was not without foundation as yellow chives needed heat, moisture and a soil enriched with manure, which were also perfect conditions for the growth of parasites. However, this could be overcome by thorough rinsing and cooking.

Chinese yellow flowering vegetable: this vegetable belongs to the cabbage family and is most closely related to the Chinese cole. Its Chinese name is *caisin* in Mandarin, *choysum* in Cantonese. Yellow flowers make this popular vegetable easily recognizable. It is eaten daily in the Chinese household, especially in the southern provinces. It can be stir fried plain in hot garlic-seasoned oil or with meat, fish or seafood; or added to noodles or soup noodles; or blanched and tossed in oil or oyster sauce or fish sauce; or served as a base for cooked meat. It is very quick cooking and quite delicious. When combined with other ingredients, it is usually stir fried first and mixed into food which has been separately cooked, to avoid overcooking it. The stalk should be stir fried for a minute before the leaves are added.

Chrysanthemum leaves: the Chinese name for this species of edible chrysanthemum is *tongkaucai*. The leaf looks rather like a lettuce leaf with rounded lobes. A wild strain which has a stronger resinous taste and herbal flavour is also eaten. Chrysanthemum leaves are eaten mainly on special occasions and feast days, either raw with cooked meat or as a vegetable for the fire pot. The leaves are separated before use. For a family soup they are put into the soup tureen and a boiling soup of meat and seafood is poured onto them and served immediately, for on contact with heat they shrink to nothingness. They are highly perishable, and should be eaten on the day of purchase.

Cucumber: the cucumber arrived in China during the first or second century AD and was named *hugua*, 'foreign gourd'. At this time the term *hu* applied to all things foreign, from the West. All kinds of foods carry this prefix, for example *hujiao*, peppercorns; *hulu*, bottle gourd; *husui*, coriander; *hudou*, walnut; and many others. The name was later changed from *hugua* to *huangua*, 'yellow gourd', by which it is now known. One of the probable reasons for changing it was to avoid sensitivity with the minority groups in the border areas during the time of their menacing robber leader Shihlo, a self-made man of Turkic descent (273–332), who carved out quite a bit of west and north-west China and assumed the title of 'King of Chao' in 319, and later proclaimed himself Emperor of the so-called Han dynasty in 328. There was and still is an etiquette of being careful not to refer to a lesser thing with the same prefix or suffix that may associate it with a greater personality, be it emperor, king, head of state, one's ancestors, parents or senior relations. What we think of as a green cucumber came to be called 'yellow gourd' because in ancient times cucumbers were picked only when they had matured to a golden yellow colour. In China today some cucumbers are still allowed to mature. This maturity gives a stronger taste and more fibrous texture, and the vegetable lends itself better to boiling and braising, thus extending its culinary scope. In China several varieties are grown. There are small cucumbers, about 5 to 8 cm (2 to 3 in) long, seedless and slender; forty of them weigh about 1 kg ($2\frac{1}{4}$ lb). This strain of cucumbers is grown both in the north and the south. In Guangdong they are known as 'tea cucumbers' and are preserved in sugar and soya sauce. In the north these little cucumbers are cooked in shrimp sauce (this may also be done with young zucchini). This strain was brought to China from the West, but it has been grown in Yangzhou for more than a thousand years. Ordinary green cucumbers are eaten raw or pickled, or finely shredded and sometimes mixed with noodles flavoured with soya bean paste and minced meat sauce. In villages raw cucumbers are dipped in sauces and eaten with rice. In Xian, in the north-west, the cucumber is sliced or scored unpeeled and slightly salted overnight. The next day it is rinsed and then seasoned with heated sesame oil flavoured with shredded spring onion, ginger, dried chilli, sugar, salt, rice wine, vinegar and a little water. This is crunchy and appetizing as a side dish or hors-d'oeuvre. In the north, cold pickled cucumbers flavoured with mustard are preferred. In the south much less flavouring is used; occasionally sugar, salt or soaked dried shrimps are added. Some favourite mixtures are shredded raw cucumbers with boiled and shredded pig's tripe, or with shredded cooked chicken meat or shredded boiled egg whites, or with boiled and sliced mung bean skin, or flavoured with a hot piquant or sweet and sour sauce. The matured cucumbers, sometimes available here, are boiled with meat in soup, or filled with meat and braised. Green cucumbers are also cooked to make soup, or stir fried with meat or seafood. Cucumbers are very much preserved in China: they are salted, or soaked in soya bean paste, sometimes with sugar and chilli powder added; some are preserved in plain soya sauce, some have chilli, sugar and ginger; another version is with sesame seeds; another has vinegar; and others have fermented rice added.

Leeks: a native of the region from western Asia to Xinjiang, these were introduced to China in the Han time (202 BC–AD 220). They are grown both in the south and in the north. In the south, leeks are in season from April to May, and in the north during August and September. They are eaten a great deal during the season. They can be sliced into strips, washed thoroughly, and stir fried plain in hot oil and salt for about 2 minutes; any longer and the sweet taste would be lost, and instead of fragrance there would be an unpleasant flavour. They may also be stir fried with shredded pork, beef or chicken, or cooked with fish. In the north, they are eaten raw with barbecued or roast meat, with pancakes or steamed bread. Leeks are also much preserved in China. They may be salted: one kind is preserved in hot salt and turns a deep red with a burnt flavour. Others are preserved in soya sauce, some with vinegar and sugar added; some are flavoured with rose petal sugar, or dried cassia flowers. These preserved leeks are eaten as a relish or used as a flavouring for meat and fish dishes. Leek buds, succulent and delicious, are also eaten as a vegetable, rather like Chinese chive flowers (see above). English leeks are equally good cooked in Chinese style.

Long beans: a native plant of India, Burma, Africa and Latin America, the long beans enjoy a warm climate and in China they are grown south of the Yellow River. These beans are about 30 to 90 cm (1 ft to 3 ft) long, tubular, and either whitish green or dark green in colour. There are twelve Chinese names for these beans: the more believable ones are 'long beans' (*changdou*), an apt name; 'belt beans' (like a Chinese fabric cord belt), and, 'apron-string beans'. They are also called 'red beans' (*hongdou*), as a common variety has red beans inside the pod. Numerous varieties with different coloured beans exist. They are related to the black-eyed beans; both are eaten as green vegetables when young, and as pulses when matured and dried. In other countries they are used mainly as pulses, but in China every part of the plant is eaten. The tender young leaves are cooked as vegetables after the stringy fibre has been removed. The young beans are broken into 4 cm (1½ in) lengths and blanched, then tossed in sesame oil, mustard, or sesame paste. Chopped ham, or soaked dried shrimps or minced Sichuan preserved vegetable may be added to give variety. Young beans may also be stir fried plain or with a little shredded pork, or with soaked dried shrimps. When matured, with tougher pods and fuller beans, they are braised with soya sauce. In the Zhejiang area rice noodles are added, or the beans are braised with pork. Rural people blanch the matured beans in the pods and dry them for winter use, particularly in Hubei province. The crisp dried beans in the pods are braised with pork; they make a plain but delicious dish which is also a useful source of protein and fibre. Also in Hubei, mature beans are preserved or fermented with chilli. Recently Hubei has produced an incredible hybrid about 80 to 110 cm (31 to 43 in) in length. Long beans were one of the famine foods included in a Ming *Manual for Salvation from Famine*, and the leaves have always been a standby food in hard times. The beans are still one of the most common and regularly eaten vegetables in the Chinese diet, inside or outside China. Needless to say, they are never included in any restaurant or banquet menu.

Lotus roots: the lotus is one of the many aquatic vegetables grown in China since antiquity. China grows three strains of lotuses for food: one for the seeds (see page 67), one with pink flowers whose roots are ground into flour, and one with white flowers whose roots are used as a vegetable. The best lotus roots come from Shandong province in the north-east. The lotus, *lian* in Mandarin, is a beautiful plant that has been the subject of painting and poetry throughout the ages. Its flower is the well known Buddhist symbol of enlightenment. The wonderful bloom with its roots in the mud also symbolizes purity and higher things in spite of a lowly background. It is often compared to a woman of humble origin who has risen to high station. Lotus flowers are not only admired but also eaten. In Sichuan, there is a dessert in which a mixture of honey date paste, crystallized melon and tangerine peel is rolled up in white lotus petals, dipped in beaten egg whites, deep fried and served with a rose-flavoured syrup. The seeds are eaten in soup or as a sweet paste in cakes and puddings. The leaves are used to wrap and steam food in, imparting a lovely fragrance. The root is also symbolic and a familiar subject for painters, for when a fresh root is cut, the pieces remain joined together by fine white threads which even survive boiling! This is a symbol of perpetual attachment or sentiment. One often sees paintings of a lotus root partly cut, with the cross-section showing the joining threads. The title would often be '*Ou-tuan si-lian*', meaning 'The lotus root is broken but the threads still hang.' This describes a situation where though people are separated the sentiment still clings. Botanically speaking, the root is not a true root but a rhizome, or underground stem. It is pinkish beige in colour, though fresh ones are covered in mud. It consists of a series of bulbous links which may be fatter than a cucumber and are joined together like a string of sausages, gradually tapering towards the end. Parallel hollow tubes run along the inside, arranged in circles so that when the root is cut it has a pleasing lacy look. To cook, first scrub and rinse, then peel thinly with a potato peeler. There are many uses in savoury and sweet dishes. One favourite dessert is whole lotus root filled with glutinous rice or mashed mung beans, steamed and served sliced with a syrup. In villages in Hubei province, whole lotus roots filled with glutinous rice steamed with whole lotus seeds and served with a syrup flavoured with cassia flower sugar are called 'two lotuses sweet as honey', *lian lian se mi*, which is a homonym to 'every year life is sweet as honey'. Hence this auspicious pudding is eaten at the New Year's Eve dinner in Hubei villages. Fresh, tender, succulent lotus roots are also eaten raw as a salad ingredient; or they may be blanched and tossed in a seasoned oil or sauce; or sliced or diced into chunks and boiled in a soup with pork; or braised with meat and peanuts, a favourite dish in Guangdong in the south; or they may be coated in batter and deep fried; or stir fried to accompany other food. A rather versatile vegetable. There are numerous other recipes for this versatile aquatic root. They are preserved in salt, or sometimes in salted soya bean paste and shredded ginger; some have sugar added. They are also dried (see page 66).

Papaya: although this is usually thought of as a fruit, it is often eaten as a vegetable. It is round, oval or pear-shaped. When immature and unripe, it is green and hard, but it turns orange and softens as it ripens. The skin is thin and the flesh is thick, smooth, sweet and delicious. It is best when still firm to the touch. Inside is a cavity filled with hundreds of caviar-like seeds which are scooped out before eating. Green, hard papayas are peeled, cored, diced and boiled in soup with pork or fish head or tail. As a sweet they are boiled or steamed with rock sugar, a favourite dish in the winter months. Unripe papayas also serve as ingredients for pickles in vinegar, sugar, salt and chilli. In China, the papaya grows in the tropical and subtropical south, whence it arrived from Mexico at the end of the Ming dynasty.

Pocai: this is a spinach. Its botanical name is *spinacia oleraced, L.* and it belongs to the goosefoot family. A native of Persia, it was introduced to China in the Tang period. *Pocai* is delicious stir fried in hot oil for 2 minutes or put into a soup. Plain stir fried *pocai* is used to line a plate and separately cooked meat is piled on top. Or it can be blanched and tossed in garlic-seasoned oil and salt, or mixed with blanched bean-curd skin and tossed in a sauce of sesame paste, vinegar and salt, an ancient recipe. The addition of soaked dried shrimps, chopped ham, rice noodles or mung-bean vermicelli turns it into a self-contained meal. *Pocai* is also used as a filling for steamed bread rolls and dumplings, on its own or with meat. The bright green colour of the vegetable is highly decorative. There is a well-known green and white dish: stir-fried purée of *pocai* with stir-fried purée of chicken breast served side by side, originally a Fujian recipe. Multi-coloured meat balls are made: pork balls rolled in a mixture of finely shredded *pocai*, bamboo shoots, black mushrooms, cooked ham and cooked chicken meat, steamed and served with a thickened sauce. Sichuan has a speciality of green meat dumplings, *pojiao*; coloured with *pocai* juice. In the north and north-west, noodles and pastry are often coloured green with *pocai* juice. The vegetable is not suitable for preserving in salt, but it is blanched and sun dried for winter use.

Swatow mustard greens: the Chinese names for this vegetable are *jiehcai* in Mandarin and *kaaichoi* in Cantonese. Another member of the cabbage family, it is related to the Sichuan mustard plant which is grown for its oil; all these mustard plants are called *hsiaoyucai* or 'lesser oil plants' in China. This plant looks like a lettuce that has gone wrong. The mustard plant has a distinctive taste unlike that of its other relations in the cabbage family: a strong, pungent, slightly bitter flavour which leaves a pleasurable and appetizing aftertaste. Many local varieties are grown in China, and even those available here defy description; but have a flat, fat stalk and are pale green in colour. It may be stir fried plain or with meat, boiled or braised in soup with pork. It can be well boiled to make a cooling soup. It is much preserved in China; when salted and fermented it has an appetizing sour tang.

Sweet potatoes: hundreds of local varieties of these are grown in the world. Some have flesh as bright orange as egg yolks, sweet and delicious; others are creamy white or white streaked with orange. Various types are grown in China: the main kinds are white, red and golden. A native of America, sweet potatoes and other New World vegetables reached China before the mid-sixteenth century, from either India or Burma, through Yunnan and Guangsi in south-west China and through the seaports of Fujian in the south. The Chinese name is *faanshu*, 'foreign tubers', the prefix *faan* meaning 'barbarian' or 'foreign'. In the Ming period (1368–1650) it was applied to foreign goods entering China by sea. Since its introduction, the sweet potato has become very popular indeed; it is grown all over China, and has become the third most important food crop after rice and wheat. Not only has it had a great effect on the Chinese diet, but it has also helped to sustain the growth of the rural population. It is used both as a staple food like a cereal, and as a vegetable. High yielding and nutritious, it has a pleasantly sweet flavour. Sometimes sweet potatoes are boiled or roasted in their jackets on an open fire, then eaten with salted fish and salted vegetables. Peeled, cut up, and boiled with rice to make a 'potato porridge', they are taken with salted fish, preserved meat or vegetables. They make a satisfying breakfast or lunch for rural people. In a year of poor harvests sweet potatoes may well be staple for dinner too. Sometimes they are boiled with salted sour vegetables for a soup, or plain boiled as a sweet snack with a piece of ginger 'to expel the wind'. They can be made into appetizing pastries and cakes. The young shoots or leaves of the potato plant are also a delicious vegetable, sweet and tasty when stir fried in hot oil with salt, or blanched and tossed in hot garlic-seasoned oil. Although this is strictly a rural delicacy and is classified as a standby famine food, it can be quite tasty. Normally the green parts of the plants are boiled as pig feed.

Taro: Chinese names for the taro are *yutau* in Mandarin and *wootau* in Cantonese. It is a brown, hairy tuber, oval in shape with encircling rings where the stems have grown. Strictly speaking, the tuber is a part of the stem and not a root. Some taros have bright pink buds on them and from these buds new bushes would grow. There are two varieties on sale in this country: the large 'areca nut' taro of about 10 to 12 cm (4 to 5 in) diameter and the smaller egg-sized ones. Taros have a delicious, subtle taste and some have a stronger fragrance than others. The colour of the flesh ranges from white to mottled purple, the Chinese liking the latter which has more taste; its flesh resembles that of a cut areca nut, hence its name. When peeled the taro is slimy, and if held it often produces rashes and itches on the hands owing to the presence of oxalate crystals. For this reason it must be thoroughly cooked, or the tongue and the throat may suffer; and for the same reason the Chinese more often than not precook taro whole, whether it is large or small, in boiling water, then peel and slice it for use in further cooking. Taro is a popular food with the Chinese. It may be eaten as a vegetable steamed or braised with meat, boiled in soup, or made into sweet or savoury puddings or cakes. Or it may be sautéd, stewed or deep fried. When sliced and deep fried it may be eaten as a snack. It can also be braised or steamed with red-cooked pork. To choose, pick one light for its size. The taro is a semi-aquatic, tropical plant, thriving in swampy soil. It is probably a native of South-East Asia. The warm, wet subtropical south of China is well suited to its cultivation. It is believed to have been domesticated in China as a staple food before rice, which was originally a weed in the taro fields. Taro and yams (a different species altogether) are surmised to be the first foods domesticated before cereals in southern China. The popularity of both taro and yam suffered a setback on the arrival of the sweet potato from America in the sixteenth century. But while the sweet potato is mainly a staple supplementing cereals, the taro and yam are more versatile foods. However, taro, yam and the sweet potato remain valuable famine foods in China, since they are less vulnerable than cereals to floods, locusts and other natural disasters. The stems of taro when peeled and chopped may be boiled in soup or braised as a vegetable, and are often eaten by the rural people. But in times of plenty the leaves and stems are usually boiled with those of the sweet potato plant as pig feed.

Water chestnuts: the bulb of a marsh plant, this is another aquatic vegetable grown in southern China. Brown, hairy, tough-skinned and the size of a walnut, it is usually sold covered in mud to prevent it from drying out. It has an agreeably crunchy texture. The Chinese name is *mati* in Mandarin, meaning 'horse's hooves', referring to its colour, texture and shape. Water chestnuts must be washed, peeled and rinsed thoroughly before eating as the rough skin harbours waterborne parasites. They are eaten raw like a fruit or sliced and stir fried in a mixed vegetarian dish, or with meat or seafood. They may also be boiled in a soup with meat or offal. But the Chinese much prefer them chopped up in a minced meat mixture as a filling for dumplings and rolls. They may be shredded, mixed with rice flour and sugar and steamed to make a cake which is a favourite with the Cantonese for the spring festival. Canned ones retain the texture but not the taste or flavour. Water-chestnut starch is a thickener and an ingredient for cakes and puddings.

Water spinach: this is one of the aquatic vegetables grown in southern China. It is related to the morning glory flower and does not taste like spinach at all. One Chinese name is *kongsincai*, meaning 'empty-stemmed vegetable', since it has a jointed hollow stem. The long stems carry leaves of an arrowhead shape. When cooked they turn slightly slimy, not unlike the tender shoots of the sweet potatoes which belong to the same family. Both have clusters of little bell-shaped white flowers reminiscent of the morning glory. One variety with smaller and more abundant leaves is grown on land, but there is no real difference in taste. Water spinach is grown in a shallow pond adjacent to the pigsty. The water used to wash the pigs and their sty fertilizes the vegetable. Usually the part near the pigsty is used for an aquatic plant for the pig's feed and the part farther away is used for water spinach. The Chinese never eat this vegetable raw, obviously because of the danger of waterborne parasites, and in any case it tastes better when cooked. The stems are broken into 2.5 cm (1 in) long pieces and stir fried for 2 minutes in hot oil seasoned with garlic and salt, sometimes with soaked dried shrimps and chopped hot red chillis. A favourite method is to stir fry them with sliced beef and shrimp sauce. One simple way is to blanch them whole and pour garlic-and-salt-seasoned hot oil over them. They are also blanched whole and served with pork stewed in fermented red bean curd, a favourite dish of Fujian province.

Winter melon: known as *donggua* in Mandarin, it is a native of Thailand, Malaya and Java and reached China some time before AD 419, through Yunnan and Guangsi in the south-west. The winter melon is huge, even larger than its relation the watermelon; some may grow to about 45 kg (100 lb) in weight. They are often sold cut up, like pumpkins. Dark skinned and hard rinded, with smooth, white flesh, the melon is covered in a layer of white powder when mature; hence is also called *baigua* or 'white melon' in Mandarin. It is a favourite for the banqueting table: skilful chefs carve appropriate scenery, symbolic flowers and birds or other designs on the outside and fill the inside, when the seeds and coarse fibre are scooped out, with meat, whole boned duck, or chicken, or pigeons, black mushrooms for contrasting colour and flavour, and presoaked lotus seeds, lily bulbs, pearl barley; or any other mixture. A favourite filling is the 'Eight Treasures' mixture (eight items of various food). 'Winter melon bowl', *dongguazhong* in Mandarin (also often translated as 'winter melon pond'), is made by steaming a filled melon till the contents are tender. To eat, the contents are served in individual bowls at table, and then the melon flesh is scooped out with a spoon and placed in each bowl. Another high table winter melon dish is *baiyu cangzhen*, 'white jade with hidden treasures'. This is a thick square of melon with corners rounded, thinly peeled so that it looks faintly green. A small hole is made on one side and filled with a deep-fried and seasoned mixture of duck's gizzards, chicken meat with soaked dried scallops, ham, black mushrooms, etc., or any other mixture. The cut-out melon pieces are replaced over the hole, and the filled block of melon is steamed in a bowl, cut side up, till tender. To serve it is turned inverted into a soup tureen and a boiling-hot stock is poured over. For ordinary family meals the winter melon is invariably a soup ingredient. It is always cut in large chunks and boiled or simmered as a soup with pork rib bones, pork meat, chicken, duck or pigeon, and flavoured with black mushrooms, or with dried shrimps, dried oysters, dried squids or salted radishes. The only limit to the variety is the imagination of the cook. The Chinese never attempt to stir fry winter melon; it would turn into a watery mush. But those grown in the south of China, dark skinned with dense white flesh, are preserved in salt and sugar. Crystallized melon is used as a confection or as filling in cakes and puddings such as winter melon cakes, or the 'Eight Treasures' pudding.

Fruits

Fresh, dried, or preserved in sugar or salt, fruits are mostly eaten as snacks. The following are commonly eaten by the Chinese:

peach, plum, pear, haw (*shanzha*, only eaten preserved), persimmon, strawberry, loquat (*pipa*), jujube, fig, grape, litchi, longan, papaya, mango, pineapple, banana, kanlan (Chinese olive), apple, many varieties of orange and tangerine including kumquat, and other citrus fruits including pomelo and Buddha's hands citron.

Preliminary Preparations

Cutting the Ingredients

Cutting ingredients thin and small is characteristic of Chinese cooking, and it is regarded as a feature of fine cuisine. Chinese culinary art in the Chou time (1027–256 BC) was known as *ge-peng* or 'cut and cook', a term incidentally still used in Japan. It is said that an expert chef once cut fish slices so thin that when a strong wind blew they flew into the sky like snowflakes. From the cooking point of view, cutting the ingredients small allows better absorption of flavourings and faster cooking. Neat slicing and cutting produce a more attractive and appetizing dish. Moreover, bite-sized food is better managed with chopsticks.

The main consideration when cutting a given ingredient is the nature of the food; how it is going to be cooked and what ingredients it is to be combined with. Tough meats are cut into chunks so as to absorb liquid when cooked and become tender. Moderately tough meat may be minced to make it tender and so that it combines well with flavourings and other ingredients. Tender cuts are better finely sliced and quickly stir fried so that their delicate texture and taste are preserved. Foods for stir frying and steaming are cut small so that the heat penetrates them well. Uniformity in size and shape is important for even cooking and for the look of the finished dish. Usually the main ingredient decides how the dish is going to appear. Shredded meat is usually stir fried with shredded vegetables, peas with similar-sized diced meat, matchstick-sized meat with shredded bamboo shoots, Chinese chives with meat slivers and so on.

With beef and lamb every trace of visible fat or sinew is removed before slicing, as the Chinese regard beef and lamb fat as malodorous. Beef is usually cut across the grain which makes it more tender. Lean good braising steak, without marbled fat, when sliced across the grain, is excellent for stir-fried or quick-fried dishes. But tender chicken meat is cut with the grain.

The Chinese cutting techniques are:

Straight vertical slicing: the knife is held vertically and straight over the

Straight vertical slicing   Roll cutting

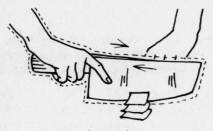

Saw cutting   Flat slicing

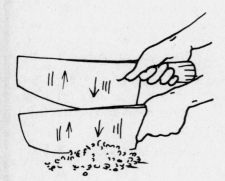

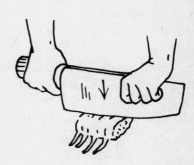

Mincing with two choppers   Hay cutting a piece of meat with small bones

Hay cutting spices

89

ingredient. This is used on soft, tender ingredients such as liver, scallops and mushrooms. (See illustration.)

Diagonal slicing: used on tough meat and fibrous vegatables. The knife is held at an angle of 60 degrees to the ingredient (for example spring onion, white, young leek, cucumber, asparagus, French beans) which is cut into 2.5 cm (1 in) pieces.

Roll cutting: a variation of diagonal cutting, but in this the ingredients are usually root vegetables such as yams, taros, carrots and turnips, to be used in slow cooking. Make a diagonal cut of about 4 cm (1⅝ in) across one end of the vegetable, roll it a quarter turn, make a second diagonal cut of the same length, and continue rolling and cutting to the end. (See illustration.)

Saw cutting: a method of finely slicing meat with a slow and gentle sawing action. The meat is frozen or chilled until firm before cutting into paper-thin slices such as are required for the Mongolian fire pot and Mongolian grill dishes. (See illustration.)

Flat slicing: done by holding the knife blade horizontally parallel to the ingredient and slicing from right to left. This is usually used on soft ingredients such as *doufu* and cold jellied meat. (See illustration.)

Dicing: the ingredient is cut into cubes. In Chinese cooking there are three sizes: cubes of about 4 to 5 cm (1½ to 2 in) are for deep frying and slow cooking; dice ranging from 0.3 to 1.3 cm (⅛ to ½ in) are usually for stir-frying; and fine dice or 'mince dice from 0.1 to 0.3 cm (1/16 to ⅛ in) are used in steaming and for fillings. The ingredient is cut into appropriate-sized strips and then cut crosswise into cubes or dice.

Shredding: similar to *julienne* in Western cuisine. The ingredient is cut into strips about 0.3 cm (⅛ in) thick and 5 to 8 cm (2 to 3 in) long. Sometimes it is called 'matchstick size'. Cut the meat into 0.3 cm (⅛ in) slices, stack these together and cut into strips.

Sliver cutting: similar to shredding but coarser. The food is sliced about 0.5 cm (⅕ in) thick, stacked together and cut into strips.

Mincing: also called fine chopping, and mostly used for meat. Either one or two choppers may be used. The meat is diced first and then chopped rhythmically from right to left and back. As the meat spreads out, flip it over with the knife and continue chopping. Repeat until it is reduced to an even, fine texture. This may be done in a food processor, but over-processing makes the mince dry. Hand-minced meat is lighter in texture. (See illustration.)

Crushing: smashing with the back of the chopper, as used for garlic, ginger and the stem of vegetables, to release their flavour or for easier penetration of seasonings.

Scoring: usually made on large cuts of meat or whole fish. Some shallow slashes are made on the surface to allow seasonings and heat to penetrate better. Often scoring lengthwise and crosswise in a regular criss-cross pattern is done on smaller ingredients such as pig's kidneys, chicken or duck gizzards, chicken breast meat, cuttlefish and squid for the same reasons, and also for decorative effect.

Hay cutting: the right hand holds the handle of the knife while the left hand holds the back of the blade towards the end and the cutting is done with a firm pressure. This gives better control and an accurate cut on foods such as crabs, boiled salted eggs in their shells or meat with small bones. Another way is to cut in a see–saw fashion, with the left and right ends going up and down alternately, as in the cutting of Sichuan peppercorns and similar spices. (See illustrations.)

Utensils in the Chinese Kitchen

Utensils for Chinese cooking are very simple. One can manage with the bare minimum of one saucepan for rice, one for boiling soup and a wok for everything else. Some equipment from the Western kitchen may be adapted for Chinese cooking: a large saucepan may be adapted for steaming; or steaming can be done by putting a sandwich cake tin in a wok; dariole moulds (castle pudding tins) can be used for Chinese cup cakes; slow-cooked dishes can be done in the oven; the possibilities are endless. However, real Chinese utensils are simple and efficient to use and give a great deal of pleasure in re-creating Chinese cuisine. Here is a list of basic equipment:

Brass mesh strainers: shallow fine brass strainers with long bamboo handles in a wide range of sizes. They are excellent for taking food out of hot oil or boiling water, so that the liquid may be used for further cooking. They also allow better control over smaller pieces of food in hot oil or boiling water. Some are large enough to hold a whole bird. The smallest are about the size of a Western soup spoon, completely made of fine brasswire, and are used for the cooking of food in the fire pot. Each diner has a strainer.

Chopper: a large, heavy knife looking like a butcher's cleaver, with a rectangular blade of tempered steel, and sometimes with a wooden handle. It is used in chopping bones and mincing. The thick, blunt top of the blade is used for pounding and tenderizing meat, crushing garlic, bruising ginger and so on. A lighter version with a thinner and narrower blade is used for slicing cooked or raw meat and vegetables. Choose a

91

carbon steel one rather than stainless steel, which is harder to sharpen.

Chopping block: a thick, sturdy, round solid piece of wood 5 to 10 cm (2 to 4 in) thick. Many sizes are available, and the large ones have stands. Chinese households usually have two: one for cooked foods and the other for raw. The raw-food chopping block is usually spread with a piece of fresh pork skin when mincing meat to protect the surface from chipping and avoid wood chips getting into the food. To season a new chopping block, rub it with water and salt, or soak it in brine.

Double saucepans: these have long handles. They are used for steaming soups, and especially for tonic food. The bottom saucepan is filled one-third full of water and the top one, with a cover, holds the food and cooking liquor.

Earthenware pot: its name, *saguo*, means 'sand pot', referring to its sandy texture on the outside; inside it is dark glazed. Some have wire netting on the outside for strengthening. *Saguo* come in various shapes and sizes; they are used for slow-cooked dishes, soup and tonic food. They can only be used on the stove or in the oven.

Fire pot: also called 'steamboat', a metal soup tureen with a built-in charcoal stove at the base. The soup is placed in the moat-shaped top round the chimney, which leads up from the stove. The cover has a hole to fit over the chimney. This is a special utensil for cooking the Mongolian fire pot or chrysanthemum fire pot dishes, in which the food is cooked by the diners at the table. Various sizes and qualities are available, and they may be made of iron, brass, stainless steel or aluminium. (Silver ones were used in the imperial palace.) Nowadays electrically heated ones are available, but the flex looks ugly and gets in the way.

Long chopsticks: special thick, long (about 35 cm, 14 in) chopsticks for the kitchen. They are useful in deep frying and other hot jobs. The Chinese use five or six ordinary chopsticks at once as an egg beater.

Metal steamers: these are a version of the bamboo steaming baskets with perforated bases, and usually comprise a set of two steamers with a bottom pot. Some are large enough to hold a whole bird.

Pot mat: a woven latticed bamboo mat put in the bottom of the pot to prevent sticking in slow-cooked dishes. A small plate may be used instead. A metal version, a round flat disc with perforated holes, is also available.

Rice pot: an ordinary metal pot, thick, heavy and with a tight-fitting lid, is perfect for the cooking of rice. Reliable automatic rice cookers are available, and may be used as a steamer or a stewing pot. But the Chinese always keep the rice pot for that purpose only.

Steaming baskets: cylindrical woven bamboo baskets with latticework bottoms which allow the steam to go through and cook the food. A lid is provided. This is a fuel saver as many baskets of food may be stacked together and steamed over a pot of boiling water – provided the food does not completely block the air holes in the latticework. The larger baskets may be used over a wok. They are completely washable, and should be dried away from heat.

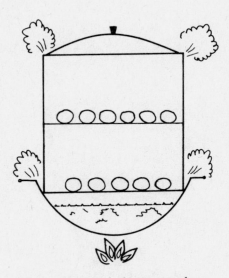

Large steaming baskets over a wok

Wok: a most versatile device – one can stir fry, sauté, deep fry, boil, braise or steam in it. It may be used for non-Chinese cooking, too, such as making omelettes or pancakes, or it can be filled with charcoal and turned into a barbecue grill. It is fat-saving, as the oil is collected at the base and the food being sautéed may be rested on the sloped sides, draining off excess oil to be used again. The high, smooth, sloping sides ensure even distribution of heat and prevent spilling when stir frying. Various qualities are available, and it may be of iron, stainless steel and aluminium. Iron is to be preferred, giving as it does better conduction and retention of heat; aluminium is not tough enough and is best avoided. The iron wok is also said to have taken care of the iron requirement in the Chinese diet. A metal ring can be used to hold the round-bottomed wok steady on a modern stove, and is often supplied with it. An iron spatula with rounded blade is sometimes also provided with the wok. When choosing a wok make sure it has a rounded bottom and the lid has a high spherical dome, the essentials of an efficient wok; particularly in steaming. For a small family a wok of 30 to 35 cm (12 to 14 in) diameter is sufficient. Most Chinese families have a large and a small one for different jobs. To season a new wok, thoroughly clean it with hot water and liquid detergent. Rinse thoroughly, dry and heat 2 tablespoons of cooking oil in it until hot. Swivel the wok round to cover the inside entirely with oil, then pour off the oil and wipe the wok with kitchen paper until it is smooth and shiny.

Cooking Methods

Chinese home cooking is mostly done on the stove. Traditionally, a large, thick iron wok, sometimes as much as 90 cm (3 ft) in diameter, is built into the top of a stove of pounded earth or bricks, heated by means of charcoal or firewood. In rural areas this arrangement still survives. Large woks are real fuel savers, as several items of food may be steamed together on a strong slatted bamboo tray which fits across the inside of the wok over boiling water. Nowadays with smaller families, and in urban areas where gas and electricity are laid on, smaller woks are popular. The oven is rarely used, except in professional cooking such as the roasting of Cantonese *charsiu*, barbecued pork, and Beijing duck. In some modern Chinese families, baking has been borrowed from the Western kitchen and some cakes are baked, as are *bao*, the buns which are traditionally steamed. This innovation is particularly true of Chinese settlers in the West, where ovens are common. These baked *bao* are now on sale in some Chinese shops here. Traditionally, baking was done only in northern China where *shaobing*, buns of yeasted wheat dough and sesame seeds, were baked, stuck to the sides of a pot-shaped oven; a method common in India, Pakistan and Iran, from which both the sesame seeds and the oven came.

Chinese cooking tends to be fast, especially the quick boiling and stir frying favoured in the southern and south-western provinces. However, in northern China slow-cooked, braised and simmered dishes prevail. These methods of cooking usually make use of residual heat, the dying fire barely kept alive after the cooking of the family meal. In the Chinese kitchen one may say that economy is the keyword. To save precious fuel food is cut into small pieces and cooked quickly. Long slow cooking tenderizes a tough cut and ensures that nothing is wasted. Most homes have besides the stove a covered terracotta urn for saving the glowing charcoal once cooking is over.

Although there are about ten thousand different dishes in the Chinese culinary repertoire, the basic cooking methods number around two dozen. Through these methods of preparation, application of heat and timing are achieved the four traditional criteria of fine Chinese cuisine:

colour, fragrance, flavour and texture. The cooking of food may be said to be applying the right amount of heat for the right length of time in the right way, which may be through the medium of heated water or oil, or by the dry heat of the oven. The subtlety of approach means that there are crucial differences from the West in sautéing, steaming, deep frying, braising and roasting. There are, in fact, no direct translations of the Chinese terms differentiating the various ways these can be employed. For example, all the various braising techniques practised by a Chinese cook end up in English as 'braising'. While the method itself is similar to braising in the West, the difference lies in the preparation of the ingredients, as well as the addition of seasonings and flavourings beforehand. Chinese terms clearly indicate to the cook or diner whether the dish is braised plain, thickened with a starch, braised with a dark soya sauce or with spices and wine, or whether it is pan fried, deep fried or raw before cooking.

*A cook in a senior official's household, Henan.
Northern Song dynasty (906–1126)*

The following are some of the cooking methods commonly employed in Chinese cuisine:

Boiling (*zhu*): boiling in water is an important process in Chinese cooking. Food, either raw or par-cooked, is put in plenty of water or stock and brought to the boil over high heat, then skimmed and allowed to cook on low heat. No thickening is needed for the soup that is produced by this method. An example of food cooked in this way is white chopped chicken.

Fast boiling (cuan): this method is boiling quickly in water or stock. The ingredients are small: sliced, shredded or made into balls. The stock or water is brought to the boil over high heat; then the ingredients are put in and the seasonings added. It is brought to the boil again and dished up immediately without thickening. Sometimes the ingredients and the cold water are put in at the same time, as in the cooking of meat balls. Another way is to cook the ingredients in boiling water or stock, drain and place them in a serving bowl, then pour over a well seasoned boiling stock, as in the cooking of noodle soup. Food cooked this way has plenty of clear soup and tastes fresh.

Plunging and rinsing (shua): this is cooking done at the table with the fire pot or 'steamboat' in the middle surrounded by raw, thinly sliced meat, fish, seafood and vegetables, raw noodles and dips and sauces. A strong, well flavoured boiling stock is put into this special pot, which has a built-in charcoal stove underneath. Each diner cooks his own food according to how well done he likes it. The food is put into a small individual brass mesh strainer and lowered into the stock; when it is done the strainer is lifted out. It is eaten with dips, sauces and seasoned salts. In northern China, it is eaten with steamed bread rolls and sweet pickled leeks. Care is taken not to put in too much food at a time, so that the temperature of the boiling stock is not lowered. When all the meat, fish and so on are eaten, the noodles or vermicelli are put in and the meal is rounded off with a noodle soup. This method of cooking originated in Mongolia and Manchuria; it was evolved from nomadic cooking and is known as 'Mongolian fire pot' in English or 'Genghis Khan fire pot' in Japan. It is an ideal cooking method in the winter months.

Meeting (hui): blending or cooking together several ingredients cut small. There are three ways of doing this: one is to heat the oil, season it with spring onion and ginger, then add other flavourings, stock or water and lastly the main ingredients, which have been sliced, diced or shredded; sometimes they have also been parboiled or deep fried. The food is then covered and simmered on low heat, and the cooking liquor is thickened before dishing up. Another way is to season the oil, add other flavourings and liquid, bring to the boil and thicken before putting in the main ingredients, par-cooked by boiling or deep frying. Food cooked this way is tender and succulent. The third way is to season the oil with spring onion and ginger, then add stock or water and seasonings. When the stock is boiling, the main ingredients are added. It is necessary to skim before dishing up. No thickening is used, for which reason the method is called 'clear meeting'. The cooking is done on high heat throughout.

Distilling (ao): the ingredients are small, sliced, diced or shredded. A little oil is put in the wok and heated – it may be seasoned with ginger and spring onion – the main ingredients are put in and briefly stir fried; then either stock or water is added. It is brought to the boil, covered and simmered on low heat until cooked. The juice is not thickened. This method is popular in home cooking.

Simmering (dun): this means simmering the food very slowly in plenty of water. The heat is conducted directly from the water but the food is cooked long and slowly with the water barely simmering, a bubble here and there. This is not unlike the French *pot au feu*. The ingredient is scalded in boiling water, refreshed in cold water, drained and placed in an earthenware pot (*saguo*) with plenty of water to cover; the proportion of food to water is 1 to 2. Seasonings are added. The water is brought to the boil, skimmed, the heat is reduced, then the pot is covered and left to barely simmer for around 2 to 3 hours. Usually the lid is sealed with moistened parchment or greaseproof paper. The soup is not thickened. The classic seasonings are spring onion, ginger and rice wine. Most tonic food is cooked in this way.

Steaming (zheng or dun): this plays an important part in Chinese home cooking as most Chinese households do not possess an oven. Reheating is done by steaming so that the original juice does not dry up and the food is not hardened by dry heat. Two methods of steaming are covered by the word *tun*, steaming in water and indirect steaming.

Indirect steaming (dun): done with the food not in direct contact with the source of heat, by a kind of *bain marie* method. The food is cooked in a closed container surrounded by boiling water, so that the liquor with the food is kept barely simmering. The food, which may be a whole piece of meat or poultry, is first scalded in boiling water to remove any odour. It is then put into an earthenware or enamel casserole or deep bowl. Seasonings (spring onion, ginger and rice wine) are added with stock or water to cover. The vessel is sealed with greaseproof paper and covered. It is placed in a larger pot, filled with water to about halfway up the side of the casserole; too much water would boil over on to the pot containing the food or cause it to float. Sometimes the inner pot sits on an upturned saucer or bowl to raise it slightly from the bottom of the steamer or outer pot. The outer pot is also covered tightly. The water is brought to the boil over a high heat and kept boiling on medium heat all through the cooking. The pot or steamer should be replenished regularly with boiling water, and should not be allowed to boil dry. The time taken is usually about 2 to 3 hours, depending on the size and nature of the food cooked (see illustration). This is quite similar to the steaming of British Christmas pudding, except that liquid is added to the food whereas the Christmas pudding is in a dry pudding basin. Food cooked in this way preserves its flavour as the liquid does not evaporate and is not diluted by the addition of any more water. The soup is clear and tasty. Tonic food with medicinal herbs is often cooked in this way. Double saucepans are also used to steam food in the same way; the only difference is that the saucepan containing the food is not entirely enclosed by the larger saucepan.

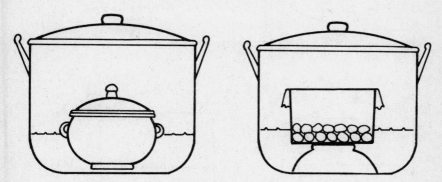

Indirect steaming: (left) *a covered pot inside a larger pot — note water level in outer pot;* (right) *food in a covered bowl steaming inside a large pot*

Direct steaming (*zheng*): in this form of steaming the food is normally exposed and comes into contact with the steam surrounding it. It is usually used for smaller ingredients such as fish, chicken, egg custard, minced meat cakes, meat balls, cakes and puddings which require a short cooking time from 5 minutes to 1 hour, depending on the size and the ingredients. This is most efficiently done in a wok, whose hemispherical domed cover allows free circulation of the steam. The food is put in a plate or bowl and stood on a rack which is placed at the bottom of the wok. The water should not be too high, which would flood the food, nor too low, so that it would not generate sufficient steam and would dry out far too quickly. There should be a space of at least about 2.5 cm (1 in) all round between the wok and the plate or bowl, so that the steam may circulate freely and cook the food. A large bamboo basket placed in a wok or saucepan is another excellent way of steaming food. A 35 cm (14 in) wok takes a 30 cm (12 in) basket nicely. Large and dry ingredients may be placed directly in the basket. It is usually lined with a damp piece of muslin to absorb excess moisture or prevent smaller pieces of food from falling through. The bamboo cover or the wok cover may be used; the latter has more room for a whole bird or a large piece of food. With steaming baskets it is possible to cook several baskets of food at once, stacking them together over a pot of boiling water, provided that airholes

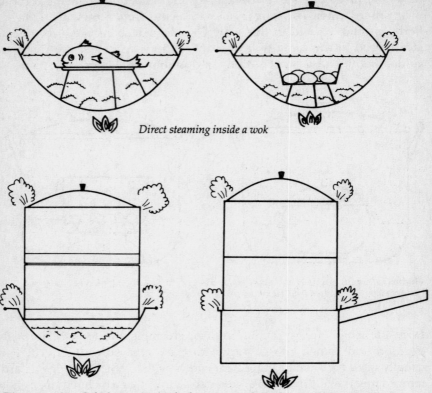

Direct steaming inside a wok

Direct steaming: (left) large steaming baskets over a wok; (right) smaller steaming baskets over a saucepan

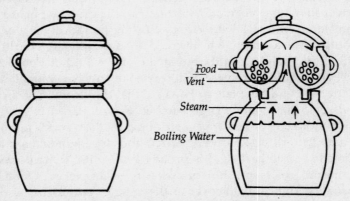

Food
Vent
Steam
Boiling Water

Steaming in a Yunnan qi-guo *on top of another pot*

are not completely blocked by food, and that the topmost basket is covered. The pot used should have a rim of a suitable width for the basket to sit on, so that it is not submerged in water. Metal steamers are also very efficient for steaming. Whatever equipment is chosen, it is important to make sure that the water in the pot or wok is replenished and not dried out during cooking (see illustrations). In the Chinese tradition there are two kinds of direct steaming: one is 'clear steaming' or *qin-zheng*, in which the ingredient is not given any kind of coating. It may be steamed with other ingredients: for example, a fish may be 'clear steamed' with shredded ginger, mushrooms, ham, and the like. In contrast, in 'floured steaming' or *fen-zheng*, the raw ingredient is marinated and then rolled in toasted, seasoned rice flour before steaming.

Braising (*men*): similar to steaming in water except that the ingredient is first brushed with a colouring such as dark soya sauce or caramel and then deep fried or pan fried till par-cooked instead of scalding in boiling water. After frying it is put into an earthenware or enamelled pot with some stock or water (not necessarily to cover), and the classic seasonings of dark soya sauce, sugar and spices (such as star anise seeds, cassia bark, and Sichuan peppercorns). It is brought to the boil, then the heat is reduced to very low, and it is covered and simmered till the meat is tender and the juice is dark red, reduced and thickened. The famous 'Tungpo meat' and its variants, and the Cantonese spiced braised beef are cooked in this way. Tough cuts of meat are most suitable for this treatment. Cooking time varies from $1\frac{1}{2}$ to 3 hours depending on the ingredients. Sometimes the meat is cut into chunks but normally it is cooked whole. This is popularly known in the West as the red-cooked method.

Waiting (*kau*): the word in the north-eastern dialect of China means waiting for a long time. In this method food is cooked through slow evaporation of the liquid. This method of cooking began among the Manchurian tribes when they led a nomadic life and had to cook in the wild where water was scarce and they could not keep adding precious water to a pot of boiling meat. Hence a long, slow cooking evolved, with some liquid which was gradually reduced to a very small amount. Originally game was cooked in this way. In this method the main ingredient is first either deep fried or sautéd, without a coating; then ginger, spring onion, seasoning and a suitable amount of stock are added. It is brought to the boil and simmered on medium heat till the liquid is reduced, then the heat is further reduced to low, and cooking continued till the juice is thickened. No extra thickening is required; instead, a little oil is added before serving. In the colder north more oil and heavier seasonings are used. In the south the seasonings tend to be on the sweet side. Food cooked in this way is dark red and shiny. Ingredients with a resilient texture are most suitable for this method, so that after long simmering they remain intact but become tender. Fish, prawns, poultry, meat and root vegetables are all suitable ingredients, but the simmering time for fish and prawns is much shorter, and very little liquid is added to these fast-cooking ingredients. Tender ingredients, for example fish, are left whole, and prawns are left unshelled. Tender chicken and fish need about 20 to 30 minutes cooking. Older birds and meat need about 40 minutes to 1 hour.

Stewing (wei): this is similar to the *tun* method of steaming in water by very slow simmering. The cooking time is around 4 to 5 hours, sometimes even longer, and the method is used for really tough ingredients such as beef tendons. Food cooked in this method usually acquires a sticky juice without thickening, as in stewed oxtail soup, where the proportion of liquid to solid is half and half. Unlike red-cooked or braised meat, which has little but thick rich sauce, stewed meat has a sticky but fresh-tasting soup and plenty of it.

Slow braising (pa): in the northern dialect *pa* means cooking through slow evaporation of the liquid, similar to *kau* ('waiting'). The difference is that the food is neatly cut and arranged in the pot after the oil is heated and seasoned with spring onion and ginger. Sometimes the ingredient has been precooked by boiling or steaming. Flavouring and stock are added. The cooking is done on low heat and the liquor is thickened with a starch.

Kau, wei and *pa*, three methods of 'braising', are prevalent in the north and north-east, as in the cooking of Shanghai, Beijing and Shandong.

Fry-stewing (shao): this means stewing after frying. A *shao* dish is normally sautéd, pan fried or deep fried, or steamed or boiled before seasoning and stock are added. It is brought to the boil over a high heat and cooked on low heat till the food is well flavoured. The heat is then raised and the juice is reduced. Sometimes the meat or fish is removed to a warmed serving dish before the juice is reduced separately.

Deep frying (zha): similar to deep frying in western cuisine. Plenty of oil is needed in proportion to the amount of food cooked. Normally the oil has to be heated to a very high temperature, at which a small cube of bread is browned immediately. In the Chinese tradition there are various ways of deep frying; sometimes the oil is not heated to a high temperature before the food is put in.

Warm oil	70–100°C (160–212°F)	no smoke, surface calm
Hot oil	110–170°C (230–340°F)	slight smoke, movements from side to centre
Very hot oil	180–220°C (360–430°F)	smoking, surface of oil is quiet, but it makes a crackling sound when stirred

Plain deep frying (*qinzha*): in this method the ingredient is marinated in soya sauce, rice wine and salt and no coating is needed. Liver, and duck or chicken liver or gizzard, are normally treated this way.

Dry deep frying (*kanzha*): the raw ingredient is marinated and then rolled in flour or coated in a batter before deep frying.

Soft deep frying (*ruanzha*): the ingredients are cut into slices or strips and then coated in batter. The oil must be moderately hot, about 180°C (360°F); if too hot the food would be burnt on the outside and uncooked inside, and if not hot enough the batter would fall off. Not too much food must be put in at once, or the temperature of the oil will fall too low. A pair of long cooking chopsticks is used to keep pieces of food separate in the oil. As soon as the coating is firm, the food is taken out and left to drain. It must not be left in the oil too long, or it will become greasy and the coating will fall off as the temperature of the oil drops. Then the oil is reheated to hot and the food is fried again till it turns golden. If the oil gets too hot, remove the wok from the heat. The first frying is to seal and firm the coating. The second frying further crisps it and cooks the food through. Food cooked in this way is crisp and golden on the outside and succulent inside; examples are deep- fried quail's eggs and button mushrooms.

Crisp deep frying (*suzha*): the food is either boiled or steamed first. A piece of meat or poultry that has been boned is coated with batter; if unboned it is left uncoated. The oil is heated very hot and the food is fried till the outer layer turns a deep golden colour. Food cooked in this way is crisp on the outside and succulent inside, for example, spicy crispy duck.

Paper-parcel deep frying (*zhibaozha*): the raw ingredients are boned and cut fine and seasoned with salt and rice wine, or other seasonings, then wrapped in clingfilm or greaseproof paper like an envelope. The oil is heated to fairly hot, 110°C (230°F). The parcels are put in, a few at a time, and when the temperature of the oil rises again and the parcels are cooked they rise to the top. An example is paper parcel chicken.

Crunchy deep frying (*cuizha*): the ingredient usually has a skin, for example, a chicken or duck; and it is sealed in boiling water first to close the pores and tighten the skin. Then it is brushed with maltose and hung up to dry in a cool, airy place. It is deep fried in hot oil, turning all the while so that the oil enters the cavity. When it is pale golden in colour the wok is removed from the heat and the food left to cook in the hot oil for a while for the heat to penetrate further but without burning the skin. An example is crispy skin chicken.

Flaky deep frying (*songzha*): sometimes raw ingredients are boned and cut into slices or diced, marinated and coated with egg batter, then slowly deep fried in *warm* oil till cooked. Ingredients cooked in this way swell and expand and become light and flaky.

Oil soaking (youjin): the ingredient used is tender and fresh. It is marinated and then put into very hot oil (220°C, 430°F). The pot is removed from the heat and the ingredient is allowed to soak in the hot oil till cooked. Food remains very moist and tender, and keeps its original colour. Fish and chicken are often cooked in this way.

Oil splashing (youfa): the raw ingredient is usually small, tender and easily cooked. It is marinated and placed in a metal colander. The oil is heated to smoking hot and ladled on to the ingredient in the colander until it is cooked, as in oil-splashed bean sprouts. Sometimes the ingredient is pre-steamed until just cooked and placed in a serving plate with shredded onion on top. Then smoking-hot oil is splashed on to the food, as in the classic oil-splashed chicken or fish – though these recipes are often translated into 'steamed chicken with spring onion' or 'steamed fish with spring onion' in English.

Quick-thickened gravy method (liu): food cooked by this method is probably one of the types of Chinese cooking best known in the West through the Chinese restaurants, apart from stir-fried dishes. There are two steps in this method: the first is to precook the ingredient by deep frying, boiling or steaming. The second step is to heat a little oil, season it with spring onion and ginger or garlic, rice wine, and so on, add stock or water and thicken it with a starch to make a smooth gravy which is poured onto the precooked food. Sometimes the gravy is made by thickening a stock without oil. Sometimes the precooked food is stirred into the gravy to heat through. If the ingredient is deep fried it is usually cut into slices, shreds, or dice. If it is boiled or steamed it may be left whole, as with a whole fish. The cooking is done on high heat and is fast work. Food cooked in this way is velvety and tender. There are three main thickened gravy methods:

Crispy and smooth method (cuiliu): the raw ingredient is coated in batter or rolled in flour and deep fried till crispy and golden, then a thickened gravy is poured over it. Sometimes sesame oil, or minced garlic, or vinegar is sprinkled on to the gravy first. Usually while the ingredient is being deep fried the gravy is made at the same time in a separate wok so that the piping hot ingredient will absorb the gravy better. If only one person is cooking, the ingredient may be kept hot in an oven; but if heated too long it may be overcooked and become dry. Food cooked by this method is crisp outside and moist inside, for example sweet and sour fish.

Slippery and smooth method (hualiu): the ingredient is boned and in small pieces. It is cut into slices, strips, shreds or cubes and coated in batter. It is then deep fried till par-cooked. Make a thickened gravy in a wok, stir in the par-cooked ingredient and heat through. Examples include the well-known sweet and sour pork, and fish slices in fermented rice. Pork is never eaten undercooked, and it is boiled first before deep frying.

Soft and smooth method (ruanliu): the ingredient is usually treated whole; this is mainly a method for fish. It is steamed or boiled in seasoned water (spring onion, ginger, rice wine and salt), drained and placed on a warmed plate, then a thickened gravy is poured over it. The gravy may be made by thickening a stock without oil. Food cooked in this way is tender and smooth, for example West Lake steamed carp in vinegar and boiled fish in piquant sauce.

Quick frying (bao): the ingredient is boned and cut into small pieces of even thickness and size. It is usually par-cooked by scalding in boiling water or oil. Next it is stir fried quickly over high heat in hot oil; then a little mixture of stock or water, seasonings and starch is stirred in. When the sauce is thickened and well mixed, it is dished up. Food cooked thus is almost dry. There are three ways of quick frying:

Quick frying in oil (youbao): the ingredient is cut small, scalded in boiling water, drained and deep fried till almost cooked. It is then stir fried in hot oil, and a mixture of water or stock, seasonings and starch is stirred in. The usual seasonings are spring onion, ginger, minced garlic, soya sauce, salt and rice wine. Sometimes the ingredient is not scalded in boiling water but coated in a batter before deep frying. Diced chicken meat or gizzards, shredded pork or shelled prawns are treated in this way.

Quick frying in salted soya-bean paste (jiangbao): this is similar to quick frying in oil but has a seasoning of salted soya-bean paste without starch. The oil is seasoned with this paste and other seasonings such as rice wine, ginger and chillies, before the par-cooked ingredient is stir fried in it and the liquid added. A dish cooked in this way is Sichuan pork with fish flavour.

Quick frying in spring onions (congbao): sometimes instead of salted bean paste, chopped spring onions are used, as in quick-fried spring onion and lamb, *congbao yangrou*, in which the fast-cooking lamb is not precooked.

Stir frying (chao): this is perhaps the method most used in Chinese home cooking to produce quickly made, nutritious and delicious everyday dishes. The fuel and oil consumption is slight and cooking time is short as the ingredient is cut small. The success of stir frying lies in the control of the heat. The amount of heat applied and the temperature depend on the ingredients. If the volume of food is large, it should be stir fried in several batches. The wok is preheated over high heat till really hot, and the oil is put in, heated and seasoned with garlic, or spring onion, ginger and salt before the main ingredient is added. Once the ingredient is in, it is tossed rapidly and vigorously. If it is too dry, a tablespoonful of water is sprinkled on to prevent sticking, charring or burning. If things get too hot, the wok should be taken off the heat, and stir frying continued. The wok is put back on the heat when it is at the right temperature again. With green vegetables a special technique is required. The vegetable must be fresh, tender and young. The stalks are separated from the leaves, peeled and sliced. The wok is preheated over high heat before the oil is put in and seasoned with garlic and salt. Salt is important here as it helps to brighten the green; if added later it does not. First the stalks are put in and tossed thoroughly and rapidly, and then the leaves; sometimes a tablespoonful of water is added, and the cover is put on immediately. After about 1 to 2 minutes the sound of boiling begins and steam comes puffing out at the sides; the cover is lifted and the food is stir fried briefly and dished up. Traditionally, the Chinese stir in a teaspoon or two of oil before dishing up to give the vegetables a glistening look. The cooking is done on high heat throughout. Beans are usually cooked slightly longer than other vegetables, for better taste and to make them more digestible. Stir frying is done so very quickly that it is necessary to have every ingredient handy, down to a mug of water for sprinkling. Small bits and pieces are best put in neat piles on a large plate so that nothing is missing when required. When mixed ingredients are stir fried together the fastest-cooking one is put in last. Normally the ingredients are cut more or less the same size for even cooking. But the fastest cooking or most fragile items may be cut larger, or the larger ones may be put in first. Stir frying is usually done minutes before eating. All the cutting and preparation are done well beforehand. Traditionally there are four main ways of stir frying:

Raw stir frying (senchao): the main ingredient is raw, and is not coated. It is stir fried in hot oil till par-cooked and the accompanying ingredients are added, or if they take a long time to cook they may be put in at the same time. Seasoning is added, and the food is rapidly stir fried till just cooked and dished up. Food cooked this way has hardly any juice and tastes fresh and tender. If the ingredients are slightly large and need more cooking, a little water is added so that it may be cooked through. But the water should only be added when the ingredients have lost their moisture.

Cooked stir frying (suchao): a large ingredient is precooked or par-cooked by boiling, steaming or deep frying. It is then sliced or diced and stir fried in hot oil. Accompanying ingredients are then added, followed by seasonings and some stock or water. It is stir fried to cook through and dished up. An example is Sichuan leek stir-fried pork.

Slippery stir frying (huachao): the ingredient is skinned, boned or shelled and cut into slices, shreds, strips or small cubes, or minced. Or it may be a small ingredient such as shelled prawns. It is then seasoned and coated with egg and starch and deep fried till par-cooked. (If a vegetable is used it is not coated but deep fried till crisp.) Then it is stir fried on high heat with accompanying ingredients, for example, stir-fried beef in oyster sauce.

Dry stir frying (kanchao): the ingredient is cut small but not coated. It is marinated and then stir fried in hot oil till the outside is brown, when accompanying ingredients and seasonings, usually hot salted soya-bean paste, or Sichuan peppercorns, or ground pepper, are added. The stir frying is continued till all the juice is evaporated or absorbed by the ingredients. Food cooked this way has no juice; it is dry, flavourful, crisp and slightly on the hot side, for example, dry stir-fried shredded beef from Sichuan.

Quick frying and stir frying in sauce (peng): the ingredient is small and may be coated in batter or uncoated. It may then be deep fried till golden, and the oil drained from the wok, which is left unrinsed and returned to the heat with a very little oil and the cooked ingredient. A mixture of a little liquid and seasonings (without starch) is added. The food is stir fried to heat through, and dished up. Prawns in their shells, or diced chicken, meat or fish are suitable ingredients.

Pan frying (jian): in this method a thick, flat-bottomed pan is heated on a low fire, and then the bottom of the pan is covered in a little oil. The ingredient is usually marinated first, and sometimes coated in batter or rolled in flour. Usually it is made into a flattened shape, arranged neatly in the pan and cooked on a low heat till one side is golden, then turned over and cooked on the other side. When both sides are golden, seasonings such as soya sauce, tomato ketchup, oyster sauce, sesame oil, or rice wine are added and mixed well. The cooking is continued for a minute and the food dished up. Sometimes no seasoning is added; instead a dip is served with the food, as with pan-fried fish. The heat must be kept low to avoid the oil being burnt or dried up and the food charred or partly uncooked. The low heat and slow frying gently cook the food through and crisp the outside.

Pan braising (guota): the ingredient is usually coated in batter and then cooked till golden on both sides on low heat in a flat-bottomed pan. Sometimes high heat is used. Then seasonings and a little stock are added. It is covered and cooked on low heat till the liquid has evaporated. The colour of food cooked this way is similar to that of pan-fried food but it is more crisp on the outside and succulent inside, for example, Beijing pan-braised *doufa* and Beijing pan-braised fish. Skinned fish fillet marinated and coated in batter may be pan braised.

Pan baking (guotie): similar to pan frying, but only one side is cooked till golden and the ingredient is usually in sandwiched layers and coated.

Roasting in the oven (kao): in the Chinese tradition there are two kinds of roasting: one is called 'closed-oven roasting', *anlukao*, in which the ingredient is hung up on a hook or threaded on to a skewer and roasted in a closed oven, as are Beijing duck and the Cantonese *charsiu* or barbecued pork. In the West, owing to the difference in design and size of ovens, it is more convenient to roast such items on a rack in a tray. The second form of roasting is 'open-fire roasting', *minglukao*. This is done over a charcoal stove on top of which is an iron grate. The ingredient is threaded on to a skewer and placed on the iron grate to cook, rather as on a Western barbecue. Examples are Mongolian grilled beef, Beijing grilled lamb and Yangzhou 'roast square'. Some special roasting methods are:

Salt roasting (yenji): the ingredient may be raw or par-cooked, then marinated, wind dried and wrapped in greaseproof paper. The wrapped ingredient is then put in a pot of preheated salt (usually course salt). This is a speciality of Cantonese cooking, as in the famous salt-roasted chicken. Food cooked this way has a crunchy skin, and is smooth and tender inside, flavourful and tasty.

Clay roasting (nikao): a unique form of roasting. The ingredient is marinated, and wrapped first in caul fat, then in lotus leaves, then in brown paper. Finally, the parcel is covered completely in moist clay. It is then put in a charcoal or wood fire to cook. Food cooked in this way has its flavour sealed in and is delicious and exotic; an example is Hangzhou 'clay chicken'.

Smoking (xun): the ingredient may be raw or cooked; raw ingredients are first marinated. The food is put on a rack (like a circular cake cooler) in a wok with the smoking materials (wood shavings, tea leaves, sugar-cane pulp, brown sugar) at the bottom of the wok. It is then placed on the stove to heat up, and the food is cooked and smoked at the same time. Normally smoking is done with food that has been steamed or deep fried first, and the smoking is only to give it colour and a smoky flavour, as with smoked eggs or smoked fish.

Steeping (lu): in this method a whole chicken or duck or a large cut of meat is cooked in spiced soya sauce or spiced and salted water. The spiced liquid is prepared first, then the food, raw or sometimes par-cooked or scalded in boiling water, is put in to cook on a very low heat, slowly simmering so that the flavour of the sauce penetrates the food. The same cooking liquor may be used for chicken, duck or other meat. It is used again and again and the spices and flavourings are renewed and adjusted from time to time. The older the spiced liquor the better is the flavour. It is known as 'master sauce'. The spices used vary slightly from region to region. In Guangdong in the south, they use a 'white' steeping liquor without the addition of soya sauce, but instead with salt; and a 'red' steeping liquor with soya sauce. In the south more spices are used; in Zhejiang and the north less spices are used but more ginger and spring onion, and also *hongqu*, red rice (a medicinal rice preparation, also used as a colouring), which gives the liquor a dark purplish tint.

Stewing in a thick sauce (jiang): this is slightly different from steeping in a master sauce. The raw ingredient is first rubbed with salt and marinated, then brushed with soya sauce before being put into a liquor made of soya sauce, sugar, rice wine and spices, and stewed on low heat. There is less cooking liquor, and it is not kept. Usually when the ingredient is cooked it is taken out, and the sauce is reduced to thicken it and used to brush the cooked ingredient or poured over it.

Cold mixing (ban): the ingredient may be raw, or cooked and cooled. Meat is always cooked, vegetables may be raw or cooked. It is cut into shreds, strips, slices or cubes, and mixed with a seasoning sauce. Normally the seasonings are soya sauce, vinegar, sesame oil and various spices. In this much depends upon personal taste: flavourings such as minced garlic, ginger juice, chilli powder, shredded chilli, ground peppercorns, sesame paste and sugar may be used.

Hot Salading (qiang): the Chinese culinary term means to boil meat or vegetables in water till just cooked and then dress them with seasonings. The raw ingredient is cut into shreds, slices, strips or little cubes and then either boiled in water or deep fried briefly in hot oil. While still hot it is tossed in a seasoning mixture, the main ingredients of which are usually Sichuan peppercorn oil, ground Sichuan pepper or fresh Sichuan peppercorns. The seasonings are mixed with the cooked hot ingredient for better penetration of flavour.

Pickling with salt (yenyan): The ingredient is either rubbed with salt or marinated in brine. This is the most basic method of pickling. When an ingredient is salted it loses its moisture, and has a salty taste but retains its freshness and crisp texture, as with salt-pickled white salad cabbage, carrots or cucumber. Many Chinese pickles are made by this method, for example, Beijing pickled cabbage.

Drunken pickling (zuiyan): the main seasonings are wine and salt. The ingredient used may be raw or cooked, and the technique is called 'raw drunk' or 'cooked drunk' respectively; or it may be 'red drunk' when soya sauce is added and 'white drunk' when salt only is used. In the 'raw drunk' method, which is used for such things as crabs, the creature is pickled alive; but this needs great professional skill and high standard of hygiene. The food is ready after three days. A simple dish easily attainable by non-professionals is 'drunken chicken', in which white chopped chicken meat is pickled in wine overnight.

Fermented rice pickling (*zaoyan*): the main seasoning ingredients are fermented rice and salt. The ingredient is boiled or steamed, cooled and then quartered and marinated in salt and wine till well flavoured, a couple of hours. It is then marinated in a mixture of fermented rice with seasonings such as 'five spices' and sugar for an hour, when it is chopped into bite-sized pieces and served. Pork, chicken and duck are suitable ingredients.

Candy flossing (*basi*): literally this means 'pulling the threads'. It is a popular method of preparing dessert in the north. Fresh and dried fruits, nuts and root vegetables such as yams, taros, sweet potatoes and lotus roots are suitable ingredients. The ingredient is cut into small pieces or made into balls, and sometimes rolled in flour or coated in batter. It is then deep fried, boiled or steamed till cooked. Meanwhile a sugar caramel is made with either water or oil till it can be drawn into threads, the hot cooked ingredient is added immediately and it is served at once. Food cooked this way is crisp, sweet and tasty; examples are candied bananas, candied apples and candied yams. Normally two persons would work together, one making the floss and the other cooking the main ingredient.

Frost coating (*guashuang*): This is bare minimum icing or frosting: a small amount of sugar is used. The ingredient is cut small or made into balls. It is then deep fried and rolled in icing sugar while still hot, or sprinkled with icing sugar. Another way is to make a sugar syrup with a little water and heat it to just before the thread stage, when the deep-fried ingredient is added, stirred to coat it and taken out. When cold it is covered in a layer of frosting. Sometimes the food is rolled in sugar again while still warm, as with frosted barbecued spare ribs and frosted egg slices.

Honeyed syrup coating (*mizhi*): this is used in the cooking of a sweet dish with a juice. Usually the sugar is stir fried briefly in a little oil and a little water or, better still, honey is added and mixed well. The main ingredient is now added and cooked in the juice on a slow heat till the syrup begins to bubble, then it is dished up. Bananas, apples, yams and taros are quick-cooking and suitable ingredients. Another way is to steam the main ingredient with either sugar or rock sugar with a little honey till cooked. The steaming liquor is drained, reduced to a thick syrup and poured over the cooked food; sometimes it is thickened with a little starch. This is usually applied to easily cooked ingredients, such as ham or lotus seeds. Food cooked in this way is most flavourful.

A Selection
of Recipes

For information on and the preparation of some Chinese ingredients, see the sections on Ingredients (pages 46–87) and on Preparation of Some Chinese Ingredients (pages 222–229).

Cold hors d'oeuvres

Chinese dinners for special occasions more often than not begin with a cold platter: an assortment of cold cooked meats, seafood, eggs both fresh and preserved, and pickled vegetables. It may be elaborate or simple consisting of only preserved eggs and pickled vegetables. The following are some suggestions:

salted eggs (steamed or boiled)
cooked ham, barbecued or white cooked pork, boiled beef
braised pig's tripe, tongue, liver
cold roast duck breast, cold cooked chicken breast
cold steamed prawns
cold steamed winter mushrooms, or braised mushrooms
salted jellyfish
'hundred-year-old eggs' (boiled, shelled and quartered)
squid (scalded, scored and sliced)
chinese sausages (steamed and sliced)
pickled vegetables: carrots, stem ginger, radishes, Chinese white radish
   (mouli), cucumbers, white cabbage, or mixed pickles
fresh vegetables: cucumbers, tomatoes
quail eggs (steamed or deep fried)
steamed egg-yolk cake (see page 112)
cold boiled lobsters
cold deep-fried crab's claws

111

SUNFLOWER COLD PLATTER (SHANGHAI)

80 g (3 oz) each of the following:
cooked chicken breast
roast duck breast
cooked ham
cooked white pork
cooked braised gizzard
cooked beef (roasted or boiled)
braised winter mushrooms
pickled cucumbers
dark braised pig's liver
cooked prawns in the shells (fried or boiled)

30 g (1 oz) each of the following:
cooked green peas
cooked button mushrooms
cooked and shelled prawns

900 g (2 lb) potatoes (boiled and diced)
4 small lettuce leaves
egg-yolk cake (see below)
mayonnaise

1. Slice the first 8 items thinly and neatly. Arrange the slices overlapping and in blocks of contrasting colours round a 36 cm (14 in) plate, leaving the rim of the plate clear.
2. Slice the liver into 20 thin slices and arrange them in an inner circle. Make a potato salad with the boiled and diced potato mixed with mayonnaise and heap it in the centre in a mound. Stick the unshelled prawns into the potato mound around the edge, with the tails out, forming a circle.
3. Carve the egg-yolk cake into semicircles and cut 25 thin slices from it for the sunflower petals. Space the lettuce leaves evenly around the rim of the plate to represent the sunflower leaves. Put the egg slices all around the rim of the plate surrounding the meat slices, and on top of the lettuce leaves.
4. Shred the rest of the egg-yolk cake finely and sprinkle it round the prawn circle; scatter some on the potato salad. Then scatter the button mushrooms, green peas and cooked shelled prawns over the potato salad.

Egg-yolk cake
5 egg yolks
5 eggs
2 tsp rice wine
½ tsp salt

Beat all the ingredients lightly in a bowl, cover and steam till cooked, about 10 minutes. Cool and use as required. It may be cut into cubes, diamonds or shreds, or carved into shapes for decorating cold platters.

Shanghai cooking excels in cold platter dishes. This one is simple to prepare and most suitable for the buffet table. There is no fixed rule as to the number and kinds of ingredients used.

BANG-BANG CHICKEN (SHANGHAI)

110 g (4 oz) cooked chicken breast (skinned)
110 g (4 oz) mung-bean skin

Sauce:
1 tbsp sesame oil
1 stalk spring onion (chopped)
1 tbsp light soya sauce
1 tbsp sugar
1 tbsp vinegar
1 tbsp sesame paste
2 tbsp chilli oil

1. Mix together all the seasoning ingredients for the sauce, and set aside.
2. Boil the mung-bean skin till cooked, about 2 minutes. Drain and cut into strips about 5 cm (2 in) long by 1.3 cm (½ in) wide. Mix in a pinch of salt and a little sesame oil. Put on a serving plate.
3. With a meat mallet or rolling pin, gently beat the meat to loosen the fibre. Tear into shreds. Place them on top of the mung-bean strips. Pour the sauce over and serve.

This is a simple and popular appetizer for all seasons. The name is not an English joke: *bang* means a wooden stick for beating meat.

CANTONESE RED STEEPED DUCK (GUANGDONG)

Mixed spice bag:
14 whole star anise seeds
4 5 cm (2 in) pieces cassia bark
3 slices liquorice root
10 cloves
3 5 cm (2 in) pieces tangerine peel
1 pod ovoid cardamom
4 slices dried ginger

1 tbsp fennel
1 tbsp Sichuan peppercorns

Seasoning for oil:
4 slices ginger (bruised)
2 stalks spring onion whites (whole)

Seasoning for sauce:
570 ml (1 pint) dark soya sauce
140 g (5 fl oz) light soya sauce
230 ml (8 fl oz) rice wine
230 g (8 oz) sugar
1 tbsp salt

1 tbsp cooking oil

1. Tie the spices in two layers of muslin. Heat a thick-based enamelled or stainless steel pot over medium heat, and stir fry the ginger and spring onion whites till fragrant. Pour in the seasonings for the sauce, 850 ml (1½ pt) water and the spice bag. Stir to dissolve the sugar. Bring to a gentle boil. Lower the heat, cover and simmer for 30 minutes. Discard the spring onion and ginger. Skim, and adjust the seasoning, which should be rich and salty.
2. Scald the duck in boiling water for 5 minutes. Drain and dry.
3. Put the duck in the steeping liquor. Bring to a gentle boil. Lower the heat, cover and simmer till cooked, about 40 minutes. Leave to steep till cold or till required. Take out the duck, chop into bite-size pieces, arrange on a plate and serve.

The steeping liquor is not served with the meat. Each time after use, it is boiled up, skimmed, cooled and stored in an airtight container in the fridge, and boiled up once a week. Renew the spice bag each time it is used. Additional light soya sauce, sugar and wine may be added according to taste. Chicken and other meats may be cooked in it. Before the days of refrigeration, this served as a way of preserving meat over feast days. Ready-mixed spices are available.

CHICKEN AND MUNG-BEAN SKIN SALAD (SHANDONG)

110 g (4 oz) raw chicken breast meat
1 piece mung-bean skin (or mung-bean vermicelli)
30 g (1 oz) coriander leaves
15 g (½ oz) dried wood ears (soaked)

Marinade:
1 egg white

½ *tsp salt*
2 *tsp cornflour with a little water*

Seasoning:
1 *tbsp light soya sauce*
1 *tbsp sesame oil*
2 *tsp wine vinegar (or to taste)*

1. Slice the chicken meat into matchsticks, mix them with the marinade, and let stand for 10 minutes. Scald them in boiling water for about 5 to 6 minutes, or till cooked. Drain and leave in cold water to cool. Drain well.
2. Pick over and rinse the coriander leaves, and cut into 2.5 cm (1 in) lengths. Scald them briefly in boiling water, refresh in cold water, and drain well. Rinse the soaked wood ears and scald in boiling water. Drain well.
3. Boil the mung-bean skin in water till softened and transparent. Cool in cold water, drain and cut into 5×1.3 cm (2×½ in) pieces. Mix them with the coriander leaves and put on a plate. Cover with the cooked chicken and sprinkle the wood ears over the top.
4. Mix the seasoning together and pour over the salad.

This is a crunchy, cooling summer dish.

DRUNKEN CHICKEN (SHANGHAI)

1 *plump chicken about 1.8 kg (4 lb)*

Seasoning for marinade:
2.5 *cm (1 in) piece cassia bark*
½ *pod star anise seed*
1 *slice ginger (bruised)*
1 *stalk spring onion (cut into 2.5 cm or 1 in lengths)*
2 *tsp salt*
80 *ml (3 fl oz) fermented glutinous rice*

2 *tbsp rice wine*
3 *tsp salt*

1. Scald the chicken in boiling water till the skin begins to tighten. Rinse in cold water.
2. Bring 2.3 l (4 pt) of water to the boil on high heat and put in the chicken. Bring to the boil again, skim and reduce the heat to low. Cover and simmer for about 25 minutes or till just cooked. Take out the chicken and put it in a large bowl. Pour the cooking liquor over it to cover, and leave to cool.

3. When cooked, bring 280 ml (½ pint) of the chicken stock to the boil, and add all the seasoning except the fermented rice. Boil for a minute or two till the stock is well flavoured; cool. Add the fermented rice, and stir well to mix. Strain the flavoured stock into an earthenware pot with a lid.
4. Quarter the chicken. Rub the chicken pieces first with the salt, then with the rice wine. Cover and leave to marinate for about 1 hour at room temperature.
5. Transfer the chicken pieces into the alcohol-flavoured stock. Cover and marinate for at least 3 hours or overnight.
6. Chop the chicken into bite-size pieces. Place the smaller, scrappy pieces first on a serving plate, then the best pieces of breast and leg meat on top. Pour over some of the flavoured stock and serve the rest separately.

This is a well-known Shanghai chicken dish, and popular summer fare. It is important not to overcook the chicken. Keep the remaining un-flavoured stock for soup.

SOYA SAUCE CHICKEN (JIANGSU)

1 plump chicken about 1.1–1.4 kg (2½–3 lb)

Seasoning for steeping liquor:
850 ml (1½ pt) dark soya sauce
30 ml (1 fl oz) rice wine
110 g (4 oz) sugar
2.5 cm (1 in) length cassia bark
1 pod star anise seed
1 stalk spring onion (tied in a knot)
1 slice ginger (bruised)
570 ml (1 pt) chicken stock or water

2 tsp sesame oil

1. Rinse the chicken and wipe dry.
2. Bring the ingredients for steeping to the boil. Put in the chicken, bring to the boil on high heat, turn the chicken over, cover it with a plate, cover the pot and take off the heat. Let it stand in the liquid for 10 minutes. Return the pot to medium heat, bring to the boil, turn the chicken over, cover with the plate and replace the lid. Remove from the heat and leave to steep for 15 minutes. Return to medium heat, bring to the boil again, and take out the chicken.
3. Cool, chop into bite-size pieces and arrange neatly on a serving dish. Spoon on a little of the cooking liquor and sprinkle on the sesame oil.

The skin glows a dark red and the meat is succulent and smooth. This is a favourite summer cold dish.

STRANGE-FLAVOUR CHICKEN (SICHUAN)

1 chicken about 1.1–1.4 kg (2½–3 lb)

Seasoning for sauce:
1 stalk spring onion (minced)
2 tsp Sichuan peppercorns (crushed)
2 tbsp light soya sauce
2 tbsp sesame oil
1 tbsp sugar
1 tbsp vinegar
2 tbsp chilli oil
1 tbsp sesame paste (or tahini*)*
1 tsp salt

2 tbsp sesame seeds (toasted)

1. Steam or boil the chicken for 30 minutes, or till cooked, and brush with some of the sesame oil. Leave till completely cold.
2. Mix together all the seasoning ingredients for the sauce. Set aside.
3. Bone the chicken, cut into neat slices and arrange on a plate. Pour the sauce over the meat, sprinkle on the toasted sesame seeds and serve.

The sauce may be varied with the addition of minced garlic or ginger juice. The chicken meat may be shredded or diced. This dish is served as an appetizer. The combination of salt, chilli oil, soya sauce, sugar, vinegar, sesame paste, Sichuan peppercorns, sesame oil, spring onion, garlic and sometimes crushed roasted peanuts is known as 'strange flavour' in Chinese culinary terminology.

WHITE STEEPED CHICKEN (HENAN)

1 chicken about 1.8–2.3 kg (4–5 lb)
3 tablespoons Sichuan pepper salt
stock (chicken and pork bone) to cover

Seasoning for steeping liquor:
30 g (1 oz) star anise seeds (crushed)
60 ml (2 fl oz) rice wine
110 g (4 oz) spring onion (slightly bruised and tied in knots)
30 g (1 oz) ginger (bruised)

1. Rub the chicken all over and inside with the Sichuan pepper salt (for the preparation of this, see 227). Let it stand for 1 hour.
2. Bring the stock to the boil, scald the chicken in it briefly and take out. Put all the seasoning for steeping in the stock, bring to the boil, cover and simmer for 30 minutes. Add the chicken, bring to the boil, lower the heat, cover and simmer for 15 minutes. Turn off the heat and let the chicken cool in the liquid, covered, for 35 minutes.
3. Chop into bite-size pieces and serve.

This chicken has a shiny, golden skin and spicy, tender meat. The steeping liquor may be used again, but discard the spices and reboil before storing. Renew the spices when reusing the liquor.

HANGZHOU STEEPED DUCK (ZHEJIANG)

1 plump duck about 2–2.3 kg (4½–5 lb)

Seasoning:
1 stalk spring onion (tied in a knot)
1 slice ginger (bruised)
1 pod star anise seed
2.5 cm (1 in) piece cassia bark
280 ml (½ pt) dark soya sauce
70 g (2½ oz) sugar
30 ml (1 fl oz) rice wine

70 g (2½ oz) sugar

1. Bring to the boil 700 ml (1¼ pt) water with the seasoning. Put in the duck. Reduce the heat to medium, cover and cook for about 40 minutes, or till the duck is cooked. Take out and cool.
2. Chop into bite-size pieces and arrange neatly on a serving plate.
3. Discard the spices. Bring the cooking liquor to the boil again and add the second lot of sugar. Boil till the liquor begins to thicken.
4. To serve, spoon some of the thickened liquor over the duck. Reserve the rest of the liquor for future cooking.

This is a popular cold dish for summer.

KIDNEY SLICES IN SESAME SAUCE (BEIJING)

3 pig's kidneys
110 g (4 oz) lettuce (or cucumber)

Sauce:
2 *tbsp sesame paste (or* tahini*)*
2 *tsp sesame oil*
2 *tsp sugar*
1 *tsp salt*

Marinade:
1 *tbsp rice wine*
1 *tsp salt*

1. Slice the kidneys in half lengthwise and core them. Slice thinly, holding the knife on a slant to the right, so that the slices are long and thin, about two-thirds the length of the kidney. Marinate them in the wine and salt.
2. Mix together all the ingredients for the sauce, and set aside.
3. Rinse and shred the lettuce, and place it on a serving plate.
4. Pour boiling water over the kidney slices, stirring with chopsticks to loosen. Drain. Repeat the process; when the colour changes and the edges roll up, they are cooked. Drain immediately. Pile the kidney slices on the lettuce, pour the sauce over and serve immediately as an appetizer.

The sauce and lettuce may be prepared in advance, but the kidney slices should be cooked only just before serving. Chilli sauce may be added to the sauce.

LOTUS-ROOT AND GINGER SALAD (SHANDONG)

450 g (1 lb) fresh lotus root
2 slices ginger (minced)

Seasoning:
1 *tbsp light soya sauce*
2 *tsp vinegar (or to taste)*
½ *tsp salt*
1 *tbsp sesame oil*

1. Mix together all the seasoning ingredients, and set aside.
2. Scrub and rinse the lotus root thoroughly. Peel the skin thinly and cut across into thin slices. Scald them in boiling water, drain, place in a bowl, and add the minced ginger and a pinch of salt. Mix well, cover with a plate and marinate for 5 minutes. Transfer on to a serving dish. Pour on the sauce, and serve.

Hot, sour, savoury and crunchy, this is a traditional lotus salad from Jinan in Shandong province, where fat, succulent and sweet lotus roots abound in the lake called *Taning Hu*.

SALTED JELLYFISH IN MUSTARD SAUCE (SHANDONG)

140 g (5 oz) salted jellyfish (shredded and soaked)
1 boiled egg white (shredded)
30 g (1 oz) coriander leaves (cut into 2.5 cm or 1 in lengths)
15 g (½ oz) dried shrimps (soaked)

Sauce:
3 tsp mustard powder
1 tbsp light soya sauce
1 tbsp vinegar
1 tbsp sesame oil

1. Drain the shredded jellyfish (see page 224 for preparation). Place it on a plate, put the shredded egg white on top, then the coriander leaves, and finally the soaked dried shrimps.
2. Mix the mustard powder with a little cooled boiled water into a thin paste. Cover and let stand for about 20 minutes for the flavour to develop. Sprinkle it on the dried shrimps.
3. Heat the sesame oil, add the vinegar and the soya sauce and pour over the jellyfish.

This is a traditional winter cold dish from Jiaodong, along the Shandong coast near Qingdao.

SALTED JELLYFISH SALAD (ZHEJIANG)

170 g (6 oz) salted jellyfish (shredded and soaked)
30 g (1 oz) cooked ham
60 g (2 oz) cooked chicken meat
110 g (4 oz) cucumber
1 sweet green pepper

Seasoning:
1 clove garlic (minced)
1 tbsp vinegar
2 tsp sugar (or to taste)
2 tsp light soya sauce
1 tbsp sesame oil

1. Peel and deseed the cucumber, and cut into matchsticks. Rub in a pinch of salt, rinse and squeeze out the water. Cut the chicken, ham

and green pepper into matchsticks. Scald the green pepper in boiling water, refresh in cold water and drain well.
2. Mix the seasoning (except the sesame oil) with the cucumber and jellyfish (see page 224 for preparation). Put these on a serving plate and cover with the shredded chicken, green pepper and ham. Sprinkle on the sesame oil.

This salad is very crunchy and colourful, a delightful appetizer for all seasons.

SALTWATER PRAWNS (SHANDONG)

450 g (1 lb) medium-sized fresh prawns

Seasoning:
30 g (1 oz) spring onions (whole)
15 g (½ oz) ginger (bruised)
60 g (2 oz) salt
1 tbsp rice wine
1 tsp Sichuan peppercorns

1. Rinse the prawns.
2. Put 850 ml (1½ pt) water in a pot with the seasoning. Bring to the boil, add the prawns, and cook till they turn pink. Pour into a bowl and let stand for about 10 minutes. Drain, discard the spices, arrange the prawns on a plate, and serve.

A delicious and simple way of cooking prawns.

Meat Dishes

Beef

BRAISED BEEF WITH *DANGKUI* (FUJIAN)

680 g (1½ lb) braising steak
15 g (½ oz) dangkui *(Chinese angelica root)*
6 caps winter mushrooms (soaked)
80 g (3 oz) bamboo shoots

Seasoning:
1 clove garlic (minced)
1 slice ginger (minced)
1 tbsp rice wine
1 tsp sugar

2 tsp light soya sauce
pepper to taste
1 tsp sesame oil
1 tsp cornflour with a little water

2 tbsp lard or cooking oil
850 ml (1½ pt) stock or water

1. Boil the beef briskly for about 15 minutes. Drain, remove any fat, and dice into cubes. Dice the bamboo shoots and mushrooms. Set aside.
2. Set the wok over high heat till hot, put in 1 tbsp lard, stir fry the garlic and ginger till fragrant, add the beef, bamboo shoots and mushrooms, and stir in the rice wine, sugar and soya sauce. Pour in the stock, bring to the boil and transfer to an earthenware pot, *saguo* or casserole. Add the *dangkui*, cover and simmer on low heat for about 2½ to 3 hours, or till tender.
3. Discard the *dangkui*. Thicken the soup with the cornflour mixture, and add the rest of the lard. Sprinkle on the sesame oil and serve.

BRAISED SPICED BRISKET (GUANGDONG)

0.9–1.1 kg (2–2½ lb) beef brisket

Seasoning for oil:
1 slice ginger (bruised)
1 clove garlic (crushed)
1 tbsp salted soya bean paste

Seasoning for sauce:
1 tsp salt
2 tsp sugar
2.5 cm (1 in) square piece tangerine peel
1 pod star anise seed
1 tbsp dark soya sauce
pepper to taste
1 tbsp rice wine

stock or water to cover
1 tbsp sesame oil

1. Remove any fat and boil the meat in stock or water to cover till half done, about 40 minutes. Drain and reserve the liquor. Cut the meat in large cubes.
2. Mix all the seasoning together, except the rice wine.
3. Put the wok on medium heat, put in 1 tbsp cooking oil, and add the

seasoning for the oil. Stir fry till fragrant, then add the beef. Stir fry for 1 minute, pour in the wine, then the stock, and the seasoning mixture last.

4. Transfer to a casserole, cover, and braise on top of the stove or in the oven for 1 hour on low heat, or till tender. Serve sprinkled with the sesame oil.

Do not remove the lid, stop cooking or add water halfway through, or the flavour will be spoilt. The gravy should be thick. Cooking this dish in an earthenware pot greatly improves the flavour. Only brisket can give the authentic taste and texture of this dish.

CHAOZHOU BEEF FIRE POT (GUANGDONG)

680 g (1½ lb) beef fillet steak
2 lettuces (any kind)

Seasoning:
110 ml (4 fl oz) sacha jiang *(barbecue sauce)*
½ tsp salt
1 tsp sugar
2 tbsp sesame paste (or tahini*)*
2 tsp chilli oil (or to taste)
2 tbsp cooking oil or lard

850 ml (1½ pt) beef stock

1. Remove any fat or gristle from the beef. Freeze till firm and saw-cut into paper-thin slices. Lay them on a plate.
2. Discard any soiled leaves from the lettuces, separate the leaves, rinse well and dry. Put them on 2 plates.
3. Mix all the seasoning ingredients together into a paste. Divide into 2 equal parts, in 2 small bowls.
4. Place the fire pot ('steamboat') on a heatproof mat on the dining table. Put in the hot stock and 1 bowl of the seasoning paste. Stir well, cover and bring to the boil.
5. To eat, dip the beef and lettuce a little at a time, cooking and eating at the same time with chopsticks and spoons or mesh wire strainers. Use the other bowl of the paste as a dip for the meat.
6. After the meat and lettuce have been eaten, the stock is drunk as an excellent soup.

A traditional winter and spring dish in Chaozhou (Teochiu) county in Guangdong, where the apparatus consists of a small earthenware stove and a cooking pot, similar to the *tapinlo* or fire pot of Guangzhou (Canton)

123

and the fire pot of Hunan. Fire pots with a built-in charcoal stove (see page 92) are used in urban areas.

DRY STIR-FRIED BEEF WITH CELERY (SICHUAN)

340 g (12 oz) lean beef
60 g (2 oz) celery
2 slices ginger (shredded)
2 stalks spring onion whites (cut into 2.5 cm or 1 in lengths)

Seasoning:
2 tsp salted soya beans (crushed)
1 tsp chilli powder
1 tsp sugar
1 tsp soya sauce
1 tsp vinegar
2 tsp rice wine

2 tbsp peanut oil
½ tsp Sichuan peppercorns (ground)

1. Cut the beef and celery into matchsticks. Mix all the seasoning together, and set aside.
2. Put the wok on high heat. When hot, add the oil, put in the beef and stir fry for 1 minute; add salt, and stir fry till cooked, when it turns a dark red.
3. Add the seasoning mixture and stir fry briefly. Stir in the celery, onion and ginger. Continue stir frying till the celery is cooked but crisp, then sprinkle on the ground Sichuan peppercorns.

If water comes out of the beef, stir fry until it is dry before adding in the seasonings.

OXTAIL IN TOMATO SAUCE (BEIJING)

1 oxtail (about 1.1 kg or 2½ lb)

Sauce:
3 fresh tomatoes (or 3 tbsp tomato ketchup)
2 tsp sugar (or to taste)
1 tsp cornflour with a little water
1 tsp salt

Seasoning for oil:
1 stalk spring onion (chopped)

1 slice ginger (minced)

2 tbsp peanut oil

1. Bring the oxtail to the boil in plenty of water with 1 tbsp of salt. Boil fiercely for about 10 minutes. Drain and rinse thoroughly. This process deodorizes the meat.
2. Put the oxtail in a clean pot with fresh water to cover and bring to the boil. Skim, lower the heat and simmer covered till tender, about 2 to 3 hours. Skim off any fat, drain and reserve the cooking liquor.
3. Skin and chop the tomatoes.
4. Heat the wok, put in 1 tbsp of peanut oil, and stir fry the spring onion and ginger till fragrant. Add the tomatoes, stir fry briefly, then add the sugar and salt, 280 ml (10 fl oz) of the cooking liquor and the oxtail. Bring to the boil, lower the heat, cover and cook for about 10 minutes. Stir in the cornflour and water mixture. Sprinkle on the rest of the peanut oil and dish up.

This satisfying winter dish originated from the cuisine of the Moslem minority groups in the north. It may be eaten with rice, steamed lotus-leaf buns (see page 156), Chinese bread (see page 128) or potatoes.

Lamb

ICED LAMB CUBES (BEIJING)

230 g (8 oz) cooked lean lamb
15 g ($\frac{1}{2}$ oz) gelatine
280 ml (10 fl oz) strong, well flavoured stock

Seasoning:
1 tbsp soya sauce
1 tbsp vinegar (or to taste)
1 tbsp sesame oil
salt and pepper

a few coriander leaves (chopped)

1. Tear the lamb meat into fine shreds. Season with a pinch of salt and pepper, and arrange in a rectangular dish.
2. Dissolve the gelatine thoroughly in the stock, over a pan of boiling water. Pour on to the shredded meat, then leave to cool and set in the refrigerator.
3. Cut into oblong cubes about 4×1.5 cm (1$\frac{1}{2}$×$\frac{1}{2}$ in). Arrange into 3 rows, 2 at the base and 1 on top. Sprinkle on the coriander

leaves. Mix the seasoning together and pour over.

A Beijing dish of Inner Mongolian origin.

LAMB FIRE POT (BEIJING)

900 g (2 lb) leg of lamb
230 g (8 oz) Chinese 'celery' cabbage (rinsed and chopped into 2.5 cm or
1 in lengths)
110 g (4 oz) mung-bean vermicelli (soaked)
1.1 l (2 pt) stock
a few dried shrimps (soaked)
a few winter mushrooms (soaked)

Dips:
60 g (2 oz) sesame paste
30 g (1 oz) rice wine
1 cube fermented bean curd (mashed)
30 g (1 oz) light soya sauce
30 g (1 oz) chilli oil
30 g (1 oz) shrimp sauce
30 g (1 oz) rice wine vinegar (or wine vinegar)
30 g (1 oz) spring onion (chopped)
30 g (1 oz) coriander leaves (finely chopped)
30 g (1 oz) preserved Chinese chives (optional)

1. Spring lamb is best, but any lean, tender leg of lamb will do. Remove any gristle, bone and fat. Freeze till well hardened.
2. With the left hand hold the meat with a clean tea towel and slice very thinly with a sawing motion, so that long thin shavings of meat are obtained. Arrange the neat, thin slices on serving plates as they are cut.
3. Put the cabbage and soaked vermicelli on separate plates, and all the dips in separate little bowls. Place the dip bowls, cabbage, vermicelli and meat plates on the table in a circle leaving a space in the centre for the fire pot.
4. Burn some charcoal until glowing red. Boil the stock with shrimps and winter mushrooms to flavour it. Strain and discard these, and ladle the stock to fill the 'moat' in the fire pot. Put pieces of the glowing charcoal in the 'stove'.
5. Place a thick mat in the middle of the table. Place the fire pot on a heatproof tray on the mat.
6. Each diner has a spoon, chopsticks and bowl, and a little wire-mesh strainer to cook the food in. The diner places the meat in

the strainer, lowers it in the boiling stock and, when the colour changes, takes it out and eats it with the dips.

7. When the meat is finished, the cabbage and the vermicelli are put in – not too much at a time, as this would reduce the temperature in the pot. Sometimes, new ingredients are introduced to extend the meal: diced bean curd, noodles, meat balls, anything that takes the fancy. The stock is replenished from the kitchen stock pot.

Only the very best odourless young lamb of about 23 kg (50 lb) weight is used, of which only about 7 to 8 kg (16 to 17 lb) is good enough for this dish of Manchurian origin.

MONGOLIAN GRILL (BEIJING)

680 g (1½ lb) lamb or beef (tender fillet)
110 g (4 oz) spring onion whites (cut into 2.5 cm or 1 in lengths)

Marinade for meat:
3 tbsp light soya sauce
1 tbsp rice wine
3 tsp ginger juice
2 tsp sugar
1 tbsp sesame oil
1 egg lightly beaten (optional)

Accompaniment:
Mandarin pancakes (see page 142) or Chinese bread (see below)
cucumbers
coriander leaves
pickles

1. Bone and trim the meat and put it in the freezer till frozen. Cut into thin slices. As the meat is to be cooked on an open fire, it must not be sliced too thin. There should be about 50 slices 15×8 cm (6×3 in). Cut each of these across into 3.
2. Marinate the meat slices for at least 20 minutes.
3. Spread the onion shreds on a fine-mesh wire rack, and lay the meat slices on top. Place the rack over the charcoal fire. With a pair of very long chopsticks (special ones about 45 cm or 18 in long are used for this), turn the pieces over and over till they turn powdery white (if lamb is used) or purple (beef). Pick them out and place on a serving plate.

In China, the choice and cut of meat for this dish is as stringent as that

127

for the lamb fire pot. The ox should be about 140 kg (300 lb) in weight, of which only about 18 kg (40 lb) of meat is suitable for this dish. The wire rack used here is an improvization. In China the grid used for cooking is circular, about 60 cm (2 ft) in diameter, with the centre slightly convex and the sides sloping down. The mesh has bars about 1.3 cm ($\frac{1}{2}$ in) wide, 0.6 cm ($\frac{1}{4}$ in) thick, closely spaced, about 0.6 cm ($\frac{1}{4}$ in) apart. Willow and pine are the favourite woods for the fire. This dish has been eaten in Beijing for nearly 300 years. At first, only cooked meat was used, but about seventy years ago raw meat was adopted. Originally, each diner cooked his own meat and ate it standing up with one foot on a bench.

CHINESE BREAD (KONGSINBING)

450 g (1 lb) strong white flour
2 eggs
30 g (1 oz) fresh yeast or 1 tsp dried yeast
1 tsp sugar
$\frac{1}{2}$ tsp salt

1. Sieve the flour and salt. Take out 30 g (2 oz), mix with 140 ml (5 fl oz) of cold water and cook over low heat till thickened. Leave to cool.
2. Make a well in the flour. Put in the eggs, yeast, 140 ml (5 fl oz) of warm water, sugar and the cooled cooked paste. Use your hand to mix the eggs, yeast and water well before drawing in the flour. Knead into a smooth, shiny dough. Leave to rest for 30 minutes in a warm place.
3. Shape the dough into a long roll, and cut into 16 equal pieces. Take one piece, and with your fingers shape it into a little round, about 8 cm (3 in) in diameter, gathering the edges together as though wrapping up a filling. Roll into a ball and place on a greased baking sheet. Shape the other pieces similarly.
4. Let them rest for 20 minutes in a warm place. Preheat the oven to hot, 220°C (425°F, gas mark 7).
5. Bake for 15 minutes, until nicely browned and golden and puffed up like balls. Cool on a rack.

Kongsinbing means 'hollow bread' in Mandarin.

QUICK-FRIED LAMB WITH SPRING ONION (BEIJING)

230 g (8 oz) leg of lamb
4 stalks spring onion whites

Seasoning:
1 tbsp light soya sauce
½ tsp salt
½ tsp sugar (optional)
2 tsp rice wine
2 tsp sesame oil

1 tbsp vegetable oil

1. Cut the lamb into thin, bite-size slices. Slice the onion diagonally into 2.5 cm (1 in) pieces. Season both together with the soya sauce, salt and sugar.
2. Heat the oil over high heat till smoking, and stir fry the meat, onion and juice together till the meat is cooked. Sprinkle on the rice wine and sesame oil, and dish up.

A favourite fast-cooking family dish; the lamb is tender and delicious.

Pork

ANHUI MEAT BALLS (ANHUI)

Pork ball mixture:
230 g (8 oz) minced pork (¼ fat)
1 egg
1 stalk spring onion (minced)
1 slice ginger (minced)
2 tsp rice wine
1 tsp sugar
1 tbsp cornflour
1 tbsp water
½ tsp salt
2 tsp light soya sauce

Sauce:
5 tbsp stock or water
½ tsp salt
½ tsp sugar
1 tsp cornflour with a little water

110 g (4 oz) glutinous rice

1. Wash the rice and soak in cold water for 30 minutes.
2. Mix together all the ingredients for the pork balls. Make into walnut-size balls.
3. Drain the rice and dry well. Roll each pork ball in the rice until completely covered. Steam in a wok over high heat for 25 minutes or till cooked.
4. Bring the sauce ingredients to the boil, pour the sauce over the pork balls and serve.

This is very popular among the people of Anhui, hence its name. It may be eaten without the sauce, as a dumpling.

CHARSIU – CANTONESE BARBECUED PORK (GUANGDONG)

1.8 kg (4 lb) shoulder of pork (skinned and boned)

Marinade:
1 tbsp salt
230 g (8 oz) sugar
2 tbsp salted soya bean paste
1 tbsp dark soya sauce
3 tbsp light soya sauce
4 tbsp rice wine

Syrup for basting:
4 tbsp maltose (or honey or sugar)
2 tbsp vinegar
1 tbsp rice wine
2 tsp cornflour

1. Cut the meat into strips about 5 cm (2 in) wide and 2.5 cm (1 in) thick. If cut too thin they get too dry and hard on cooking.
2. Marinate for 1 hour at room temperature, or several hours in the refrigerator. Dissolve the maltose in the vinegar and wine over a low heat. Cool and mix in the cornflour. Preheat the oven to very hot, 250°C (475°F, gas mark 9).
3. Place the meat on a rack standing in a roasting tin containing 0.6 cm (¼ in) of hot water. Roast for 15 minutes. Turn the meat over and continue roasting for another 15 minutes. When the meat oozes clear oil, it is cooked.
4. Take out the meat and leave to cool for 3 minutes. Brush all over with the syrup mixture. Put it back in the oven for 3 more minutes; when the meat is nicely glistening take it out, cool and cut diagonally into thin slices. Serve with sliced cucumber. Boil up any juice with the marinade as a dip.

The meat is sweet and salty and has that charred taste where the fat has been burnt and the sugar caramelized. For best results the meat should be 80 per cent lean and 20 per cent fat. It should not be overcooked, which would make it dry and hard. In Guangzhou (Canton) the strips of meat are threaded on to a rotating roasting hanger and roasted over a charcoal fire (see illustration).

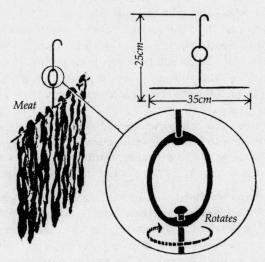

This roasting hanger, available in the West, is too tall for a normal western oven, but it is all right over a charcoal fire

CRAB MEAT LION'S HEAD (JIANGSU)

Pork ball mixture:
680 g (1½ lb) minced pork (¼ fat)
110 g (4 oz) crab meat
30 g (1 oz) shelled raw prawn meat (minced)
2 tbsp spring onion and ginger juice
1 tsp salt
2 tbsp rice wine
1 tbsp cornflour

Topping for meat balls:
30 g (1 oz) crab yolk
6 lettuce leaves (or any greens)
1.1 kg (2½ lb) Chinese 'celery' cabbage (or any kind of lettuce)
1 tbsp dried shrimps soaked (optional)

170 g (6 fl oz) stock or water
1 tbsp lard or cooking oil

1. Mix together all the ingredients for the pork balls and divide into 12 portions.
2. Discard any soiled outer leaves from the cabbage. Trim the cabbage stem. Rinse the cabbage well and quarter it lengthwise. If it is too long to fit the wok, cut the quarters in half cross wise.
3. Put the wok over a high heat. When hot, put in the lard, stir fry the cabbage till it changes colour, and add the soaked shrimps, salt and stock. Bring to the boil and take the wok off the heat.
4. Grease a casserole, arrange the cooked cabbage neatly at the bottom, then gently pour in the juice. Take a portion of the pork mixture, and roll into a large ball between your palms. Flatten it slightly, press a little crab yolk on to it and place it on the cabbage. Do this with all the meat balls. Finally, cover each with a piece of lettuce (or other) leaf.
5. Cover the casserole, and bring the contents to the boil on medium heat. Reduce the heat to low and simmer for 30 minutes, or till cooked. Take the casserole to the table, remove the leaves from the meat balls and discard them. Serve straight from the casserole.

These large meat balls resemble the wrinkled look of the lion's face, hence its name. In Yangzhou this traditional favourite is cooked with the tender hearts of Chinese cole (*bokchoi* in Cantonese), but Chinese 'celery' cabbage or any lettuce are good substitutes. If crab yolk is not available, boiled salted egg yolks may be used for colour, texture and a reasonably similar taste.

FIVE-SPICE ROLLS (GUANGDONG)

3 sheets bean-curd skin

Filling:
340 g (12 oz) minced pork
110 g (4 oz) prawns (raw or cooked, peeled and chopped)
110 g (4 oz) cooked liver (diced)
60 g (2 oz) water chestnuts (peeled and diced)
110 g (4 oz) dressed crab meat
2 eggs

Seasoning:
1 tbsp sugar
2 tbsp light soya sauce
1 tbsp dark soya sauce
1 tbsp cornflour with a little water
pepper to taste

2 tsp five-spice powder
2 stalks spring onions (chopped)

Egg paste:
1 egg white with 2 tsp cornflour and a little water
cornflour for dusting
850 ml (1½ pt) cooking oil

Accompaniments:
cucumber slices
plum sauce or tomato ketchup

1. Mix together all the ingredients for the filling, add the seasoning and mix well. Divide into 6 portions.
2. Beat the egg white lightly and mix in the cornflour and water to a thin paste.
3. Dip the bean-curd skin in hot water to soften, drain and pat dry with kitchen roll. Cut into 6 pieces each about 13×20 cm (5×8 in) and trim off any hard edge. Spread one piece on a flat surface, and brush it all over with the egg paste. Put a portion of the filling along one long side about 2.5 cm (1 in) from the edge in a row. Fold up three sides and roll up, sealing the opening with more paste. Put on a plate fold side down. Make another 5 in the same way. Steam all the rolls for 10 minutes in the wok on high heat.
4. Take out the rolls, drain off any liquid and dust them thoroughly with cornflour. Deep fry till golden in hot oil. Cut diagonally into 2.5 cm (1 in) slices and serve with the cucumber slices and plum sauce or tomato ketchup.

This is very popular in both Guangdong and in Fujian in the south, though here very often caul fat rather than bean-curd skin is used as wrapping.

'LITCHI' KIDNEYS (YUNNAN)

450 g (1 lb) pig's kidneys
2 tomatoes

Seasoning:
1 tbsp light soya sauce
2 tsp sugar
2 tsp vinegar
1 tsp rice wine
60 ml (2 fl oz) stock or water
1 tsp cornflour

133

Egg coating:
1 egg white
1 tbsp cornflour

Seasoning for oil:
1 stalk spring onion (chopped)
1 slice ginger (minced)

850 ml (1½ pt) cooking oil
2 tsp melted lard

1. Split the kidneys in half lengthwise and core them. On the smooth side make criss-cross scorings, and cut each half into 3 pieces. Marinate them with a little salt and some rice wine.
2. Skin the tomatoes, deseed and chop into pieces the size of rice grains.
3. Mix together all the seasonings and stock. Set aside.
4. Drain the kidneys, reserve the marinade and add to the seasoning mixture. Mix together the egg white and cornflour and add to the drained kidneys. Mix well.
5. Deep fry the kidneys till just cooked, take out and drain well.
6. Heat the wok, put in 2 tsp of oil, stir fry the ginger and spring onion till fragrant, and add the seasoning mixture. Stir well and then add in the chopped tomatoes and the kidneys. Mix well and, when heated through, stir in the lard and dish up.

Truly delicious, this is slightly sweet and sour with a reddish sauce. The kidneys covered in red sauce are reminiscent of the crimson shells of fresh litchi, hence the Chinese name. One of Yunnan's banquet dishes, it may be eaten with drinks or rice.

PIG'S TROTTERS IN BLACK VINEGAR (GUANGDONG)

3 or 4 pig's trotters (prepared)
6 eggs (boiled and shelled)

Seasoning:
570 ml (1 pt) black vinegar (sweet vinegar)
230–450 g (½–1 lb) green ginger
140 ml (5 fl oz) white rice vinegar (optional)
110 ml (4 oz) sugar (or to taste)
1 tsp salt

1. Bring the black vinegar to the boil in an enamelled or earthenware pot, add the white rice vinegar, if used, dissolve the sugar in it, and add the salt.

2. Soak the ginger in boiling water, scrape off the skin, bruise it slightly and dry fry (without oil) in a pan till slightly parched and fragrant. Add to the vinegar pot. Bring to the boil, cover and simmer for about 30 minutes.
3. Add the prepared trotters (see page 225) and simmer on a very low heat till tender, about 2 to 3 hours. Add the eggs and marinate for several hours, or overnight, before serving. Serve at room temperature.

This dish is not sour, nor the ginger hot. The Cantonese variety of black vinegar sometimes has sugar added and is also known as 'sweet vinegar'; it is quite different from the Zhejiang and Zhenjiang vinegars (see page 60). The white vinegar is to give zest to the dish. The seasonings are entirely to personal taste.

PORK WITH FISH FLAVOUR (SICHUAN)

230 g (8 oz) lean pork
15 g (½ oz) dried wood ears (soaked)
2 stalks spring onions (chopped)
30 g (1 oz) pea shoots (optional)

Seasoning:
1 slice ginger (minced)
1 clove garlic (minced)
6 dried red chillis (or to taste)

Sauce:
1 tbsp light soya sauce
½ tsp salt
1 tsp sugar
1 tsp vinegar
4 tbsp stock or water
1 tsp cornflour

2 tbsp vegetable oil

1. Shred the pork into matchsticks, and season with salt and a little cornflour and water.
2. Soak the chillis in hot water, deseed and chop finely. Add the minced ginger and garlic.
3. Mix the sauce ingredients and set aside.
4. Pick over and rinse the bean shoots, and add the spring onion and wood ears.
5. Heat the wok over high heat, put in the oil and, when smoking,

135

quick fry the pork till white. Add the seasoning. Continue stir frying till fragrant and red, then add the vegetables. Stir well to mix. Give the sauce mixture a stir and pour it in. Stir well and dish up.

The taste of sweet, sour, hot and salty combined with spring onion, ginger and garlic is the classic 'fish flavour' from Sichuan. The bean shoots are the tender tips, with young leaves and tendrils, of mange-tout plants, not to be confused with mung bean sprouts or soya bean sprouts. It is called *doumiao* in Mandarin and also known as *longxicai*, dragon's whiskers vegetable, referring to the tendrils.

PORK STEAMED IN FERMENTED RICE (SHANDONG)

680 g (1½ lb) belly pork (with skin)

Seasoning:
2 tbsp fermented glutinous rice
4 tbsp stock or water
2 tbsp dark soya sauce
1 tsp salt
2 stalks spring onion (shredded)
1 slice ginger (shredded)

1.1 l (2 pt) peanut oil

1. Cut the pork into slices about 8 cm (3 in) long and 1.3 cm (½ in) thick. Deep fry them till golden. Arrange them skin side down in a bowl. Sprinkle on the spring onion and ginger.
2. Mix together the fermented rice and the stock, strain and add the soya sauce and salt. Pour over the meat. Steam in the wok for 2 hours or till tender. Turn out on to a serving dish.

This meat is dark red with a strong alcoholic flavour. It may be parboiled or roasted and then sliced, instead of deep fried in slices.

RED-COOKED PORK KNUCKLE WITH HAIRWEED (GUANGDONG)

1 pork knuckle about 900 g (2 lb)
30 g (1 oz) hairweed
450 g (1 lb) lettuce (any kind)

Seasoning for oil:
2 shallots (minced)
1 clove garlic (minced)

Seasoning for braising:
1 tbsp red fermented bean curd (mashed)
1 tbsp rice wine
2 tbsp dark soya sauce
½ tsp salt
1 slice ginger (bruised)
1 pod star anise seed
2 tsp sugar

425 ml (15 fl oz) stock or water
1 tbsp cooking oil
1 tsp cornflour with a little water
1 tbsp cooling oil.

1. Do not wash the knuckle. Rub it with some dark soya sauce and salt. Let stand for about 20 minutes. Preheat the oven to hot, 220°C (425°F, gas mark 7).
2. Roast the knuckle for 25 minutes on each side, until the skin is golden and crisp. Take out and wash in hot water. Rinse in cold water and put in a pot with a tea plate at the bottom.
3. Heat the wok on medium heat, put in the oil, stir fry the shallots and garlic till fragrant, and add the fermented bean curd, wine and stock, then the rest of the seasoning. Bring to the boil.
4. Pour the flavoured stock over the knuckle. Bring to the boil again, and reduce the heat. Skim, cover and simmer for about 1½ hours, or till tender.
5. Prepare the hairweed. Twenty minutes before the end of cooking discard the spices, put in the hairweed and continue simmering.
6. Blanch the lettuce (whole leaves) and arrange it round a plate. Put the knuckle in the centre. Strain the cooking liquor and reserve. Spread the hairweed over the meat. Reduce the cooking liquor if necessary, and thicken with the cornflour. Pour over the meat.

The name of this dish is a homonym for 'prosperity is at hand', so it is an auspicious food for the Cantonese for New Year's Eve dinner and on other special occasions.

RED CRISPY PORK (HENAN)

900 g (2 lb) shoulder of pork (boned)

Seasoning for steaming:
1 tbsp spring onion (in 5 cm or 1 in lengths, bruised)
1 tbsp ginger slices (bruised)
2 tsp rice wine

1 tsp salt
1 tsp Sichuan peppercorns (crushed)

vinegar for brushing

Accompaniment:
spring onion whites (shredded)
sweet salted soya bean paste
Mandarin pancakes (see page 142) or lotus-leaf buns (see page 156)

1. Cut the pork into two pieces. Boil for 5 minutes. Drain and rinse in cold water.
2. Place the meat in a plate, skin side up, and sprinkle on the seasoning for steaming. Steam in the wok till cooked, about 1½ hours. Discard the spices. Wipe dry and leave to cool. Preheat the oven to very hot, 230°C (450°F, gas mark 8).
3. Roast the pork for about 10 minutes. Take out and brush the skin with vinegar. Repeat this twice, till the skin is crisp and golden.
4. Cool, cut into thin bite-size slices, and serve with the accompaniment.

Originally, the meat was deep fried instead of roasted, which is a British innovation. The colour is a beautiful rich red brown. When cold it slices paper-thin. It tastes more like a smoked and preserved meat, and is excellent for sandwich filling or the cold table.

ROCK SUGAR PORK KNUCKLE (SHANGHAI)

1 pork knuckle about 900 g (2 lb)

Seasoning:
60 g (2 oz) rock sugar (or granulated sugar)
30 ml (1 fl oz) rice wine
30 ml (1 fl oz) dark soya sauce
½ tsp salt
1 stalk spring onion (tied in a knot)
1 slice ginger

1. Boil the knuckle till the skin tightens, about 10 minutes. Drain and rinse in cold water.
2. Put a tea plate in the bottom of the pot to prevent sticking, and place the meat on it. Add water to cover. Put in the seasoning and bring to the boil on high heat. Reduce the heat, cover and cook on low heat for about 30 minutes. Turn the meat over and continue cooking till tender, about 1 hour.
3. Raise the heat to high and cook till the liquid is reduced and sticky

and the oil begins to run out of the meat. Take out the meat and place in a serving bowl. Discard the ginger and spring onion, pour the thickened juice over the meat and serve.

For best results use only rock sugar, and do use a knuckle – do not be tempted to replace it with a better cut.

SPARE RIBS STEAMED IN SALTED BLACK BEANS (GUANGDONG)

450 g (1 lb) pork spare ribs

Seasoning:
1 slice ginger (minced)
1 clove garlic (minced)
1 tbsp salted black beans (ground)
½ tsp sugar
1 tbsp dark soya sauce
1 tbsp light soya sauce
2 tsp cornflour
1 tbsp cooking oil

1. Trim any fat and gristle from the spare ribs. Chop into 2.5 cm (1 in) lengths. Rinse and dry.
2. Combine the seasoning with the spare ribs. Add the cornflour and mix well. Transfer on to a plate.
3. Sprinkle on the oil and steam in a wok on high heat for 35 minutes, or till cooked.

This is a very simple yet delicious family dish. Chopped chilli pepper may be sprinkled on before steaming.

STEAMED PORK IN FERMENTED BEAN CURD (SHANGHAI)

900 g (2 lb) thick belly pork (with skin)

Seasoning for steaming:
1 tbsp strong red rice water (hongqu)
1 tbsp rice wine
1 tbsp red fermented bean curd
½ tsp salt
½ tsp sugar
1 stalk spring onion (tied in a knot)
1 slice ginger
2.5 cm (1 in) piece cassia bark

139

80 ml (3 fl oz) stock
1 tsp cornflour with a little water

1. Burn away any hair on the pork skin, and rinse well. Boil the pork till par-cooked, about 15 minutes, then take it out and remove the rib bones. Score on the skin side, the full depth of the fat, then score on the meat side, as far as a quarter of the thickness of the meat.
2. Mix together all the seasoning for steaming with the stock, except for the last three items. Put the pork in a bowl skin side down, pour the seasoning mixture over it, add the rest of the spices and cover the bowl with cling film to prevent moisture getting in. Steam in a wok or pot on high heat for about 1½ hours.
3. Take out the pork, discard the spices, drain and reserve the juice. Slice the meat and arrange on a serving dish. Bring the juice to the boil, thicken with the cornflour mixture and pour over the meat.

This pink, aromatic meat is delicious with plain boiled rice or steamed lotus-leaf buns, *heyehjia*, (see page 156).

STEAMED SANDWICHED PORK (SICHUAN)

900 g (2 lb) fatty pork (belly or shoulder)
170 g (6 oz) red bean paste
230 g (8 oz) sweet potatoes (optional)

Seasoning:
2 tbsp light soya sauce
30 g (1 oz) sugar

1. Choose a fairly flat piece of meat. Cut it into 6 cm (2½ in) wide pieces. Boil till par-cooked, about 15 minutes. Take out, cool and dry. Remove the ribs if belly pork is used.
2. Peel and slice the sweet potatoes into 1.3 cm (½ in) thick slices.
3. Cut the meat into 'butterfly' slices: cut into 2 cm (¾ in) thick slices, then cut each from the meat side to the skin, forming two slices joined by the skin.
4. Sandwich some red bean paste between each pair of slices. Place the slices skin side down in a bowl (or an 850 ml or 1½ pt soufflé dish), tightly packed in one layer. Sprinkle on the soya sauce and the sugar. Cover the meat completely with the sliced sweet potatoes (if used). Steam on high heat for 2 to 3 hours or till tender, topping up the steamer regularly. Turn on to a serving dish and serve hot.

This is a highly popular sweet meat dish in some parts of Sichuan, especially at weddings, funerals, births and similar festive occasions. If preferred it may be oven baked in a *bain-marie*. It should be so tender that the fat melts in the mouth. Taros may be used instead of sweet potatoes.

TUNGPO PORK (JIANGSU)

1.1 kg (2½ lb) belly pork in one piece
140 g (5 oz) bamboo shoots
6 caps winter mushrooms (soaked)

Seasoning:
1 stalk spring onion (tied in a knot)
1 slice ginger (bruised)
½ tsp salt
1 tbsp dark soya sauce
2 tsp rock sugar (or granulated sugar)
1 tbsp rice wine

1. Cut the belly pork into 10 squares. Make criss-cross slashes on the skin side, and a cross on the meat side, but do not cut right through the skin. Scald in boiling water and rinse in cold water.
2. Roll cut the bamboo shoots into wedges. Drain the mushrooms and reserve the water.
3. Put a bamboo mat or tea plate at the bottom of the pot. Lay the pork on it, skin side down. Add the seasoning with the mushroom soaking water, the vegetables and cold water to cover. Bring to the boil on high heat, skim, reduce the heat to low, cover and simmer for about 2 hours.
4. Skim off the fat, take out the meat and put the pieces skin side up on a serving dish. Discard the onion and ginger. Place the vegetables round the meat.
5. Boil the cooking juice till well reduced and thick, pour over the meat and serve.

Named after the poet-official Su Tungpo, who took pleasure in preparing favourite dishes for himself and his friends during his exile in Huangzhou in Hubei province from 1080 to 1084. Later he was transferred to Hangzhou where his braised pork was so admired that local restaurants started to include it on their menus. Today Tungpo pork is eaten everywhere with slight variations here and there; this recipe is a Huaiyin and Yangzhou version.

WHITE SLICED PORK (BEIJING)

1.1 kg (2½ lb) belly pork or shoulder (boned)

Dip:
2 tbsp soya sauce
2 cloves garlic (minced)
1 tsp preserved Chinese chives (optional)
3 tsp fermented bean curd juice
3 tsp chilli oil

1. Put the pork in a pot with water to cover, bring to the boil, reduce the heat and simmer for about 1 hour, or till tender.
2. Take out, cool, peel off the skin, and cut the meat into thin slices, about 8 to 10 cm (3 to 4 in) long and 0.6 cm (¼ in) thick.
3. Mix together all the ingredients for the dip, and serve separately with the Mandarin pancakes.

   Mandarin pancakes:
   170 g (6 oz) flour

   Seasoning oil:
   1 tbsp sesame oil
   ½ tsp salt
   ½ tsp Sichuan peppercorns (ground)

1. Mix together all the ingredients for the seasoning oil, and set aside.
2. Make a well in the flour and pour in 80 ml (3 fl oz) of boiling water. Mix into a smooth dough. Divide into 30 pieces. Roll each piece into a circle 5 cm (2 in) in diameter. Brush one side with a little of the seasoning oil. Place one on another, oiled sides together. Roll each pair of pancakes into a 10 cm (4 in) circle.
3. Cook each pair in a dry thick frying pan or griddle on medium heat, till bubbles appear. Turn over, and when bubbles appear again they are ready. Take them out, separate them and stack together oiled side up. Cover with a tea towel to keep soft. Steam on a plate to reheat.

WRINKLED PORK (SHANDONG)

680 g (1½ lb) shoulder of pork (boned)
caramel or sweet salted bean paste (as required)

Seasoning:
2 pods star anise seeds (crushed)
4 tbsp stock or water
1 tbsp dark soya sauce

2 tsp rice wine
1 stalk spring onion (whole)
1 slice ginger (bruised)

1.1 l (2 pt) vegetable oil
2 tsp sugar
1 slice ginger (minced)

1. Boil the pork till par-cooked, about 20 minutes. Take it out and score a cross on the skin side, half the depth of the skin. Rub on some caramel or sweet salted bean paste.
2. Deep fry the pork till reddish golden. Take out and drain.
3. Place the star anise seeds in the bowl, and put in the pork skin side down. Add the stock and the rest of the seasoning. Steam in the wok till tender, about 45 minutes. Strain the juice, discard the spices and turn the meat on to a serving dish.
4. Add the sugar and minced ginger to the cooking juice and dissolve the sugar on a low heat. Pour the juice over the pork and serve.

The dark red skin of the pork appears wrinkled, hence the name. The meat may be braised instead, in which case increase the amount of stock. It may also be browned (skin side only) under the grill instead of deep fried.

YUNWU SMOKED PORK (ANHUI)

900 g (2 lb) belly pork
570 ml (1 pt) stock or water

Seasoning for meat:
3 pods star anise seeds
10 fennel seeds   } *(tied in a piece of muslin)*
3 peppercorns
1 tsp salt
1 stalk spring onion (tied in a knot)
1 slice ginger (bruised)

Smoking ingredients:
60 g (2 oz) dried cooked rice (guoba)
2 tbsp tea leaves
1 tbsp brown sugar

Dips:
light soya sauce
black vinegar (or vinegar)
sesame oil

1. Choose a square piece of meat. Grill the skin till bubbles appear. Soak in water (or better still rice water, water in which rice has been washed) for 15 minutes. Scrape off any charred part. Rinse in cold water.
2. Put the meat in a pot, add the stock or water, bring to the boil on high heat, and put in the seasonings. Skim, reduce the heat to low and simmer till the meat is cooked, about 40 minutes (if ready, the meat can be pierced with a chopstick). Take out.
3. Put the smoking ingredients in the wok (for the preparation of *guoba*, see page 224). Place a rack (a round wire cake cooler) in the wok. Put the meat on the rack, skin side up. Cover the wok and set it on high heat. The smoking mixture will start to smoulder, and smoke will come out under the lid. Take off the heat. Do not open the lid. Leave (off the heat) till the smoke is spent, about 8 minutes.
4. Take out the meat and cut into thin bite-size slices. Arrange them neatly on a plate. Serve with the dips in separate saucers.

This meat is suitable for the cold platter. *Yunwu* means 'cloud and mist', referring to the smoke. The smoke coming out of the wok is no more than the steam in ordinary cooking.

Poultry and Game

Chicken

CRISPY CHICKEN DRUMSTICKS (HENAN)

12 chicken drumsticks

Marinade:
2 tsp rice wine
2 tsp sugar
1 tsp salt

Seasoning for steaming:
2.5 cm (1 in) piece cassia bark (crushed)
1 pod star anise seed (crushed)
1 stalk spring onion (cut into 2.5 cm or 1 in lengths)
1 slice ginger (minced)

Batter mixture:
3 egg whites (lightly beaten)
1 tbsp cornflour

1.1 l (2 pt) peanut oil
a few parsley or coriander leaves (chopped)

Dips:
soya sauce
chilli sauce

1. Make slashes across the drumsticks. Rub in the marinade and let them stand at room temperature for 2 hours. Add the seasoning for steaming and steam in a wok on high heat for about 20 minutes, or till cooked. Take out and cool.
2. Make the batter. Dip each drumstick into the batter and deep fry till golden. Drain well on kitchen roll. Cover each drumstick end with paper frills and garnish with chopped parsley or coriander. Serve with the dips.

An aromatic, crisp, succulent and delectable dish for the buffet table.

HOT AND SPICY CHICKEN (HUNAN)

680 g (1½ lb) chicken meat on the bone

Seasoning for oil:
1 dried red chilli pepper (or 1 tsp chilli powder)
1 stalk spring onion (chopped)

Seasoning for sauce:
1 tbsp light soya sauce
2 tsp vinegar
½ tsp salt
110 ml (4 fl oz) chicken stock or water
1 tsp rendered chicken fat (optional)

550 ml (1 pt) chicken stock or water
1 tbsp sesame oil
a few coriander or parsley leaves (chopped)

1. Bring the chicken to the boil in the stock, reduce the heat and simmer for about 20 minutes, or till just cooked. Drain and cool. Remove the bones and cut the meat into neat bite-size pieces.
2. Mix together the seasoning for the sauce and set aside. Pour hot water over the dried chilli to soften it, then mince it fine.
3. Set the wok on high heat, put in the sesame oil and, when it is almost hot, stir in the chilli and the spring onion. Stir fry till fragrant and add in the seasoning mixture. Mix well and take off the heat.
4. Pour one-third of the seasoned sauce into a pudding basin, and put a few of the chicken pieces neatly in it, skin side down. Pour on a little sauce, and build up alternate layers of meat and sauce. Finally pour the rest of the sauce in. Turn out on to a serving plate. Garnish with the coriander leaves.

The chicken must not be overcooked but moist and tasty. Pack the meat tightly in the basin so that when turned out it has a round shape.

SPICY CHICKEN IN PUMPKIN (SICHUAN)

900 g (2 lb) tender chicken meat
1 pumpkin about 1.6–1.8 kg (3½–4 lb)

Marinade:
½ tsp salt
2 tsp rice wine
2 tsp fermented glutinous rice (optional)
1 tbsp light soya sauce
1 tbsp sugar
1 tbsp fermented red bean curd (mashed)
1 stalk spring onion (minced)
1 slice ginger (minced)

Seasoned rice flour:
2 tbsp long-grain rice
1 tsp Sichuan peppercorns

2 tbsp cooking oil
3 tbsp stock or water

1. Cut a piece from the top of the pumpkin to form a lid. Scoop out the seeds and fibrous part. Stand it in a bowl.
2. Mix together the seasoning for marinade. Chop the chicken into bite-size pieces. Marinate for 20 minutes.
3. Rinse the rice and dry fry with the Sichuan peppercorns till the rice is pale yellow and the spice fragrant. Cool and grind into powder. Coat the marinated chicken with the spiced flour.
4. Set the wok on high heat and put in the oil. When hot, stir fry the chicken till par-cooked, then add the stock or water. Fill the pumpkin with the chicken, replace the lid and steam in the wok for about 45 minutes to 1 hour on high heat. Serve hot with plain boiled rice.

This dish is a rural delicacy from Sichuan. It has a slightly sweet flavour. The pumpkin may be baked in a *bain-marie*, but protect the top with a piece of foil. The cooking time for pumpkin varies; a stored pumpkin needs at least 30 minutes longer. Though a pumpkin of this weight is not big, it needs a large wok which is not commonly found in Western households; the *bain-marie* method is a good alternative.

SPICY STEAMED CHICKEN (HUNAN)

340 g (12 oz) raw chicken meat (boned and skinned)
80 g (3 oz) pork fat

Marinade:
1 tbsp rice wine
½ tsp salt

Seasoning:
1 tbsp light soya sauce
1 tsp ginger (minced)
1 tsp sugar

Rice flour mixture:
30 g (1 oz) glutinous rice
30 g (1 oz) long-grain rice
½ pod star anise seed

1. Cut the chicken meat into *julienne* strips about 4 cm (1½ in)×1 cm (⅜ in). Marinate for about 15 minutes.
2. Shred the pork fat finely and mix with the marinated chicken and the seasoning. Mix well.
3. Dry fry the 2 kinds of rice and the star anise seed till the rice is a pale yellow. Cool and grind into powder.
4. Stir the rice flour into the meat mixture, and add 1 tbsp of water. Mix well and put in a bowl. Steam in a wok for about 1½ hours, till the pork fat dissolves. Halfway through cooking, sprinkle on 1 tbsp of cold water. Take out and turn on to a serving dish.

STEAMED SLIPPERY CHICKEN (GUANGDONG)

1 tender chicken about 0.9–1.1 kg (2–2½ lb)
6 caps winter mushrooms (soaked and shredded)
4 thin slices ginger (shredded)
1 tsp salt
1 tbsp cornflour
1 tbsp peanut oil
3 stalks spring onions (shredded)

1. Chop the chicken into bite-size pieces. Rub them with the salt and then the cornflour. Mix in the shredded mushroom and ginger.
2. Arrange them in a dish skin side up in one layer. Sprinkle on the oil and steam in the wok on high heat for 20 minutes; when the juice is clear, the chicken is cooked. Sprinkle on the spring onions and serve hot.

If preferred, sesame oil may be sprinkled on before serving.

147

TANGERINE PEEL CHICKEN (SICHUAN)

450 g (1 lb) chicken meat (boned and skinned)

Marinade:
½ tsp salt
1 tbsp rice wine
1 tbsp light soya sauce
1 stalk spring onion (minced)
1 slice ginger (minced)

Seasoning for oil:
2 tsp Sichuan peppercorns
1 tbsp dried tangerine peel (soaked and diced)
8 dried chillis (deseeded, cut into 2.5 cm or 1 in lengths)
2 stalks spring onion (cut into 2.5 cm or 1 in lengths)
2 slices ginger (bruised)
1 tsp chilli powder (or to taste)

Ingredients for sauce:
1 tbsp rice wine
2 tbsp light soya sauce
1 tbsp vinegar
2 tbsp sugar
½ tsp salt
280 ml (½ pt) stock

850 ml (1½ pt) cooking oil
4 tbsp sesame oil

1. Dice the chicken into 2.5 cm (1 in) cubes and marinate for 1 hour.
2. Mix together all the ingredients and stock for sauce.
3. Deep fry the chicken till golden. Drain well.
4. Heat the sesame oil and stir fry the Sichuan peppercorns till fragrant. Discard the peppercorns. Stir fry the tangerine peel and the dried chillis; when the chillis turn dark purple, add the spring onions, ginger and chilli powder. Stir fry briefly. Put in the chicken and the sauce mixture. Cover and cook till dry, on medium heat. Discard the spring onions and ginger.

This traditional Sichuan dish may be eaten hot or cold. If preferred the deep frying may be left out, and the chicken stir fried in step 4 with the spices.

YUNNAN *QI-GUO* (STEAM POT) CHICKEN (YUNNAN)

1 plump chicken about 1.6–1.8 kg (3½–4 lb)

Seasoning:
1 tsp salt
2 slices ginger (bruised)
2 stalks spring onion white (slightly bruised)
pepper to taste

1. Chop the chicken into 5 cm (2 in) square pieces.
2. Put the chicken pieces into the steam pot. Add the salt, spring onions and ginger. Put on the lid. No water or stock is needed for this dish.
3. Set the steam pot in another pot which should be filled with water to within 5 cm (2 in) of the top (see illustrations on page 100).
4. Bring the water in the lower pot to the boil on high heat, reduce the heat to medium and steam for 2 to 3 hours. Replenish the water in the lower pot every now and again with boiling water. The boiling water in the lower pot sends up steam through the vent in the steam pot to cook the meat (see illustrations on page 100).
5. When the chicken is cooked, discard the spring onion and ginger, and sprinkle with pepper. Take only the steam pot to the table.

Mainly winter fare, this traditional Yunnan dish is deemed a nutritious food. Sometimes tonic herbs such as *dong-chongcao* (Chinese caterpillar fungus) or Chinese wolfberries (red medler berries) are added to enhance the medicinal value. There is very little juice in this dish as no water has been added. The meat is tender and moist and all the flavour is conserved. For a soup, stock may be added before steaming.

Alternatively, the steam pot may be placed directly on the bottom of a larger pot without being raised. The water should be filled to just below the handles of the steam pot (see illustration on page 99). Bring the water to the boil in the outer pot, take off the heat and then put in the steam pot and proceed as usual.

Duck

BEIJING DUCK (BEIJING)

1 plump duck 2–2.3 kg (4½–5 lb)
1 tbsp maltose (or honey or sugar)

Accompaniment:
Mandarin pancakes (see page 142)
spring onion brushes (see page 227)
minced garlic (optional)
sweet salted soya-bean paste
radishes (or sliced cucumber)

149

1. *Scalding the duck*: hold the duck upright with the left hand, neck end upwards. Pour boiling water over it, turning it slowly. Do this only for a few seconds; too much hot water could cause the skin to exude oil, so that it will not crisp or colour easily. Wipe dry.
2. *Sousing with maltose water*: Mix the maltose with 280 ml (10 fl oz) water. Heat slightly to dissolve the maltose if necessary, but cool before use. Souse the duck with the maltose water, as above.
3. *Cooling the skin*: Put the duck on a meat hook and hang it up in a cool and airy place to dry. In the winter this will take about 10 hours. In summer, it may be left in the refrigerator on a rack, but take it out 2 hours before roasting. When airing it is important that the air is not too warm or the skin will run oil and it will not crisp well. To ensure it is thoroughly covered, souse the skin with more maltose mixture just before roasting.
4. *Roasting*: roast in a very hot oven, 230–250°C (450–475°F, gas mark 8–9) for about 45 minutes or till cooked, turning over halfway through cooking.
5. Cool slightly. Take off the skin, cut into bite-size pieces and arrange on a serving dish. Bone the duck, cut into bite-size pieces and place on a separate plate.
6. To eat, put a piece of pancake on the plate, brush on a little sweet salted bean paste (see page 228 for preparation) with a spring onion brush, add a piece of skin or meat (usually the skin is enjoyed first), a little garlic and a radish, roll up and eat.

This is a simplified version of the cooking of this famous dish. The preparation begins with the breeding of the duck. The duck is fed with special food from the time it is hatched for sixty days, when it reaches 2.3 to 2.7 kg (5 to 6 lb) in weight, and develops a meaty breast. The slaughtering is done in such a way that the skin is intact from head to tail. Air is pumped into the space between the skin and the meat and the aperture is tied up to keep the air in. Inside, the breast is held up by a piece of wood to keep it in shape when cooking. Then comes the sousing and cooling. Just before roasting the rear end of the duck is sealed with a wooden plug the size of a cork. Hot water is poured into the cavity through a hole in the duck's side previously made to disembowel it and this is also sealed. This hot water serves to keep the temperature inside the duck even, and by boiling it inside while it roasts outside, it cooks faster. This has the added advantage of replacing the moisture lost during roasting. The carcass is made into a stock to which either Chinese 'celery' cabbage or winter melon is added, which is served as a soup at the end of the meal. The liver, gizzard, wings and feet are cooked as a separate dish or dishes with vegetables, and served at the same table either hot or cold. The sliced breast meat may be served as an hors d'oeuvre or used in dishes where cooked duck meat is called for.

CONGCAO DUCK (SICHUAN)

1 duck about 1.8 kg (4 lb)
10 sticks Chinese caterpillar fungus (congcao)

Seasoning:
1 tsp salt
1 tbsp rice wine
pepper to taste
2 stalks spring onion
2 slices ginger (bruised)

1.4 l (2½ pt) clear stock or water

1. Remove the glands from the parson's nose. Scald the duck in boiling water for 1 minute, then rinse in cold water. Rinse the caterpillar fungus in water twice, then soak it briefly in a little water. Drain and reserve the soaking liquor. Split the spring onions and chop into 2.5 cm (1 in) lengths.
2. Put the spring onions and ginger inside the duck cavity and place the duck with the caterpillar fungus in a casserole, breast side up. Add in the stock and the soaking liquor. Put in the rest of the seasoning, cover the casserole and steam in a pot or wok till tender, about 2 hours.
3. Discard the spring onion and ginger and serve the duck in the casserole.

Western Sichuan is the main producing area of the Chinese caterpillar fungus, a medicinal herb, *congcao* or *dong-congcao* in Mandarin. This is a winter tonic food.

FIVE-SPICE DUCK (GUANGDONG)

1 duck about 1.8–2.3 kg (4–5 lb)
2.5 cm (1 in) piece galangal ginger (optional)

Marinade:
2 shallots or spring onions (minced)
1 slice ginger (minced)
4 tbsp five-spice powder

Seasoning for sauce:
110 ml (4 fl oz) dark soya sauce
110 g (4 oz) sugar
2 tbsp rice wine
1 tsp salt

¼ cucumber (sliced)

1. Mix together the ingredients for the marinade. Rub it all over the duck and inside the cavity. Scrape and bruise the galangal ginger, if used. Put the duck, giblets and ginger in a roaster, cover and let stand for at least 30 minutes.
2. Preheat the oven fairly hot, 190–200°C (375–400°F, gas mark 5–6). Roast the duck with the giblets and spices for 30 minutes in the covered roaster. When the oil begins to run and the spices smell fragrant, take the roaster out.
3. Mix the sauce seasoning with 100 ml (4 fl oz) of water. Pour the sauce mixture over the duck. Baste thoroughly, but there is no need to turn it over. When the sugar is completely dissolved, cover and roast for about another 45 minutes, or till just cooked.
4. Take out the duck and pour away excess fat. Baste it with the sauce. Leave it to cool completely in the sauce, covered. Chop and arrange in a plate. Heat up the sauce, reduce if necessary, and serve with the meat, poured over or separately. Garnish with the cucumber slices.

This dish is best cooked a day in advance for better flavour. It is eaten on feast days in Guangdong, especially in the rural areas. The oven method is a British innovation and a Western roaster is used. When roasting the aim is to avoid a crisp skin; it should be like a braised duck, with the meat still firm and not falling apart.

NANJING SALTWATER DUCK (JIANGSU)

1 duck about 2–2.3 kg (4½–5 lb)

Spiced salt mixture:
130–140 g (4½–5 oz) salt (according to size of duck)
2 tsp Sichuan peppercorns (ground)
1 tsp five-spice powder

Seasoning for duck cavity:
2 stalks spring onions
2 slices ginger (bruised)
1 pod star anise seed

Seasoning for cooking liquor:
4 slices ginger
4 stalks spring onions (each tied in a knot)
1 pod star anise seed
110 g (4 oz) salt
2 tsp black vinegar (Zhenjiang vinegar)

1. *Salting the duck*: dry fry the salt, ground Sichuan peppercorns and the five-spice powder till fragrant. Rub the cavity of the duck with half the salt mixture, and the outside of the duck with the rest. Leave it overnight in the refrigerator.
2. Put the seasonings inside the duck cavity.
3. *Boiling the duck*: bring about 2 l (or 4 pt) of water (or enough to cover the duck totally) to the boil with the seasoning for the cooking liquor. Reduce the heat, cover and simmer for 30 minutes till the water is well flavoured. Put in the duck, cover and simmer for about 45 minutes or till cooked.
4. Take out, cool, remove the spices inside the cavity and discard. Chop the duck into bite-size pieces and serve at room temperature with plain boiled rice.

Eaten cold only, Nanjing's famous duck looks creamy white.

SPICY CRISPY DUCK (HUNAN)

1 duck about 1.8–2.3 kg (4–5 lb)

Marinade:
1 stalk spring onion (minced)
1 slice ginger (minced)
1 tbsp rice wine
2 tsp Sichuan peppercorns (crushed)
1 pod star anise seed (crushed)

1.1 l (2 pt) tea oil or other vegetable oil
cornflour for dusting
a little sesame oil
a few more Sichuan peppercorns (ground)
a few coriander or parsley leaves (chopped)

Dip:
tomato ketchup

1. Rub the duck with the spring onion, ginger and wine and let stand for 30 minutes. Add the 2 tsp of crushed Sichuan peppercorns and the crushed star anise seed. Steam in the wok for about 1 hour or till cooked, but not overdone. Discard the spices. Drain well and dust thoroughly with the cornflour. Reserve the juice for other cooking.
2. Deep fry the duck till golden. Drain well on kitchen roll. Cool. Chop into bite-size pieces and arrange on a serving dish. Sprinkle with a little sesame oil and ground Sichuan peppercorns. Garnish with coriander or parsley leaves. Serve with tomato ketchup as a dip.

If preferred the duck may be roasted after dusting with cornflour in a hot oven, 220°C (425°F, gas mark 7) for 25 minutes on each side. Normally a bird is served with the pieces of meat rearranged into a bird shape in a flat layer on the dish, with head, tail, feet and wings, to denote that the dish is cooked from a whole bird. Tea oil is sometimes used in cooking in the tea-producing areas.

SUZHOU DUCK (JIANGSU)

1 duck about 2–2.3 kg (4½–5 lb)
230 g (8 oz) pork fat

Seasoning:
1 tbsp dried red fermented rice (hongqu)
80 ml (3 fl oz) dark soya sauce
1 tbsp salt
60 ml (2 fl oz) rice wine
60 g (2 oz) rock sugar (or granulated sugar)
2.5 cm (1 in) length cassia bark
1 pod star anise seed
3 stalks spring onion (each tied in a knot)
3 slices ginger (bruised)

Sauce:
2 tbsp sugar
1 tsp cornflour with a little water
2 tsp sesame oil

1. Rinse the duck and pork fat. Put a bamboo mat or tea plate at the bottom of a pot. Put in the pork fat and the duck. Pour in cold water to cover the duck. Cover and bring to the boil, skim and add the seasoning. Put another plate on top of the duck to make sure that it stays submerged during cooking. Cover the pot and bring to the boil. Reduce the heat to medium and cook for 30 minutes. Reduce the heat again to low, and simmer for about 45 minutes or till cooked. Take out and cool.
2. Remove the pork fat and discard all the spices. Strain the cooking liquor and bring to the boil. Take out 140 ml (5 fl oz) and reserve the rest for future cooking. Bring this liquor to the boil, add the 2 tbsp sugar and boil till it becomes sticky, then stir in the cornflour mixture and, when it has thickened, sprinkle on the sesame oil. This is the sauce.
3. Chop the duck into bite-size pieces, and arrange neatly in a serving plate. Pour the sauce over.

This is a traditional duck recipe from Suzhou. It is mahogany red, with succulent meat and a sweet, salty taste.

TEA-SMOKED DUCK (SICHUAN)

1 duck 1.8–2.3 kg (4–5 lb)

Smoking ingredients:
2 tbsp poplar-wood shavings (or 1 tbsp dried cooked rice)
1 tbsp tea leaves (jasmine tea)
1 tbsp soft brown sugar

Marinade:
1½ tbsp Sichuan pepper salt
2 tbsp rice wine

Seasoning for steaming:
2 stalks spring onions (cut into 2.5 cm or 1 in lengths)
2 slices ginger (bruised)

1.4 l (2½ pt) peanut oil
cornflour for dusting

Accompaniment:
spring onion whites (cut into 8 cm or 3 in lengths)
sweet salted soya bean paste
steamed lotus-leaf buns (see below)

1. *Marinating*: rub the duck all over and inside with the Sichuan pepper salt and wine. Leave to stand for 2 hours at room temperature, or overnight in the refrigerator. Wipe with kitchen paper and hang in a cool and airy place to dry the skin.
2. *Smoking*: put the poplar shavings or rice, tea leaves and sugar in a thick pot or wok. Place a rack over them, about 13 cm (5 in) off the bottom. Place the duck on the rack, breast up. Cover and place the wok over heat. When the wok is sufficiently heated, smoke will start coming out. Do not open the lid. Turn off the heat and leave for 5 minutes. The duck will turn a saffron colour.
3. *Steaming*: put the spring onions and ginger inside the duck cavity. Steam it in the wok for about 1½ hours. Discard the spices and drain the duck well in a colander. Dust it all over with the cornflour.
4. *Deep frying*: deep fry in hot oil till the skin is crisp. Take out, cool slightly, and chop into bite-size pieces. Arrange on a serving plate in the form of a bird.
5. Steam the lotus-leaf buns to reheat them and place round the duck. Serve with the spring onion whites and the sweet salted bean paste.

This is a traditional Sichuan banquet dish, full flavoured, rich and tasty, dark red in colour. In Sichuan it is smoked with camphor wood and tea, and the proper name is 'camphor tea duck', *zhangcha-ya*. It may be roasted after steaming and dusting with cornflour, about 30 minutes each side in a hot oven. The meat is sandwiched inside the 'leaves' of the buns and the two eaten together.

Steamed lotus-leaf buns, *heyehjia*

340 g (12 oz) flour
20 g (¾ oz) fresh yeast or 1 tsp dried yeast
1 tsp sugar
230 ml (8 fl oz) warm water
½ tsp salt
sesame oil for brushing

1. Make a basic bread dough with the ingredients. Leave to rise to twice its volume.
2. Knock down the risen dough and knead lightly. Form into a long roll and break into 20 pieces of equal size.
3. Roll each piece into a round about 8 cm (3 in) across. Brush on a little sesame oil and fold into a semicircle. With a blunt knife make some criss-cross designs on one surface and cut 2 dents on the rounded edge, forming 3 scallops, a lotus leaf. Make all the buns in this way.
4. Line the steaming basket or metal steamer top with a folded damp cloth. Bring the water in the wok or lower steamer to a fast boil on high heat. Place the buns on the cloth in the basket or metal steamer top, cover and steam for 10 minutes. Take out and cool slightly on a rack, to let excess moisture dry off. To reheat, steam for 5 minutes before serving.

Goose

CHAOZHOU STEAMED GOOSE (GUANGDONG)

1 goose (or large duck) about 2.7 kg (6 lb)

Seasoning for oil:
3 cloves garlic (minced)
2 slices ginger (minced)
2 stalks spring onions (minced)

Seasoning paste for goose:
4 tbsp salted soya bean paste
1 tsp star anise seed powder
*1 tsp dried tangerine peel powder or 2.5 cm (1 in) square piece of tangerine
peel, soaked and minced*
1 tsp salt
2 tsp sugar
2 tsp sesame paste
1 tbsp hoisin *sauce (or plum sauce)*
2 tbsp stock or water
1 tbsp rice wine
2 tsp dark soya sauce

1 tbsp cooking oil
dark soya sauce for brushing
1 tsp cornflour with a little water

1. Mix all the seasoning ingredients for the paste (except the rice wine and dark soya sauce) together, and set aside.
2. Put the wok on medium heat, put in the oil and, when hot, stir fry the seasoning for the oil till fragrant. Add the seasoning paste mixture and stir fry briefly. Add the rice wine and dark soya sauce. Take out and cool.
3. Fill the goose cavity with the seasoning paste mixture. Rub all round inside. Sew up the neck and tail opening with thread.
4. Steam in a wok, large steaming basket or steamer on medium heat for 2 hours or till cooked. Test with a skewer on the thigh; if the juice runs clear it is cooked.
5. Take out the goose and, while still hot, brush all over with the dark soya sauce. Pull out the thread, and pour out the juice into a bowl and reserve. Chop the goose into bite-size pieces and arrange on a serving dish in the shape of a bird in one layer.
6. Bring the reserved juice to the boil. Stir in the cornflour and water to thicken. Pour over the goose and serve.

A duck cooked this way is just as delicious. If preferred the bird may be roasted in the oven instead.

Quail

QUAILS IN SWEET AND SOUR SAUCE (ZHEJIANG)

4 quails (dressed)
30 g (1 oz) cooked carrots (diced)
30 g (1 oz) cooked peas

1 small onion (diced)

Seasoning:
2 tsp rice wine
2 tsp sugar
2 tsp vinegar
1 tbsp light soya sauce

flour for dusting
1.1 l (2 pt) rape-seed oil or other vegetable oil
2 tsp sesame oil
60 ml (2 fl oz) stock or water

1. Rinse, dry and quarter the quails. Cover them with the flour.
2. Deep fry the quails in hot oil for about 2 minutes, or till golden. Drain well.
3. Put the wok on high heat, add 2 tsp of oil, stir fry the onion briefly, put in the carrots, peas and quails, and mix well. Stir in the seasoning and water, mix well and dish up. Sprinkle on the sesame oil and serve.

The quail is succulent and tender; this is a colourful and tasty dish.

Rabbit

HOT AND SPICY STIR-FRIED RABBIT (HUNAN)

230 g (8 oz) rabbit meat (boned)
30 g (1 oz) young leeks (or spring onion whites)

Marinade for rabbit:
2 tsp light soya sauce
2 tsp rice wine
½ tsp salt
1 tsp cornflour with a little water

Seasoning for oil:
60 g (2 oz) red chilli peppers (or to taste)
1 tsp Sichuan peppercorns (crushed)

Seasoning for sauce:
2 tsp light soya sauce
2 tsp vinegar

1 tsp cornflour with 2 tbsp water
1 kg (2¼ lb) lard (or 1.1 l or 2 pt cooking oil)
2 tsp sesame oil

1. Score the meat in a criss-cross pattern, then dice it into small cubes, about 1.3 cm (½ in). Marinate for about 30 minutes.
2. Slice the chillis in halves, deseed and cut into 1.3 cm (½ in) pieces. Roll cut the leeks into 1.3 cm (½ in) lengths.
3. Deep fry the rabbit meat till light golden. Drain well.
4. Set the wok on medium heat, put in 1 tbsp lard or oil, and when hot stir fry the red chillis, Sichuan peppercorns and a pinch of salt briefly. Add the rabbit meat, mix well, then stir in the vinegar, soya sauce and leeks. Stir in the cornflour mixture. When thickened take off the heat, sprinkle with sesame oil and dish up.

Fish and Seafood

Abalone

ABALONE IN OYSTER SAUCE (SHANDONG)

1 tin abalone (460g; 15½ oz)
1 tbsp oyster sauce

Seasoning:
2 tsp light soya sauce
2 tsp rice wine
1 tsp cornflour with a little water

1. Drain and reserve the abalone juice. Slice the abalone thinly.
2. Measure 5 tbsp of the reserved abalone juice and put in the wok. Bring to the boil, and add the seasoning, cornflour mixture, abalone slices and oyster sauce. Mix well and dish up.

The abalone is just heated through; overcooking would toughen it. In Shandong fresh abalone is normally used.

Crab

SCRAMBLED EGGS WITH CRAB MEAT (FUJIAN)

230 g (8 oz) dressed crab meat
5 duck eggs (or chicken eggs)
60 g (2 oz) pork fat
60 g (2 oz) bamboo shoots
5 caps winter mushrooms (soaked)
60 g (2 oz) water chestnuts (peeled)
4 stalks spring onion whites

Seasoning:
2 tsp rice wine
pepper to taste
1 tsp salt

2 tbsp lard or cooking oil
a few coriander leaves (chopped)

1. Beat the eggs with the salt till blended, and set aside.
2. Shred the pork fat, mushrooms, bamboo shoots, spring onion whites and water chestnuts finely. Put them in the eggs with the crab meat and mix well.
3. Set the wok on high heat, put in the lard and swish it round. When it is smoking hot, pour in the crab meat mixture and stir fry for about 5 to 7 minutes. Take off the heat and sprinkle on the rice wine and pepper. Dish up, garnish with the coriander leaves and serve hot.

STIR-FRIED CRABS WITH GINGER AND SPRING ONION (ZHEJIANG)

2 live crabs about 900 g (2 lb) each
2 eggs
1 tsp cornflour with a little water

Seasoning:
2 stalks spring onions (cut into 2.5 cm or 1 in lengths)
2 slices ginger (minced)
2 tsp rice wine
1 tbsp light soya sauce

2 tbsp rape-seed oil or other vegetable oil
2 tsp melted lard

1. Pierce the crabs with a chopstick through the mouth. Scrub well with a stiff brush. Rinse thoroughly. Pull off the shells and remove the spongy parts. Cut each half down the middle, then in half the other way to make 4 pieces of each. Trim the legs and crack the claws with the back of a chopper.
2. Beat the eggs lightly and mix in the cornflour mixture, then set aside.
3. Set the wok on high heat, put in the oil, stir fry the spring onion and ginger till fragrant, and add in the crab pieces. Stir fry for about 2 minutes. Pour in the rice wine and soya sauce, cover and cook for 2 minutes. When the crabs turn red they are cooked. Stir in the egg and flour mixture. Mix well. Stir in the lard and dish up.

This is a tasty local dish from Xiangshan in Zhejiang, near the coast by the river mouth. Smaller crabs are used for stir frying.

Fish

CHRYSANTHEMUM FISH (JIANGSU)

1 piece white fish fillet about 250–280 g (9–10 oz) (with skin)

Gravy:
1½ tbsp vinegar
3 tbsp sugar
1 tsp salt
3 tbsp tomato ketchup
4 tbsp pork stock or water
1 tsp cornflour with a little water

Seasoning for gravy:
1 tbsp lard or oil
1 stalk spring onion (chopped)
1 clove garlic (minced)
2 tsp sesame oil

cornflour for dusting
1.1 l (2 pt) cooking oil

1. Place the fish fillet skin side down on the chopping board. With a sharp knife, slice the meat on a slant almost to the skin, and cut through the skin only on every fourth slice, so that every piece has 4 slices joined by the skin. Cut 10 pieces altogether. Then slice each piece lengthwise at about 0.6 cm (¼ in) spacing, but do not cut through (see illustrations). Dust each piece well with cornflour and shake off any excess.

2. Mix together all the ingredients for the gravy, and set aside.
3. Deep fry the fish pieces till golden, drain well and place them on a serving dish.
4. Heat the wok and put in 2 tsp of the lard. Stir fry the spring onion and garlic till fragrant. Give the gravy mixture a stir and add to the wok; when thickened, stir in the rest of the lard and the sesame oil and pour over the fish.

This dish gets its name from the way the strips of fish spread out like the petals of a chrysanthemum.

CLEAR-STEAMED FISH (GUANGDONG)

1 whole fish about 680 g (1½ lb) (carp, sea bass, pomfret or trout)
60 g (2 oz) cooked ham or smoked back bacon (shredded)
4 caps winter mushrooms (soaked and shredded)
2 stalks spring onions (whole)
8 thin slices ginger

Seasoning for sauce:
1 tsp salt
4 tbsp stock or water
pepper to taste
1 tbsp rice wine
1 tsp cornflour
2 tsp sesame oil

3 tbsp cooking oil
1 tbsp coriander leaves (in small sprigs)

1. Mix together all the seasoning for the sauce (except the sesame oil), and set aside.
2. Scale, gut, rinse and dry the fish. Make a slash on the thick part of each side of the fish. Rub a little salt all over and inside.
3. Place the 2 whole spring onions across the plate and lay fish across them at right angles.
4. Arrange the shredded mushrooms, ham and ginger slices neatly on top of the fish in any design. Sprinkle on 1 tbsp of the oil and steam in the wok on high heat for 20 minutes. When the juice looks clear, the fish is cooked.
5. Drain off the juice, and discard the onions. Slide the fish on to a heated serving dish. Keep warm.
6. Heat the rest of the oil and pour over the fish. Bring the sauce mixture to the boil; when thickened, pour over the fish and sprinkle on the sesame oil. Place the coriander leaves by the tail end and serve immediately.

This is one of the 'great ten' in Cantonese seafood preparation.

FISH SLICES IN FERMENTED GLUTINOUS RICE (BEIJING)

280 g (10 oz) white fish meat (skinned and boned)
1 tbsp dried wood ears (soaked and cleaned)

Marinade:
1 tbsp rice wine
1 tsp salt
1 egg white (lightly beaten)
2 tsp cornflour with a little water

Seasoning for oil:
1 stalk spring onion (chopped)
2 slices ginger (minced)
1 tbsp fermented glutinous rice

Sauce:
½ tsp salt
1 tsp sugar
1 tsp cornflour
80 ml (3 fl oz) stock or water

1 tbsp cooking oil

1. Boil the soaked and cleaned wood ears in water for 1 minute, drain and set aside. Mix together the ingredients for sauce mixture.
2. Slice the fish into 1.3 cm (½ in) thick slices (fish available here is too soft to slice thinner). Marinate with the wine and salt for 20 minutes. Then mix in the egg white and cornflour mixture.
3. Steam the fish in the wok for 10 minutes, or till cooked. Drain away any water.
4. Heat 1 tbsp oil, and stir fry the ginger and spring onion and the fermented rice till fragrant. Add the wood ears and the sauce mixture, and mix well. Stir in the fish and dish up.

The fish is often deep fried. Cod and haddock are best cut in thick slices.

MOCK CRAB (SHANDONG)

230 g (½ lb) white fish fillet (skinned)
4 egg yolks

Seasoning for oil:
1 stalk spring onion (chopped)
1 slice ginger (minced)
1 clove garlic (minced)

Sauce:
2 tsp rice wine
1 tsp salt
2 tsp ginger juice
5 tbsp stock or water
1 tsp cornflour with a little water

2 tbsp lard or cooking oil

1. Steam the fish till cooked. Cool slightly and flake. Beat the egg yolks, and set aside.
2. Mix together the ingredients for the sauce, and set aside.
3. Heat the wok, put in the lard, stir fry the spring onion, ginger and garlic till fragrant, pour in the egg yolks, stir well, and add the flaked fish. Stir in the sauce mixture, mix well and dish up.

This dish looks and tastes like crab, hence the name. It makes an excellent filling for *vol-au-vent* cases and pastry flans.

GRAPE FISH (ANHUI)

450 g (1 lb) fish fillet (any firm white fish, with skin)

Marinade:
1 stalk spring onion (cut into 2.5 cm or 1 in lengths)
1 slice ginger (shredded)
½ tsp salt
2 tsp light soya sauce

Coating:
1 egg (lightly beaten)
flour for dusting

Sauce:
60 ml (2 fl oz) grape juice
3 tbsp sugar (or to taste)
3 tsp vinegar
1 tbsp light soya sauce
½ tsp salt
1 tsp cornflour with a little water
2 tsp sesame oil

550 ml (1 pt) vegetable oil
4 lettuce leaves (trimmed to look like vine leaves)

1. Choose a thick piece of fish fillet. Score the flesh side of the fillet in a criss-cross pattern at about 2 cm (¾ in) spacing, as far as

the skin, but not cut through it. Marinate for 20 minutes.

2. Discard the ginger and spring onion. Cover the fish with the beaten egg. Then roll it in the flour, making sure that both the surface and the cuts in the flesh are well dusted.

3. Mix together all the ingredients for the sauce, and set aside.

4. Deep fry the fish in hot oil for about 3 minutes, until it turns pale golden, the skin begins to shrink, and the flesh opens out to look like a bunch of grapes. Take out and drain well. Keep warm.

5. Give the sauce mixture a stir and bring to the boil. Pour it over the 'grape fish'. Place the trimmed lettuce leaves at the fat end of the 'bunch of grapes'.

This is an exotic form of sweet and sour fish.

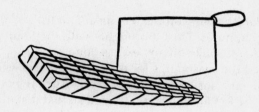

SQUIRREL FISH (JIANGSU)

1 whole fish about 680–900 g (1½–2 lb) (grouper, haddock or whiting)

Marinade:
1 tbsp rice wine
1 tsp salt

flour for dusting

Sauce:
4 tbsp sugar
3 tbsp vinegar
3 tbsp tomato ketchup
60 ml (2 fl oz) pork stock or water
1 tsp salt
2 tsp rice wine
1 tsp cornflour with a little water

Seasoning for oil:
2 stalks spring onion whites (cut into 2.5 cm or 1 in lengths)
1 clove garlic (minced)

Accompanying ingredients:
1 tbsp raw shelled prawns (optional)
1 tbsp bamboo shoots (diced)

1 tbsp garden peas
3 caps winter mushrooms (soaked and diced)

1.4 l (2½ pt) cooking oil
2 tsp lard
2 tsp sesame oil

1. Scale and gut the fish, and rinse well. Wipe dry. Cut off the head and split it in halves. Fillet the fish from the head end towards the tail but leave about 2.5 cm (1 in) of the tail end joined. Remove the back bone, cutting it through at the join.
2. Score on the flesh side lengthwise at about 1 cm (⅜ in) spacing, then score crossways at an angle and about 2.5 cm (1 in) spacing, but do not cut through the skin (see illustrations 1 and 2).
3. Rub the salt and the wine on the fish meat and fish head and leave to stand for 20 minutes. Dust thoroughly with the flour, pick up the fish by the tail and shake off any excess flour.
4. Mix together all the seasonings for the sauce, and set aside.
5. Heat the oil to very hot, about 190°C (375°F). Turn the fish flesh side up, and with the left hand pick up the tail so that it stands up; then with a pair of chopsticks pick up the other end, holding the two pieces together, and lower the fish into the hot oil (see illustrations 3 and 4). Hold the fish for about 20 seconds till the shape firms, then let go and ladle some hot oil over the tail. Add the fish head to the oil. Cook both till a pale yellow and take out.
6. Reheat the oil to the original temperature and fry the fish again till golden and crisp. Take it out and drain well on kitchen paper. Place it on an oval plate.
7. Heat an (empty) wok, put in 1 tbsp of oil, stir fry the spring onion whites till yellow and fragrant, then take them out and discard. Add the garlic to the oil and stir fry the prawn meat and the vegetables for 1 minute. Stir in the sauce mixture and, when thickened, add the lard and the sesame oil. Mix well and pour over the fish.

This is a local dish of Jiangsu province.

STEAMED FISH IN THE SNOW (ANHUI)

1 whole fish about 900 g (2 lb) (firm white fish)
170 g (6 oz) chicken breast meat (skinned and boned)
30 g (1 oz) winter mushrooms (soaked)
60 g (2 oz) cooked ham (sliced) + 2 tsp (minced)
4 egg whites

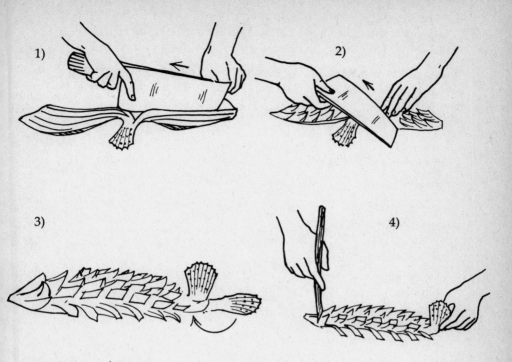

Marinade:
1 tsp salt
3 tsp rice wine

Seasoning for steaming:
1 stalk spring onion (cut into 2.5 cm or 1 in lengths)
2 tsp ginger (sliced)
½ tsp salt
2 tsp rice wine
1 tbsp stock

1. Scale, gut and rinse the fish. Cut off the head and about 8 cm (3 in) of the tail end. Reserve them. Fillet the rest of the fish. Cut the fish, chicken meat and 60 g (2 oz) ham into similar-sized slices. Marinate the fish and chicken meat together for 15 minutes.
2. Cut the soaked mushrooms into thin slices.
3. Choose an oval plate, and place the fish head at one end and the tail at the other. In the middle, in 2 rows, place the ham, fish, mushroom and chicken slices in sandwich fashion, to form the body of the fish. Scatter the spring onions and ginger slices on top. Mix together the rest of the seasoning for steaming and sprinkle on the 'fish body'. Steam in the wok for 20 minutes on high heat, or till cooked. Discard the spring onions and ginger.

167

4. Whisk the egg whites to a soft foam, and pour over the 'fish body', leaving the head and tail uncovered. Steam again on high heat for 3 minutes. Take out, sprinkle on the minced ham and serve hot.

This is rather fun to cook. The combination of chicken, mushroom, ham and fish gives an excellent flavour. If preferred the head and tail may be omitted.

WEST LAKE VINEGAR FISH (ZHEJIANG)

1 carp about 680 g (1½ lb) (or seabass, or grey mullet)

Seasoning for boiling fish:
1 tbsp light soya sauce
2 tsp rice wine
1 slice ginger (bruised)

Seasoning for gravy:
2½ tbsp sugar
2 tbsp vinegar
1 slice ginger (minced)
1 tsp cornflour with a little water

1. Scale, gut and rinse the fish well. Starting from the tail end, split the fish into left and right halves, stopping just behind the head. Leave the head on, but split it in half, so that you have two complete half fish. Leave the backbone in one half; the Chinese culinary term for this is the 'male half', and the boneless side is the 'female half'. Make 5 slashes about 4.5 cm (1¾ in) apart starting from the head end and cut through on the third slash on the 'male half' only, to make 2 pieces. Slash the 'female half' but leave whole.
2. Bring a generous 1 l (2 pt) of water to the boil, and put in the 'male half' head end first, then the tail end, and finally the 'female half', skin side up. Cover and bring back to the boil. Lift the cover, skim and bring to the boil again, cooking the fish altogether for about 3 minutes, or till it is done. Take out 110 ml (4 fl oz) of the cooking liquor, and set aside. Add the seasoning to the fish, heat through, and discard the ginger. Take out the fish and place on a warm serving dish, skin side up, with the two halves side by side and back to back.
3. Mix together the seasonings for gravy and stir into the reserved cooking liquor. Cook on medium heat, and when thickened pour over the fish and serve.

In China a carp is usually bought alive and kept in a bamboo cage which is lowered into clean clear water. It is left unfed for 1 to 2 days before cooking. This fasting process helps to clean out the muddy taste, and also firms the flesh. This is a traditional dish from Hangzhou in Zhejiang province.

Oysters

OYSTER OMELETTE (FUJIAN)

12 oysters (fresh or frozen)
4 duck eggs (or chicken eggs)
4 tbsp flour
½ tsp baking powder

Seasoning:
1 tsp salt
2 tsp light soya sauce
pepper to taste
2 tsp ginger juice
4 stalks spring onions (cut into 1.3 cm or ½ in lengths)
3 tbsp lard or cooking oil

Dip:
Zhejiang vinegar (red) with chilli, garlic and salt to taste

1. Open fresh oysters, or defrost frozen oysters thoroughly. Drain, and reserve the juice. Cut each oyster into 3 or 4 pieces.
2. Beat the eggs, and mix in the oysters and the seasoning ingredients.
3. Sift the flour with the baking powder, and mix in the reserved oyster juice. Add this to the egg mixture. Mix well.
4. Heat the wok on medium heat till hot, put in 2 tsp of oil, and swish it round to cover an area of about 20 cm (8 in) in diameter.
5. Give the oyster batter a stir. Ladle a quarter of it into the wok. Lower the heat, and swing the wok round so that the batter is spread evenly. When it is almost dry turn over and cook for 1 minute to brown, then take out.
6. Make 3 more omelettes in this way, re-oiling the wok each time. The mixture can be made into one large omelette if preferred.

Oyster pancakes and omelettes are the specialities of Xiamen (Amoy) along the coast.

SOFT-FRIED OYSTER AND CRAB-MEAT OMELETTE (FUJIAN)

230 g (8 oz) oysters (fresh or frozen; weight without shells)

169

110 g (4 oz) dressed crab meat (red and white mixed)
30 g (1 oz) minced pork
4 caps winter mushrooms (soaked and diced)

Egg batter:
2 duck eggs (or chicken eggs)
2 tbsp flour

Seasoning for oil:
1 clove garlic (minced)
1 slice ginger (minced)
4 stalks spring onions (chopped)
1 tsp salt

3 tbsp cooking oil
1 tbsp rice wine
a little sesame oil

1. Open fresh oysters, or thoroughly defrost frozen ones. Drain, and reserve the juice.
2. Beat the eggs, mix in the flour and make a batter. Add the crab meat.
3. Put the wok on high heat, add 1 tbsp oil, and when hot put in the garlic and ginger. Stir fry till fragrant, then add the spring onions, mushrooms, pork, oysters and salt. Stir fry till cooked, about 3 minutes. Take out, strain off the cooking juice and add to the reserved oyster juice. Mix the cooked oyster mixture into the crab and egg batter.
4. Add the rice wine to the oyster juice mixture.
5. Rinse the wok, replace on low heat, and when hot add 1 tbsp oil. Stir the batter mixture and pour it all into the wok, swinging the wok about to make a large round of roughly 20 cm (8 in) diameter. Cook for 3 minutes, then take off the heat for 2 minutes. Turn over. Drip in 1 tbsp oil all round the edge of the omelette. Put the wok back on the heat. Cook for another 5 minutes.
6. Dribble the wine and juice mixture round the edge of the omelette, and heat through. Transfer to a serving dish, sprinkle on some sesame oil and serve hot.

This is a popular snack from Xiamen (Amoy), and is served with drinks.

Prawns

LONGJING TEA PRAWNS (ZHEJIANG)

680 g (1½ lb) raw prawns

1 tsp Longjing tea leaves
2 tsp rice wine

Marinade:
1 egg white (lightly beaten)
½ tsp salt
2 tsp cornflour with a little water
900 g (2 lb) lard, or 850 ml (1½ pt) cooking oil

1. Shell the prawns and discard the heads. Rub them with a little salt, and rinse well.
2. Mix together the egg white, salt, cornflour and prawns. Marinate for 1 hour.
3. Pour 60 ml (2 fl oz) of boiling water on to the tea leaves. Do not cover. Set aside.
4. Heat the oil on medium heat and, when hot, deep fry the prawns for about 15 seconds, separating them with a pair of chopsticks. Drain immediately.
4. Return the prawns to the wok on medium heat, pour in the tea leaves and tea, and stir in the rice wine. Mix well and dish up.

A traditional dish from Hangzhou, this is usually cooked with newly picked Longjing tea leaves around *Qingming* festival time, in early April.

PAN-FRIED PRAWN CAKES (HENAN)

Prawn mixture:
170 g (6 oz) raw prawn meat (minced)
1 egg (lightly beaten)
1 tbsp cornflour + more for dusting
1 tsp salt
1 stalk spring onion white (minced)

Seasoning:
1 slice ginger (shredded)
1 stalk spring onion (shredded)
½ tsp Sichuan peppercorns (ground)
1 tbsp lard or cooking oil

1. Mix together all the ingredients for the prawn mixture into a firm dough. Form into a ball with a spatula, and dust with some cornflour.
2. Set a frying pan on medium heat, and put in the lard, then the prawn mixture, lowering it in with a fish slice. Reduce the heat to low. With the spatula flatten the mixture into a disc, and cook gently, turning once, till both sides are golden.

171

3. Mix together the spring onion, ginger and Sichuan peppercorn and sprinkle on to the cake. Continue cooking until fragrant. Take out, drain well, cut into bite-size pieces and serve.

Golden and tasty, this prawn cake has a spongy and resilient texture. It may be sliced thin and stir fried with Chinese chives, mung-bean sprouts or noodles, and is excellent eaten with salad.

STEAMED PRAWN ROLLS (ANHUI)

Prawn mixture:
170 g (6 oz) raw prawn meat (minced)
110 g (4 oz) raw fish meat (skinned and minced)
15 g (½ oz) cooked ham or smoked back bacon (minced)
1 stalk spring onion (minced)
1 slice ginger (minced)
½ tsp salt
2 tsp light soya sauce
2 tsp rice wine
1 egg white
2 tsp cornflour with a little water
2 tsp lard (or cooking oil)

Sauce:
½ tsp sugar
80 ml (3 fl oz) chicken stock
1 tsp cornflour with a little water
2 tsp rendered chicken fat

3 pieces bean-curd skin each about 20×13 cm (8×5 in)
1 tbsp bamboo shoots (shredded)
15 g (½ oz) cooked ham (shredded)
30 g (1 oz) pea shoots (or parsley, coriander)

1. Mix together all the ingredients for the prawn mixture, and divide into 3 equal portions.
2. Dip the bean-curd skins in hot water briefly, drain and pat dry. Spread a piece of bean-curd skin on a flat surface, and trim away any hard edges. Spread a portion of the prawn mixture to cover the skin. Roll up into a cylinder, and put on a plate folded side down. Make another 2 in the same way.
3. Steam in the wok over high heat for 10 minutes, take out, cool slightly and cut diagonally into 2.5 cm (1 in) lengths. Arrange neatly on a serving plate.
4. Bring the chicken stock to the boil, add the vegetables and ham, and

bring back to the boil. Stir in the sauce ingredients and pour over the prawn rolls.

Squid

HOT AND SOUR SQUIDS (HUNAN)

110 g (4 oz) dried squids (body only)
60 g (2 oz) lean pork
2 tbsp Hunan pickled vegetables (see below)
1 tbsp bamboo shoots
1 tbsp leek or garlic
1 tsp chilli powder (or to taste)

Seasoning:
1 tbsp light soya sauce
1 tsp salt
1 tbsp vinegar
4 tbsp stock or water
1 tsp cornflour with a little water

1 tsp lye water
1.1 l (2 pt) cooking oil
1 tsp sesame oil

1. Soak the squids in cold water for 1 hour, then remove the membrane and bone. Cut in halves lengthwise. On the inside (bone side) make criss-cross slashes, then cut into 4×2 cm (1½×¾ in) oblongs (see illustrations).

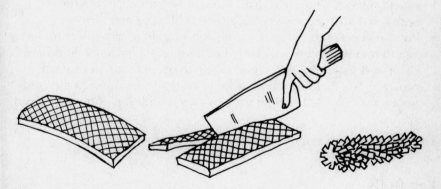

2. Put the squid pieces in a bowl and pour boiling water over them. When they curl up, drain at once and put them in cold water to cover with a teaspoon of lye water. Let them soak for about 30 minutes to soften. Rinse twice in warm water to remove the lye

water completely. Drain, rub with a little salt and dust with some cornflour.

3. Shred the pork, bamboo shoots, leeks and the pickled vegetables finely.
4. Mix the seasoning together, and set aside.
5. Deep fry the squid for 30 seconds. Drain well on kitchen paper.
6. Heat the wok till hot, put in 1 tbsp of oil and stir fry the pork. When it turns white, add the vegetables and chilli powder. When well mixed, add the squid and the seasoning mixture. When the sauce is thickened, dish up, sprinkle with a little sesame oil and serve.

The cooking should be done very fast, as overcooking toughens the squid.

Hunan pickled vegetables

vegetables (see step 2 below)

Pickling mixture:
2.3 l (4 pt) cooled boiled water
80 g (3 oz) salt
1 tsp Sichuan peppercorns
1 pod star anise seed
60 ml (2 fl oz) rice wine
30 g (1 oz) sugar
30 ml (1 fl oz) vinegar

1. Put the pickling mixture ingredients with 2.3 l (4 pt) cooled boiled water in a clean, dry enamelled or glazed earthenware pot large enough to leave some space at the top.
2. Rinse, dice and dry any or all of the following vegetables: white salad cabbage, Chinese radish, French beans, radishes, runner beans, red and green sweet peppers, chilli peppers, carrots.
3. Put the vegetables, when they appear limp, in an airy place in the sun to remove excess moisture. Put them in the pickling liquid, cover and seal tight. After 1 or 2 days they are ready to be used in cooking. The pickling liquid, if kept clean and not mixed with cold water, may be used several times with the addition of more salt and spices.

This pickle keeps for months in the refrigerator.

Egg Rolls

STEAMED EGG PURSES (SHANDONG)

Egg skins:
4 eggs

30 g (1 oz) cornflour with a little water
½ tsp salt

Pork filling:
80 g (3 oz) minced pork
1 stalk spring onion (chopped)
1 slice ginger (minced)
½ tsp salt
1 tsp light soya sauce
1 tsp rice wine

Sauce:
3 tbsp stock
½ tsp salt
1 tsp rice wine

110 ml (4 fl oz) stock (for steaming)

1. Mix together all the ingredients for the pork filling. Divide into 8 portions.
2. Beat the eggs lightly to blend well, add the cornflour and water mixture and salt. Mix well.
3. Heat a small wok or 18 cm (7 in) frying pan on medium heat. Grease it with a little oil. Pour one-eighth of the egg mixture into the wok to make a 5 cm (2 in) round. Remove the wok from the heat if it gets too hot. Put one portion of the filling in the centre of the egg skin when it is still liquid on top but cooked underneath. Quickly, before the egg hardens, use chopsticks to pick up the edges and gather them together so that they meet and stick together. Take out the 'egg purse'. Make 8 in the same way.
4. Arrange the 'purses', gathered sides down, in a bowl. Add the stock and steam in the wok for about 10 minutes on high heat, till the meat is cooked. Drain and reserve the cooking juice. Turn the 'egg purses' on to a serving dish.
5. Mix the reserved cooking juice with the sauce ingredients, bring to the boil and pour over the 'egg purses'.

If you have difficulty forming the 'purses' over the top of the filling, you will find it easier to put the filling on one side of the circle and fold the skin over it to make a semicircle.

STEAMED EGG ROLLS AND CABBAGE (YUNNAN)

Pork filling:
230 g (8 oz) minced pork (¼ fat)
1 egg white

1 tsp cornflour with a little water
½ tsp salt

Egg skins:
2 eggs
1 egg yolk
2 tsp cornflour with a little water

Soup:
½ tsp salt
pepper to taste

425 ml (15 fl oz) strong stock
450 g (1 lb) Chinese 'celery' cabbage
2 tsp melted lard or oil
½ tsp salt
140 ml (5 fl oz) stock
1 tsp sesame oil

1. Cut the cabbage into 8 cm (3 in) lengths. Blanch in boiling water, refresh in cold water, and drain. Mix in the melted lard, salt and 140 ml (5 fl oz) stock. Set aside.
2. Mix together all the ingredients for the pork filling.
3. Beat together the eggs and egg yolk, add the cornflour, and mix till smooth. Heat a greased frying pan, pour in one-third of the egg batter, and swirl it round to make an egg skin. Make 3 skins in this way.
4. Spread an egg skin on a flat surface, and spread one-third of the pork filling evenly over it. Roll up into a cylindrical shape. Make 3 rolls. Place them on a plate folded side down and steam in the wok on high heat for 20 minutes. Take out and cool. Cut each roll into 2.5 cm (1 in) lengths and arrange them neatly in a bowl, in 3 rows, side by side. Put the prepared cabbage on the egg rolls. Steam on high heat for 20 minutes.
5. Bring the strong stock to the boil, and add the seasoning. Turn the steamed egg rolls and cabbage into a soup tureen so that the egg rolls are uppermost. Pour the boiling and seasoned stock over them. Sprinkle with sesame oil.

This Yunnan dish is for both banquets and family meals.

Vegetables

Aubergines

STUFFED AUBERGINES (YUNNAN)

450 g (1 lb) aubergines

Pork filling:
230 g (8 oz) minced pork (¼ fat)
1 egg
2 tsp cornflour with a little water
½ tsp salt

Egg paste:
1 egg
2 tsp cornflour

Sauce:
1 clove garlic (minced)
2 tsp dark soya sauce
2 tsp light soya sauce
80 ml (3 fl oz) strong stock
1 tsp sugar
1 tsp cornflour with a little water

salt for sprinkling
1.1 l (2 pt) cooking oil
80 ml (3 fl oz) stock (for steaming)
2 tsp lard

1. Thinly peel the aubergines. Cut each into 2 lengthwise. Sprinkle with salt and let stand for 30 minutes. Rinse and dry. On the round side make cuts about 1.3 cm (½ in) apart, about two-thirds of the way through.
2. Mix together all the ingredients for pork filling, and set aside.
3. Beat the egg and mix in the cornflour. Rub the cuts in each aubergine half with the egg paste, and fill each cut with the pork mixture, patting it into the shape of the aubergine.
4. Deep fry the aubergines till golden, take out and drain. Put them in a bowl, meat side down. Pour in the stock for steaming and a little salt. Steam in the wok on high heat till cooked, about 20 minutes. Take out, drain, reserve any liquor and turn on to a plate.
5. Mix together the sauce ingredients (except garlic) with the liquor.
6. Heat 2 tsp of oil in the wok, and stir fry the garlic till fragrant, then pour in the sauce mixture. When thickened, stir in the lard and pour on to the aubergines.

The stuffed aubergines may be pan fried till golden instead of deep fried.

STIR-FRIED AUBERGINES WITH SALTED YOLKS (HUNAN)

680 g (1½ lb) tender aubergines
4 salted eggs

Seasoning:
1 stalk spring onion (chopped)
4 tbsp stock or water
1 tsp cornflour with a little water

salt for sprinkling
680 ml (1 pt) cooking oil
2 tsp sesame oil

1. Peel the aubergines thinly. Quarter lengthwise and cut diagonally into 5 cm (2 in) long pieces. Sprinkle on some salt and let stand for about 30 minutes. Rinse well and dry.
2. Boil the salted eggs for 10 minutes, or till cooked. Cool in cold water, shell and discard the whites. Dice the yolks finely. Mix together the seasoning ingredients, and set aside.
3. Deep fry the aubergines till golden. Drain well.
4. Heat the wok, put in 1 tbsp oil, and stir fry the yolks. When bubbles appear, stir in the aubergines. Mix well, then add the seasoning mixture. When thickened, sprinkle on the sesame oil and dish up.

The aubergines may be boiled instead of deep fried, in which case leave out the stock and cornflour.

Bean curd (and similar products)

HAKKA *JONGTAUFU* – STUFFED *DOUFU* (GUANGDONG)

1 block doufu about 550 g (1¼ lb)

Filling mixture:
170 g (6 oz) minced pork (¼ fat)
60 g (2 oz) white fish meat (cod or haddock, minced)
1 tbsp dried shrimps (soaked and pounded)
1 stalk spring onion (chopped)
2 tsp cornflour with a little water

Seasoning for filling:
1 tsp salt
2 tsp rice wine
2 tsp light soya sauce

Seasoning for gravy:
1 tbsp light soya sauce
1 tsp cornflour with a little water

cornflour for dusting

3 tbsp cooking oil
230 ml (8 fl oz) stock
1 stalk spring onion (chopped) or a few coriander leaves

1. Wrap the *doufu* in a piece of muslin and weight it with a dinner plate for about 2 hours to remove excess water. (The firm type of *doufu* does not need this treatment, but is not easily available here.) Cut the *doufu* into 4 squares and each of these into 2 triangles. Leave them in a colander to drain.
2. Mix together all the ingredients for the filling with the seasoning for the filling and a little of the soaking liquor from the shrimps to make a sticky paste. Divide into 8 portions.
3. Cut a slit in the longest side of the *doufu* triangle, sprinkle some cornflour in the cut, put in a portion of the meat filling and dust the meat side with a little cornflour. Fill all the triangles.
4. Heat a flat-bottomed frying pan with 2 tbsp of oil over high heat, put in the stuffed *doufu* meat side down and cook till that side is pale golden, about 2 minutes. Pour in the stock, reduce the heat to medium, cover and cook for about 4 minutes. Carefully take out the *doufu* with a perforated spoon and put in a serving dish.
5. Stir the seasoning for the gravy into the cooking liquor. When thickened, sprinkle on the rest of the oil and the chopped spring onion and pour over the *doufu*.

A speciality of the Dapo clan in Guangdong.

LOHANCAI – 'SOFT IMMORTAL FOOD'

15 g (½ oz) mung-bean vermicelli (soaked)
10 caps small winter mushrooms (soaked)
60 g (2 oz) bean-curd sticks
1 tbsp wood ears (soaked)
30 g (1 oz) dried lily flowers (jinzhencai)

Seasoning:
2 tbsp red fermented bean curd (mashed)
1 tbsp light soya sauce
1 tbsp sesame oil

280 ml (10 fl oz) vegetable stock
2 tbsp peanut oil or other vegetable oil

1. Break the bean-curd sticks into 5 cm (2 in) pieces. Pour boiling water over to cover, and soak for 1 hour. Rinse and drain.
2. Pour hot water over the lily flowers and soak for 5 minutes. Drain, cut off any stems. Discard any spoilt flowers. Rinse well.

179

3. Drain the wood ears and mushrooms. Reserve the mushroom water and add to the stock.
4. Set the wok on high heat. When hot, put in the oil, and stir fry the mushrooms and wood ears, till fragrant. Add the lily flowers and bean-curd sticks, and stir fry briefly. Stir in the soya sauce and fermented bean curd, then the stock. Mix well. Cover and cook on medium heat for about 20 minutes.
5. Stir in the vermicelli, lower the heat, cover and cook for 5 minutes, when the liquid should be almost dried up. Take out and sprinkle with the sesame oil.

This is a variant of the Buddhist vegetarian dish known as 'lohan's vegetable'. Lohan means 'Buddha's disciple'. Hence it is eaten on every first and fifteenth day of the month, the vegetarian days, in some Chinese households. Onion and garlic, being classified as 'meat food', are not allowed.

MAPO DOUFU (SICHUAN)

1 block doufu about 450 g (1 lb)
2 young leeks or spring onion whites (chopped)
110 g (4 oz) lean minced beef

Seasoning:
2 tsp salted soya beans
2 tsp salted black beans (crushed)
1 tsp chilli powder
2 tsp light soya sauce
2 tsp rice wine

salt
3 tbsp peanut oil
4 tbsp stock
1 tsp cornflour with a little water
½ tsp Sichuan peppercorns (ground)

1. Cut the doufu into 2 cm (¾ in) cubes. Pour on boiling water with a little salt added. Let stand.
2. Heat the wok, add the oil and, when hot, stir fry the minced beef till dry, when the oil runs out. Add the salted soya beans and the crushed black beans, cook till fragrant, stir in the chilli powder, and stir fry briefly. Drain the doufu cubes. Add to the wok the soya sauce and wine, stock and doufu cubes. Reduce the heat and cook till the doufu is well flavoured, about 6 minutes. Stir in the cornflour mixture and the chopped leeks. Dish up and sprinkle with the ground Sichuan peppercorns.

There are many variants of this excellent *doufu* dish invented by a pockmarked lady – which is what *mapo* means.

PAN-FRIED *DOUFU* (BEIJING)

230 g (8 oz) doufu

Seasoning for doufu:
1 stalk spring onion (minced)
1 slice ginger (minced)
1 tsp salt
1 tsp rice wine

Seasoning for sauce:
1 stalk spring onion (minced)
1 slice ginger (minced)
½ tsp salt
1 tsp rice wine
4 tbsp chicken stock

5 tbsp cooking oil
flour for coating
1 egg (lightly beaten)
1 tsp sesame oil

1. Cut the *doufu* into 1.3 cm (½ in) thick slices. Arrange in one layer on a plate. Sprinkle on the seasoning for the *doufu*. Let stand.
2. Set a flat-bottomed frying pan on medium heat. When almost hot, put in the oil, dip each piece of *doufu* in the flour, then in the egg, and neatly arrange in the pan in one layer. Cook till golden, then turn over and cook the other side. When both sides are golden, add the seasoning and the stock. Bring to the boil, reduce the heat, cover and simmer till the liquid is dried up. Sprinkle with sesame oil and dish up.

SMOKED VEGETARIAN DUCK (SHANDONG)

230 g (8 oz) bean-curd skins (dry weight)

Seasoning:
30 ml (1 fl oz) dark soya sauce
140 ml (5 fl oz) sesame oil

Smoking ingredients:
1 tbsp brown sugar
1 tbsp tea leaves (jasmine tea)

2 tbsp guoba *(dried cooked rice)*

1. Soften the bean-curd skins in hot water for 5 minutes. Drain and save 3 whole pieces. Shred the rest finely.
2. Mix the soya sauce and sesame oil. Mix the shredded bean-curd skins thoroughly with 110 g (4 oz) of this seasoning mixture.
3. Spread one of the reserved whole skins on a flat surface, and brush on a layer of the seasoning mixture. Put one-third of the shredded and seasoned skin on this in a line, and roll up into a cylinder. This is the 'duck roll'. Make another 2 in the same way. Preheat the oven to moderate, 180–190°C (350–375°F, gas mark 4–5).
4. Place the 'duck rolls' on a roasting rack, with the joined side down. Stand the rack in a roasting tin containing the brown sugar, tea leaves and *guoba* (for its preparation, see p. 224). Roast in the oven for 30 minutes, till they turn a dark golden brown and become crisp. Cool slightly and slice.

In Shandong the smoking is done with poplar and pine-wood shavings. If preferred, this dish may be plain roasted. It is delicious with plum sauce or tomato ketchup.

SNOWFLAKE *DOUFU* (SHANGHAI)

230 g (8 oz) doufu
15 g (½ oz) cooked ham (minced)

Chicken and egg mixture:
60 g (2 oz) raw chicken
4 egg whites
1 tsp salt
2 tsp rice wine

110 ml (4 fl oz) chicken stock
1 tsp cornflour with a little water
3 tbsp lard or cooking oil

1. Dice the *doufu* into 1.3 cm (½ in) cubes. Put them in boiling water and cook for 30 seconds. Drain.
2. Mix the minced chicken with 1 tsp of cold water, the salt and rice wine. Beat the egg whites to a soft foam and pour on to the chicken mixture. Mix gently.
3. Put the *doufu* and the chicken stock in the wok, bring to the boil, and adjust seasoning. Cook till the *doufu* is well flavoured, then take the cubes out with a perforated spoon. Bring the stock to the boil again, and thicken with the cornflour mixture. Slowly pour in the

chicken and egg mixture, stirring all the while, and at the same time add the lard gradually to prevent sticking. When the chicken is cooked, put in the *doufu*, mix well and dish up sprinkled with minced ham.

VEGETARIAN GOOSE (ZHEJIANG)

230 (8 oz) bean-curd skins (dry weight)

Seasoning:
1 tbsp dark soya sauce
1 tsp sugar

140 ml (5 fl oz) rape-seed oil or other vegetable oil
1 tbsp sesame oil

1. Mix the soya sauce and sugar with 110 ml (4 fl oz) of cold water.
2. Dip the bean-curd skins in hot water briefly, drain and dry with kitchen paper. Reserve 1 whole sheet for wrapping. Soak the rest, with the trimmings, in the seasoning mixture till well absorbed.
3. Spread out the reserved skin on a flat surface, fold each of the seasoned skins in half and pile them one on top of the other on the reserved skin. Finally, place all the broken bits and trimmings in a row on the top. Fold three times to form a flattened roll, about 5 to 6 cm (2 to 2½ in) wide.
5. Put on a plate, and steam for 5 minutes on high heat. Take out and cool.
6. Heat the oil and pan fry the roll till both sides are golden. Take out, drain, brush on the sesame oil, cut into 1.3 cm (½ in) slices and serve.

This may be garnished with tomato wedges, parsley or coriander leaves. Plum sauce or tomato ketchup make good dips.

Beans (fresh)

BROAD BEANS AND BAMBOO SHOOTS (SICHUAN)

450 g (1 lb) broad beans (in the pod)
110 g (4 oz) bamboo shoots
1 tbsp cooked ham (or grilled smoked back bacon) (minced)

Seasoning:
1 tsp salt
2 tsp rice wine

½ tsp sugar
pepper to taste
1 tsp cornflour with a little water

1 tbsp cooking oil
80 ml (3 fl oz) stock or water
2 tsp rendered chicken fat

1. Slice the bamboo shoots into bite-size pieces. Shell the broad beans, and put them in boiling water for 1 minute. Drain and cool in cold water. With a sharp knife make a slit in the tough skins, and peel the beans. Discard the skins and reserve the jade-green beans.
2. Put the wok on high heat, add the oil, and stir fry the bamboo shoots and broad beans for 1 minute, pour in the stock, cover and cook for 3 minutes. Add in the seasoning, and mix well. Stir in the chicken fat, and transfer to a dish. Sprinkle on the minced ham and serve.

This is a dish made in Sichuan in the spring, when broad beans and bamboo shoots are in abundance. Winter mushrooms may be used instead of bamboo shoots. The broad beans are not only more tender and tastier when skinned, but also look very attractively green.

DRY-FRIED LONG BEANS (JIANGSU)

450 g (1 lb) long beans (or French beans or young runner beans or Kenya beans)
15 g (½ oz) dried shrimps (soaked)
15 g (½ oz) Sichuan preserved vegetable (zhacai)

Seasoning:
2 tsp rice wine
½ tsp sugar

850 ml (1½ pt) peanut oil
2 tbsp sesame oil
140 ml (5 fl oz) stock

1. Top and tail the beans, and rinse well. If they are long, break them into 13 cm (5 in) lengths. Pound or mince the soaked dried shrimps. Rinse the Sichuan preserved vegetable to remove any grit and excess chilli powder, and mince it finely.
2. Deep fry the beans in hot oil for about 5 minutes and drain well.
3. Set the wok on high heat, put in 1 tbsp sesame oil and, when hot, stir fry the shrimps and Sichuan vegetable briefly. Add the beans, rice wine, sugar and stock. Cover and cook till the liquid has been

absorbed. Sprinkle on the rest of the sesame oil and dish up.

If preferred the deep frying may be left out; instead, stir fry the raw beans in step 3 and cook slightly longer. One version has 30–60 g (1–2 oz) minced pork added.

Bitter gourds

STUFFED BITTER GOURDS (GUANGDONG)

450 g (1 lb) bitter gourds

Pork filling:
8 oz pork mince ($\frac{1}{4}$ fat)
$\frac{1}{2}$ tsp salt
1 tbsp cooked salted fish (soft meat type)
1 stalk spring onion (chopped)
2 tsp ginger juice

1 tbsp cornflour with a little water + extra for dusting
2 tbsp soya beans
2 whole leaves salted mustard greens
1 clove garlic (minced)
2 tbsp cooking oil
340 ml (12 fl oz) stock or water

1. Rinse the bitter gourds, and cut off both pointed ends. Cut into 2.5 cm (1 in) rounds, and deseed.
2. Mix together all the ingredients for the pork filling.
3. Dust the inside of the bitter gourd rounds with cornflour and fill each completely with pork mixture, level the top and dust both ends with cornflour.
4. Rinse the salted mustard greens and the soya beans. Put the cooking oil in a pot, and cook the garlic till fragrant. Add the soya beans and stir fry till the beans crackle, then pour in the stock. Lay in the salted greens. Arrange the stuffed bitter gourd upright on the salted leaves. Cover, bring to the boil on high heat, lower the heat to medium and cook for 30 minutes, or till tender. Serve with the juice and the salted greens.

The soya beans serve to flavour the stock and may be eaten. The stuffed bitter gourd is a rural speciality of the Hakka clan.

Mushrooms

BUTTON MUSHROOMS WITH CRAB-MEAT SAUCE (GUANGDONG)

450 g (1 lb) button mushrooms
110 g (4 oz) dressed crab meat
1 egg white (lightly beaten)

Seasoning for blanching mushrooms:
1 tsp ginger juice
1 tsp rice wine
½ tsp salt

Seasoning for cooking mushrooms:
1 tsp rice wine
½ tsp salt
1 tsp cornflour with 3 tbsp stock or water

Seasoning for crab meat:
1 tsp salt
pepper to taste
½ tsp sugar
2 tsp sesame oil
4 tbsp cooking oil
1 tsp cornflour with 4 tbsp stock or water

570 ml (1 pt) stock or water for blanching

1. Rinse the mushrooms, leaving small ones whole and quartering any large ones. Set the wok on medium heat with 1 tbsp of oil. When hot, put in the seasoning and the stock, and add the mushrooms. Cook for 2 minutes, then drain.
2. Reheat the wok, and put in 1 tbsp oil, the seasoning and the mushrooms. Add the cornflour mixture. When it thickens, take the mushrooms out, drain and put on a serving dish.
3. Rinse the wok, replace on medium heat, put in 1 tbsp oil, add in the seasoning for the crab meat, stir in the crab meat, then the egg white, and take off the heat immediately. Stir in 1 tbsp oil and pour over the mushrooms.

Wheat gluten

SWEET AND SOUR VEGETARIAN SPARE RIBS (BEIJING)

110 g (4 oz) raw wheat gluten
110 g (4 oz) bamboo shoots
15 g (½ oz) wood ears (soaked and shredded)
½ each green and red peppers (deseeded and shredded)
1 slice ginger (minced)

Sauce:
2 tbsp sugar
1 tbsp vinegar
2 tbsp light soya sauce
1 tsp cornflour
3 tbsp vegetable stock

Seasoning for cooked gluten:
1 tbsp light soya sauce
2 tbsp cornflour

550 ml (1 pt) sesame oil or other vegetable oil

1. Roll the gluten into a piece 0.6 cm (¼ in) thick, and slice into 2.5 cm (1 in) wide strips. Wind a strip of gluten evenly on to a pair of chopsticks held together, beginning from the top; do not let it get loose. Proceed till all the strips are wound up. Leave to rest for 5 minutes. Put the gluten-covered chopsticks in boiling water and simmer for 10 minutes. Take out and cool in cold water. Gently slip the cooked gluten off the chopsticks.
2. Cut the cooked gluten into pieces 2 cm (¾ in) long. Mix in the light soya sauce, then roll in the cornflour.
3. Boil the bamboo shoot for 5 minutes, or till cooked. Cut into strips 4×1.3 cm, (1½×½ in), shaved to look like spare-rib bones. Slip one into each gluten tube, with both ends protruding, forming a 'spare rib'.
4. Mix together the seasoning for the sauce and add the shredded wood ears. Set aside.
5. Heat the sesame oil, and deep fry the 'spare ribs' till dark red. Drain well.
6. Put the wok on high heat, add 2 tsp of sesame oil, stir fry the ginger and peppers till fragrant, and put in the wood ear mixture and the 'spare ribs'. Cook briefly, stir in 1 tsp sesame oil and dish up.

If preferred the 'spare ribs' need not be deep fried, in which case leave out the dusting with cornflour. Fried gluten tastes deceptively like meat.

Soups

In alphabetical order of the recipe name

BIRD'S-NEST SOUP (JIANGSU)

20–30 g (¾–1 oz; dry weight) bird's nest (soaked and cleaned)

Seasoning:
1 tsp salt
2 tsp rice wine
pepper to taste

1.1 l (2 pt) clear chicken stock

1. Steam in the wok the prepared bird's nest (see page 222) in some chicken stock to cover, for 20 to 30 minutes. Pour into a soup tureen.
2. Bring the rest of the stock to the boil, flavour with the seasoning, adjust to taste and pour over the steamed bird's nest.

This is a most expensive soup which the Chinese family indulges in only occasionally. In some areas beaten eggs or shredded cooked chicken breast, or both, are added.

CANTONESE BEEF BALL SOUP (GUANGDONG)

Beef balls:
680 g (1½ lb) beef (lean braising steak or fillet steak)
60 g (2 oz) pork fat

Seasoning:
2 tsp salt
1 tsp sugar
1 tbsp light soya sauce
2 tbsp sesame oil
60 g (2 oz) pork fat
1 tbsp cornflour
pepper to taste

1. Remove any fat or gristle from the beef, and dice into small pieces. The beef must be completely lean; bought mince is not suitable. Mince the meat and the pork fat separately to a fine texture, then mince them together. Mix them thoroughly with the seasoning and 2 tbsp of cold water. Or put the meat and fat (minced separately first) and the seasoning in a food processor and grind to a fine, pale pink paste.
2. Gather the mixture into a neat ball and throw it against the inside of the mixing bowl several times till it is smooth and firm. The throwing process gives the meat balls a compact texture.
3. Fill the wok three-quarters full with cold water and put on a low heat. Take a piece of the meat mixture the size of a walnut, and roll between the palms till smooth and round. Put it in the water in the wok. Continue till all the mixture is used up. Make about 30. Keep

the water barely simmering; when cooked, the beef balls float to the top. Take them out as they float with a perforated spoon and leave them in a fresh bowl of cold water. When all are done drain and they are ready for further cooking. The beef balls are poached rather than boiled.

Soup:
beef balls (amount required)
3 stalks spring onion whites (chopped)
1 tbsp cooking oil
2 tsp light soya sauce
salt and pepper to taste
570 ml (1 pt) stock

1. Bring the stock to the boil.
2. Add in the beef balls, spring onion whites and cooking oil. Bring to the boil again. Take off the heat, add the soya sauce, salt and pepper, adjust to taste and serve. If boiled too long the onions will be overdone; they should be crisp.

CASSEROLED FISH SOUP (YUNNAN)

1 carp about 900 g (2 lb) (or sea bass, grey mullet)
1 dried cuttlefish (soaked)
1 dried sea cucumber (soaked)
4 caps dried winter mushrooms (soaked)
230 g (8 oz) doufu
30 g (1 oz) Yunnan ham (or smoked back bacon)
15 g (½ oz) dried shrimps (soaked)
60 g (2 oz) carrot
110 g (4 oz) cabbage heart
30 g (1 oz) bamboo shoots

Seasoning:
1 stalk spring onion (minced)
1 slice ginger (shredded)
½ tsp salt
pepper to taste

1 tsp salt
850 ml (1½ pt) strong chicken stock
1 tsp sesame oil

1. Scale and gut the fish. Rinse and cut into halves. Rub them with a teaspoon of salt and let it stand.

2. Cut the *doufu* into 1.3 cm (½ in) cubes. Scald in boiling water and drain well.
3. Cut the ham, sea cucumber, cuttlefish, carrot, bamboo shoots, mushrooms and cabbage hearts into slices.
4. Heat a 1.7 ml (3 pt) capacity heatproof casserole in a warm oven, to keep the casserole as hot as possible.
5. Bring the stock to the boil, and put in the marinated fish. When cooked, about 8 minutes, put in the rest of the ingredients (the next 9 items) and the spring onion and ginger. Bring to the boil on a medium heat, skim, add the salt and pepper, adjust to taste, and sprinkle on the sesame oil.
6. Put the heated casserole on a straw mat or heatproof plate. Pour the fish soup into the heated casserole and take to the table bubbling.

The numerous ingredients enhance the taste of this fish soup, one of the famous Yunnan banquet dishes.

CHICKEN SOUP STEAMED WITH CHINESE WOLFBERRIES (SICHUAN)

1 chicken about 1.4 kg (3 lb)
1 tbsp Chinese wolfberries (red medler berries)
1.1 l (2 pt) stock

Seasoning:
1 tsp salt
2 tsp rice wine
1 slice ginger (bruised)
1 stalk spring onion (whole)

1. Scald the chicken in boiling water for 2 minutes. Rinse in cold water and wipe dry.
2. Put the berries inside the chicken. Put the chicken in a casserole, breast up. Place the ginger and spring onion on the chicken. Pour in the stock down the side of the casserole, and add salt and wine. Cover and steam in a wok or pot on a medium heat for 2 hours. Do not open the casserole, but replenish the water in the steamer from time to time.
3. Discard the spring onion and the ginger, and serve hot in the casserole.

This is deemed a tonic food for general well being, particularly for the elderly. For more information on these berries, see page 16.

CHRYSANTHEMUM FIRE POT (ANHUI)

1 chicken gizzard
110 g (4 oz) raw white fish meat
30 g (1 oz) winter mushrooms (soaked)
60 g (2 oz) mung-bean vermicelli
110 g (4 oz) chrysanthemum greens (or lettuce)
6 eggs
110 g (4 oz) lean pork
110 g (4 oz) raw prawns

Marinade:
1 tbsp mixed spring onion and ginger juice
1 tbsp rice wine

Soup:
60 g (2 oz) bamboo shoots
30 g (1 oz) cooked ham
15 g (½ oz) dried shrimps (soaked)
1 tbsp preserved 'red-in-the-snow' (xuelihong)
1.4 l (2½ pt) chicken stock

Dips:
sesame oil
light soya sauce

1. Clean and rinse the gizzard, and cut into thin slices. Cut the lean pork, fish and mushrooms into thin slices. Arrange each separately on a small plate. Shell the prawns but leave the tail on, remove the vein, rinse and arrange on a small plate. Sprinkle the meat, fish and prawns with the marinade mixture and let stand.
2. Deep fry the dried vermicelli briefly and put on a plate. Rinse the greens and place on a separate plate. Put the eggs, unbroken, on another plate. Altogether there are 8 plates.
3. Slice the bamboo shoots, ham and preserved 'red-in-the-snow'. Put them in a pot together with the soaked dried shrimps and chicken stock. Bring to the boil, and cook for a few minutes. Ladle the soup into the fire pot. Put some pieces of burning charcoal inside the stove. Take to the table with the 8 plates of prepared ingredients and the 2 dips in separate saucers.
4. Put the pot in the middle of the table, on a heatproof mat or tray. Place the other dishes round the pot in a circle.
5. When the soup comes back to the boil, each diner uses chopsticks to put one of the 6 meats or vegetables (not the vermicelli or eggs) in a little brass mesh strainer and lower it into the soup. When cooked, it is taken out and eaten with the dips. Add some more boiling stock

if required. When all the meats and vegetables are eaten, put in the vermicelli and break in the eggs whole. Ladle the eggs into individual bowls first, then put vermicelli and soup on the eggs.

The ingredients can be varied according to taste and what is available.

CLEAR SCALLOP SOUP (HENAN)

Chicken mixture:
110 g (4 oz) raw chicken breast meat
1 egg white
1 tbsp cornflour
1 stalk spring onion white (minced)
2 tsp ginger juice
1 tsp lard or cooking oil
½ tsp salt

Garnish:
3 pieces of dried scallops (soaked)
2 tsp cooked ham (minced)
1 tbsp mange-tout shoots (or lettuce, parsley, coriander)

Soup:
570 ml (1 pt) chicken stock
2 tsp rice wine
1 tsp salt

cooking oil for greasing

1. Mince the chicken breast finely and mix with the rest of the ingredients for the chicken mixture.
2. Grease 24 Chinese wine cups, or improvize with dariole moulds. Divide the mixture equally into the cups. Place a little shredded scallop in a fan shape, to represent chrysanthemum petals, on top of the mixture in each cup. Dot a little minced ham in the centre to make the middle of the flower. Steam in the wok for 20 minutes, or till cooked. Slip them out and put into a soup bowl, flower side up.
3. Bring the stock to the boil, add the rice wine and salt and pour gently into the soup bowl. Sprinkle the greens on top.

DUCK BUNDLES IN SOUP (BEIJING)

230 g (8 oz) duck breast meat (raw or cooked)
80 g (3 oz) bamboo shoots
80 g (3 oz) cooked ham

30 g (1 oz) dried gourd (soaked)

Seasoning for steaming:
1 stalk spring onion (cut into 2.5 cm or 1 in lengths)
1 slice ginger (bruised)
3 tsp rice wine
4 tbsp chicken stock

Soup:
850 ml (1½ pt) stock
½ tsp salt
pinch of pepper
1 tsp rendered chicken fat

1. Slice the duck meat, bamboo shoots and ham into thin strips about
   6×1 cm (2½×¾ in), 24 pieces each.
2. Cut the soaked gourd into strips and tie one of each slice of duck,
   ham and bamboo shoot into a bundle. Make 24 bundles.
3. Place them in a bowl, and add in the seasoning for steaming. Steam
   on high heat for 20 minutes, or till cooked, or 10 minutes if cooked
   meat is used. Take out and discard the spring onion and ginger.
   Transfer the bundles to a soup tureen.
4. Bring the stock to the boil, adjust the seasoning and pour gently on
   to the duck bundles.

If dried gourd is not available, any stringy vegetable stem may be used
instead.

EGG *FURONG* SOUP (SHANDONG)

For the egg furong:
4 egg whites
110 g (4 fl oz) strong clear stock
½ tsp salt

8 leaves pocai *(New Zealand spinach), or watercress or lettuce*
570 ml (1 pt) strong clear stock
1 tbsp light soya sauce

1. Lightly beat the egg whites to blend, and add in the stock and salt.
   Mix well and steam in the wok for about 5 minutes, till just cooked,
   when the centre is set. Do not overcook. This is the egg *furong*. Take
   out and cool.
2. Rinse the *pocai* and blanch, drain and put in a soup bowl.
3. Bring the stock to the boil, add the soya sauce, and pour into the

soup bowl. Slice the *furong* with a spoon into petal-like pieces and slip into the soup one by one.

Steamed egg whites in petal forms are called *furong*, 'white lotus petals' in Chinese culinary terminology. The greens form the lotus leaves; the effect is simple yet aesthetic.

GLUTEN MEAT-BALL SOUP (SHANDONG)

6 oz raw wheat gluten

Meat filling:
110 g (4 oz) lean pork
30 g (1 oz) bamboo shoot
30 g (1 oz) mange-touts
1 stalk spring onion (minced)
1 slice ginger (minced)
1 tsp rice wine
½ tsp salt
1 tsp cornflour with a little water
2 tsp light soya sauce

Soup:
1 stalk spring onion (minced)
1 slice ginger (minced)
1 tsp light soya sauce
425 ml (15 fl oz) stock
1 tsp cornflour with a little water

2 tsp lard or cooking oil
1 tsp sesame oil

1. Mince the pork, finely dice the mange-touts and bamboo shoots and mix them with the seasoning. Mix well and divide into 25 equal portions.
2. Rinse the raw gluten and cut into 25 equal parts. Flatten one into an oblong, place a meat ball on one end, fold up 3 sides and roll up tightly into a 2.5 cm (1 in) ball. Make 25. Space them out on a plate.
3. Bring a pot of water to the boil, take off the heat, put in the gluten balls, replace the pot on low heat and cook for 5 minutes, or till they float, then drain and put them in a bowl.
4. Set the wok on medium heat, and put in the lard. Stir fry the spring onion and ginger till fragrant, put in the soya sauce and stock. Bring to the boil, pour over the gluten balls and steam in a wok for 15

minutes. Drain and reserve the liquor, and place the gluten balls in
a soup bowl.
5. Bring the reserved liquor to the boil, skim, add the cornflour
   mixture, and sprinkle on the sesame oil. Pour over the gluten balls.

The gluten is tasty and tender but has a resilient texture, which makes a
change from pastry.

HOT AND SOUR *DOUFU* SOUP (HUNAN)

170 g (6 oz) doufu
110 g (4 oz) lean pork
3 caps winter mushrooms (soaked)

Soup:
1 stalk spring onion (chopped)
2 tsp wine vinegar (or to taste)
pepper to taste
1 tsp salt
1 tbsp lard or cooking oil
1 tsp rendered chicken fat
850 ml (1½ pt) stock or water
2 tsp cornflour with a little water

1 egg (lightly beaten)

1. Wrap the *doufu* in a piece of muslin and weight it with a dinner
   plate to firm it, which will take about 1 hour.
2. Cut the *doufu* and lean meat into 4 cm (1½ in) long *julienne* strips.
   Shred the soaked mushrooms finely.
3. Bring the stock to the boil. Put in the *doufu*, pork and mushrooms.
   Bring to the boil again, skim, and add the cornflour and water
   mixture. Stir well; when thickened, take off the heat. Dribble in the
   egg so that it streaks and floats to the top, take off the heat
   immediately. Add the seasonings, and adjust to taste. Pour into a
   soup tureen and serve.

The original recipe includes 60 g (2 oz) of coagulated chicken blood which
gives a contrast in colour and texture, being dark brown, firm and
crunchy.

HOT AND SOUR FISH BROTH (HENAN)

450–680 g (1–1½ lb) white fish

195

Vegetables:
60 g (2 oz) Chinese water chestnuts (peeled and shredded)
15 g (½ oz) winter mushrooms (soaked and shredded)
30 g (1 oz) green peas

Seasoning:
1 tsp salt
1 tbsp rice wine
4 tbsp wine vinegar
1 tbsp light soya sauce
2 tsp ginger juice
pepper to taste

570 ml (1 pt) stock or water
1 tbsp cornflour with a little water
2 tsp sesame oil
a few coriander or parsley leaves (chopped)

1. If a whole fish is used, scale, gut and rinse. Poach it in the stock or water till cooked. Drain and reserve the cooking liquor. Remove the bones, break the flesh in chunks and discard the skin.
2. Bring the reserved liquor to the boil, and add in the seasoning ingredients, the shredded vegetables and peas, and the fish. Bring to the boil again, and stir in the cornflour and water mixture. When thickened, sprinkle on the sesame oil. Pour into a soup bowl, scatter on the coriander leaves and serve.

An appetizing soup, this is also deemed to help clear up a hangover.

HOT AND SOUR SEA CUCUMBER SOUP (YUNNAN)

80 g (3 oz) dried sea cucumber (soaked)
60 g (2 oz) lean pork
4 caps dried winter mushrooms (soaked)
30 g (1 oz) bamboo shoots
30 g (1 oz) carrots

Seasoning:
2 tsp light soya sauce
2 tsp dark soya sauce
2 tsp sugar
1 tbsp vinegar
1 tsp salt
2 tsp ginger juice
½ tsp ground pepper (or to taste)

570 ml (1 pt) strong chicken stock
1 tsp lard

1. Cut the soaked and prepared sea cucumber (see page 226) into 8 cm (3 in) long strips the thickness of a chopstick. Soak them in hot water.
2. Cut the pork, mushroom, bamboo shoots and carrot into matchsticks.
3. Boil the mushrooms, bamboo shoots and carrot in the stock till cooked. Add the pork, skim, then add the sea cucumber and the seasoning. Bring to the boil and cook for 1 or 2 minutes, stir in the lard and dish up.

This soup is amber-coloured, piquant and delectable.

HOT-WATER CHINESE 'CELERY' CABBAGE (SICHUAN)

900 g (2 lb) Chinese 'celery' cabbage

Seasoning:
1 tsp salt
2 tsp rice wine
pepper to taste

850 ml (1½ pt) strong clear chicken or pork stock

1. Choose very fresh, young Chinese 'celery' cabbage. Use only the tender hearts, and save the outer leaves for other dishes. Separate the leaves, rinse and leave whole.
2. Scald the cabbage hearts in boiling water. Drain and put in cold water. Drain and gently press the water out. Arrange neatly in a pile in a soup bowl.
3. Bring the stock to the boil, add the seasoning, adjust to taste, and pour into the soup bowl from the side so as not to disturb the cabbage.
4. Steam in the wok or steaming basket on high heat till thoroughly heated, about 30 minutes.

This soup depends entirely on its strong, crystal-clear stock and the freshness of the cabbage. It is called 'hot water' because the soup looks like water; the cabbage is a creamy yellow.

LIVER CUSTARD SOUP (BEIJING)

450 g (1 lb) pig's liver

1 egg (lightly beaten)
700 ml (1¼ pt) strong chicken or pork stock

Seasoning:
1 tsp salt
¼ tsp ground pepper (or to taste)

1. Grind the liver to a paste (a food processor is good for this). Add 5 tbsp of warm chicken stock. Strain through a fine sieve into a bowl, discarding the solids. Beat in the egg, salt and pepper, and pour into a lightly greased soup bowl. Steam in the wok on high heat till cooked, about 15 to 20 minutes.
2. With a knife slice the liver custard in the bowl (without unmoulding) into diamond shapes, but leave these in place.
3. Bring the stock to the boil, and gently pour into the liver custard down the side of the bowl so as not to disturb the pattern.

A fine way of eating liver; the soup is crystal clear and the custard a beige colour.

LOTUS-SEEDPOD SOUP (HENAN)

Chicken mixture:
170 g (6 oz) chicken breast meat (finely minced)
30 g (1 oz) pork fat (finely minced)
3 egg whites (lightly beaten)
1 tbsp mixed spring onion and ginger juice
1 tsp salt
2 tbsp spinach juice from 6 leaves

72 garden peas
2 tsp lard or cooking oil

Soup:
2 tsp rice wine
2 tsp light soya sauce
850 ml (1½ pt) clear strong chicken stock

1. Mix together all the ingredients for the chicken mixture and beat well (or blend in a food processor) till creamy and pale green.
2. Fill 12 greased Chinese wine cups (or dariole moulds) half full with the mixture. Tap each cup on the table to level the contents. In each cup put 5 peas in a circle and 1 in the middle. Press them lightly to form a 'lotus seedpod'. Steam in the wok on a plate till cooked, about 10 minutes. Take out and turn into a soup tureen, pea side up.

3. Bring the stock to the boil, add the seasoning, and pour gently into the soup tureen from the side, so that the 'lotus seedpods' float.

A very attractive soup for a dinner party. When cooked the 'seedpods' puff up; the texture is light and spongy. Without the pork fat the chicken would be dry and pulpy.

MILKY FISH-HEAD SOUP (ZHEJIANG)

½ *fish head about 1.4 kg (3 lb) (cod, haddock or salmon)*

Seasoning:
1 tbsp rice wine
1 stalk spring onion (tied in a knot)
1 slice ginger (bruised)
1 tsp salt

2–3 tbsp lard or cooking oil
1 tbsp green pea shoots (or parsley)
1 tbsp lean cooked ham (shredded)
1 tsp rendered chicken fat

1. Remove the gills and rinse the fish head well. If a smaller whole head is used, split in halves.
2. Scald the fish head in boiling water, and drain well. Dry with kitchen paper.
3. Put the wok on high heat, add the lard, put in the fish head, cut side up, and fry briefly. Add the rice wine, spring onion and ginger. Then turn the fish head over, and add in 1.7 l (3 pt) of boiling water. Cover and cook on high heat for about 6 minutes. Do not lift the cover or the soup will lose the milky colour which is typical of a fish-head soup).
4. Take out the fish head, and put in a soup tureen. Add the pea shoots or parsley.
5. Discard the spring onion and ginger, and strain the cooking liquor. Bring to the boil, adjust the seasoning, and pour over the fish head. Sprinkle on the ham and the chicken fat.

This delicious soup is a Chinese favourite. This recipe is from Hangzhou. The green pea shoots are the tender leaves with tendrils from the garden pea plants, not to be confused with bean sprouts.

MOCK BIRD'S NEST SOUP (SICHUAN)

1 Chinese white radish (mouli) about 450 g (1 lb)

Seasoning:
1 tsp salt
2 tsp rice wine
pepper to taste

850 ml (1½ pt) strong clear chicken or pork stock
cornflour for dusting

1. Peel the radish. Cut into 5 cm (2 in) long cylinders. Stand each cylinder upright. Then slice very thinly from the top downwards, but do not cut right through – leave 1.3 cm (½ in) or so at the bottom so that the slices are joined together. When the whole is done, turn the cylinder round through 90 degrees and slice thinly from the top downwards right through, so that each is a thin, comb-like slice (see illustration).
2. Cover each radish comb completely in cornflour. Cook a few at a time in boiling water, take out with a perforated spoon and soak in cold water.
3. Drain the radish slices, and boil them in 140 ml (5 fl oz) of the stock. Drain.
4. Bring the rest of the stock to the boil, add the seasoning, and adjust to taste. Put in the drained radish slices, bring to the boil again, and serve.

This soup looks beguilingly like real bird's nest soup, transparently clear and slippery, with a delicate flavour.

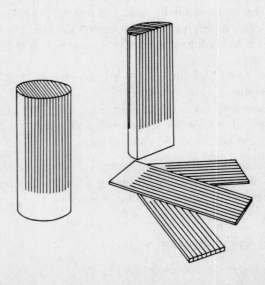

POCAI DUMPLINGS AND CUTTLEFISH SOUP (SICHUAN)

4 dried cuttlefish, body only (soaked)
2 tomatoes

Dumpling filling:
110 g (4 oz) pork mince
1 tsp ginger juice
½ tsp salt
2 tsp light soya sauce
1 tsp sesame oil
2 tsp rice wine
½ egg white (lightly beaten)
2 tsp cornflour with a little water
3 peeled water chestnuts (chopped)
pepper to taste

Dumpling skin:
110 g (4 oz) plain flour
110 g (4 oz) pocai (or spinach leaves without stalks)

Seasoning for oil:
1 stalk spring onion (cut into 2.5 cm or 1 in lengths)
1 slice ginger (bruised)

850 ml (1½ pt) milk stock
1 tbsp lard or cooking fat
2 tsp rendered chicken fat

1. The cuttlefish should be soaked till quite spongy. Cut each across into 2 or 3 oblong pieces.
2. Skin and deseed the tomatoes, and cut into wedges. Set aside in cold water.
3. Mix together the ingredients for the dumpling filling. Divide into 24 portions.
4. Make the dumpling skin: make spinach juice. Mix the juice with the flour to make a firm but pliable dough. Cover with a bowl and leave to rest for 20 minutes.
5. Divide the dumpling skin into 24 portions. With the fingers, or a rolling pin, shape each into a round about 5 cm (2 in) in diameter. Put a portion of filling in the centre, fold the pastry in half and pinch to seal, forming a half-moon shape. Make a few pleats along the sealed edge by gathering and pressing. Make 24 dumplings. Put them in boiling water in batches. When they float, take out and drain.
6. Heat the wok, put in the lard, stir fry the spring onion and ginger till fragrant, add in the stock. Boil for 1 minute, discard the spring

201

onion and ginger. Adjust the seasoning, then add the tomatoes, dumplings and cuttlefish. Bring to the boil, skim, add the chicken fat, and dish up.

This is a traditional autumn and winter soup. The dumplings are a luxuriant green. If preferred, the cuttlefish may be left out, or the dumplings eaten without soup as a pasta.

RED BRAISED SHARK'S FIN (HUNAN)

60 g (2 oz) dried processed shark's fin (prepared)
1 chicken about 0.9–1.1 kg (2–2½ lb)
450 g (1 lb) belly pork

Seasoning for braising:
1 stalk spring onion (tied in a knot)
1 slice ginger (bruised)
1 tbsp rice wine
1 tbsp light soya sauce
1 tsp salt

1 tbsp cornflour with a little water
2 tsp sesame oil
pepper to taste

1. Prepare the dried processed shark's fin.
2. Quarter the chicken. Cut 4 slices from the belly pork and quarter the rest.
3. Place a bamboo mat or a tea plate in a pot. Lay the 4 pork slices on it. Spread the prepared shark's fin on the pork slices and add the spring onion and ginger. Place a mat on top of the shark's fin. Arrange the chicken and pork pieces on the second mat, and cover them with a tea plate to prevent the meat from moving about in cooking. Pour in 1.1 l (2 pt) of water down the side of the pot.
4. Bring to the boil on high heat, then reduce to low and braise for about 2 hours, when the shark's fin should be tender.
5. When cooked, remove the top mat with the chicken and pork. Discard the chicken skin and shred the meat. Put the shredded chicken meat in a soup tureen. (Keep the belly pork for another dish.) Remove the second mat, and discard the spring onion and ginger. Put the shark's fin on top of the chicken in the soup tureen.
6. Bring the cooking liquor to the boil, add the rest of the seasoning, adjust them, thicken with the cornflour and pour over the shark's fin. Sprinkle on the sesame oil and pepper, and serve.

SHARK'S FIN AND CRAB-MEAT SOUP (GUANGDONG)

60 g (2 oz) dried processed shark's fin (prepared)
110 g (4 oz) dressed crab meat
30 g (1 oz) cooked ham (shredded)

Seasoning for shark's fin:
2 tbsp lard or cooking oil
4 tbsp strong stock
1 tbsp cornflour with a little water

1.1 l (2 pt) strong stock
1 tbsp rice wine

Accompaniment:
Zhejiang vinegar (red vinegar)

1. Place the dressed crab meat at the bottom of a soup tureen.
2. Heat the wok on medium, put in 1 tbsp of the lard, add 4 tbsp of strong stock and, when boiling, stir in the shark's fin (see page 226 for its preparation). Thicken with the cornflour and water mixture. Add the rest of the lard. Mix well, and put the shark's fin on top of the crab meat. Scatter on the shredded cooked ham.
3. Bring 1.1 l (2 pt) of strong stock to the boil with the rice wine. Pour gently into the soup tureen down the side. Serve with the vinegar.

The vinegar is served in a little bowl passed round the table; the amount added depends on individual taste.

WINE CUP *DOUFU* SOUP (FUJIAN)

280 g (10 oz) doufu
1 tbsp cornflour
1 tsp salt
1 tsp cooking oil

Filling:
110 g (4 oz) minced pork
1 duck egg (or chicken egg)
½ tbsp dried shrimps (soaked and minced)
2 caps winter mushrooms (soaked and diced finely)
30 g (1 oz) peeled water chestnuts (diced finely)

Seasoning for filling:
1 tsp salt
2 tsp light soya sauce
pepper to taste

203

½ tsp sugar
1 stalk spring onion (chopped)

lard or cooking oil for greasing + 1 tsp for stock
850 ml (1½ pt) stock

15 g (½ oz) cooked ham (minced)
1 cap winter mushroom (soaked and shredded finely)

1. Put a dinner plate on the *doufu* for about 1 hour to remove excess water. Mash the *doufu*, and mix with the cornflour, salt and cooking oil. Blend till smooth (or put all in a food processor and blend).
2. Lightly beat the egg and mix with the rest of the ingredients for the filling. Add the seasoning and mix well.
3. Grease 24 Chinese wine cups or 12 dariole moulds and half fill them with *doufu* mixture. Make a hole in the centre and press the *doufu* on to the sides. Fill the hole with the pork filling. Cover with more *doufu*. Top with a sprinkling of minced ham and mushrooms.
4. Steam the *doufu* cups in a wok or steaming basket for 20 minutes on high heat. Cool and turn out on to a serving dish. Re-steam on medium heat for 10 minutes to heat through.
5. Boil the stock, adjust seasoning, stir in 1 tsp lard and pour carefully around the *doufu* cups in the tureen.

Cakes and Desserts

In alphabetical order of the recipe name

ALMOND *DOUFU* (ZHEJIANG)

Milk mixture:
60 g (2 oz) sweet almonds
30 g (1 oz) bitter almonds
570 ml (1 pt) fresh milk
110 g (4 oz) sugar

Jelly:
7 g (¼ oz) agar-agar

Syrup:
110 g (4 oz) sugar

Flavourings:
peppermint essence (optional)
1 tsp dried rose petals (optional)
1 tsp cassia-flower sugar (or vanilla sugar)

1. Rinse the agar-agar in cold water and drain. Bring to the boil in 425 ml (15 fl oz) of water, reduce the heat and simmer for about 15 minutes, stirring every now and again till the agar-agar is dissolved completely. Strain through a fine sieve into a clean pot, and keep on a very low heat.
2. Blanch and skin the sweet almonds. Grind all the almonds finely. Heat the milk fairly hot, stir in the almonds, take off the heat, and let them infuse for about 10 minutes. Squeeze through a piece of muslin into a pot. Add the sugar and heat to dissolve.
3. Gradually pour the hot almond and milk mixture into the agar-agar jelly on a low heat, stirring all the time, and bring to almost boiling. Pour into a bowl, cool and then leave to set in the refrigerator till required.
4. Dissolve the sugar in 425 ml (15 fl oz) of water, bring to the boil and cool.
5. To serve, pour the syrup into a bowl, cut the almond *doufu* into cubes or diamonds and put them into the syrup. Sprinkle on the crushed rose petals and cassia-flower sugar (for preparation see page 222) or peppermint essence if used.

This is an old favourite Chinese summer dessert which has no artificial flavourings. There are many variants; some are served with fruits or made without milk.

CANDIED YAM (SHANDONG)

570 g (1¼ lb) yam (or taro)
110 g (4 oz) sugar
850 ml (1½ pt) peanut oil

1. Peel and rinse the yam. Roll cut into wedges. Scald in boiling water, and drain.
2. Heat the oil on medium heat and deep fry the yam till golden. Drain well on kitchen paper and keep hot.
3. Put 2 tsp oil in the wok, on low heat, and add the sugar. Cook till it is golden and bubbling, and stir in the yam. Take off the heat and stir to mix well, until the sugar begins to pull threads. This happens quite quickly; when it does, quickly tip out on to a plate and serve immediately with individual bowls of clean cold water.
4. To eat, pick up a piece of yam and dip in the water briefly to cool it down and make it less sticky before eating.

If preferred, the yam may be steamed instead.

CHERRY AND BROAD BEAN SALAD (JIANGSU)

450 g (1 lb) fresh cherries
110 g (4 oz) shelled broad beans
110 g (4 oz) pearl sago
230 g (8 oz) sugar
1 tsp cassia-flower sugar (or vanilla sugar)

1. Rinse and stone the cherries. Cover them with some of the sugar.
2. Boil the shelled broad beans till cooked, refresh in cold water and peel off the skin. Set aside in cold water.
3. Bring 1.4 l (2½ pt) of water to the boil, and drop in the sago a little at a time. When all the sago floats on top of the water, it is cooked, and the water is slightly gluey. Add the sugar, cherries and the drained broad beans. Cook till both the cherries and the broad beans float on top of the sago. Pour into a bowl and serve sprinkled with cassia-flower sugar (see page 222 for its preparation).

Broad beans and garden peas are often used in desserts.

EIGHT TREASURES RICE

Rice pudding:
230 g (8 oz) glutinous rice
1 tbsp lard
60 g (2 oz) sugar

Mixed fruits and nuts:
1 dried persimmon (soaked)
10 red dates (soaked and stoned)
3 dried apricots (rinsed)
1 tbsp walnuts
30 g (1 oz) chestnuts
1 tbsp pine nut kernels (rinsed)
1 tbsp crystallized orange peel
60 g (2 oz) crystallized melon

110 g (4 oz) red bean paste

Syrup:
60 g (2 oz) sugar

1. Rinse and boil the glutinous rice as you would long-grain rice. When still hot, mix in the sugar and the lard. Set aside.
2. Dice all the fruits except 3 dates; halve these. Pour boiling water on to the walnuts, skin with a toothpick from the flat side and dice

them. Boil the chestnuts for 10 minutes, remove any red skin, then dice them.

3. Grease a pudding basin with some lard. Arrange 5 date halves cut side up in a circle and 1 in the middle. Place other fruits round them and up the sides of the basin any way you like. Mix the rest of the fruits and nuts with the rice.
4. Put half the rice in the basin, spread the red bean paste on it, leaving 1 cm (½ in) edge all round. Put the rest of the rice on top, and smooth to cover completely. Cover with cling film and secure with a rubber band.
5. Steam in a pot on high heat for 45 minutes or longer; it can never be overcooked. Turn out on to a plate. Dissolve the sugar in 60 ml (2 fl oz) of water, bring to the boil, and pour the syrup over the pudding. Serve hot.

Eight Treasures rice is a classic dessert for festive occasions, and every village and town has its own version. The choice of fruits and nuts is entirely regional. The above is a British variant.

FRUIT SALAD IN ROCK-SUGAR SYRUP (HUNAN)

450 g (1 lb) fresh loquat (pipa)
15 g (½ oz) dried longan
30 g (1 oz) canned cherries
30 g (1 oz) cooked garden peas

Syrup:
140 g (5 oz) rock sugar (or granulated sugar)
1 tsp rose-petal sugar (or vanilla sugar)

1. Wash, peel and deseed the loquats. Scald them in boiling water briefly. Drain and refresh. Pour hot water over the longan, rinse and drain.
2. Crush the rock sugar and bring to the boil in 570 ml (1 pt) of water. When the sugar dissolves add in the fruits and peas. Bring back to the boil and stir in the rose-petal sugar (for the preparation of this, see page 226). Pour into a bowl and serve.

Longan may be replaced by a dried fruit of your choice.

HONEYED LOTUS-ROOT CAKE (HENAN)

450 g (1 lb) fresh raw lotus root
80 g (3 oz) glutinous rice

80 g (3 oz) honey
80 g (3 oz) sugar (cassia flower or vanilla flavoured)
2 tsp lard or cooking oil

1. Soak the glutinous rice in cold water for 3 hours. Drain.
2. Scrub, wash and rinse the lotus root well. Cut away one end.
3. Fill the lotus root with the rice through the cut end. A little funnel and a chopstick are helpful here. Steam in the wok on high heat till cooked, about 35 to 40 minutes for a large root, or 30 minutes for 2 smaller ones. Cool in cold water briefly, peel off the outer skin, and pat dry. Cut off the other end of the root.
4. Slice the root into rounds about 1 cm (⅜ in) thick, arrange neatly on a plate, and sprinkle on 60 g (2 oz) of the sugar (for how to flavour sugar, see page 222). Steam for 10 minutes, drain and reserve the juice, and turn the lotus rounds on to a serving dish.
5. Heat the reserved juice with the honey and the rest of the sugar; when the sugar dissolves, stir in the lard and pour over the lotus slices. Serve hot.

The lotus root is cooked before peeling to minimize contact with metal, which discolours it. A fat root has large air holes and is easier to fill.

KAOLI BANANAS (YUNNAN)

900 g (2 lb) bananas

Egg batter:
3 egg whites
30 g (1 oz) flour
2 tsp cornflour with a little water

Syrup:
110 g (4 oz) sugar

1.1 l (2 pt) cooking oil
15 g (½ oz) sugar
30 g (1 oz) sesame seeds (toasted)

1. Beat the egg whites lightly, and beat in the flour and cornflour to make a smooth batter.
2. Peel and roll cut the bananas into wedges, about 4 cm (1½ in) long. Add them to the batter.
3. Deep fry them in hot oil: with a spoon drop in one piece of banana at a time with a little batter. Cook about half a dozen at a time till golden. Drain well on kitchen paper and keep hot.

4. Dissolve the sugar in 110 ml (4 fl oz) of water and boil till bubbles appear all over and it becomes syrupy. Stir in the bananas and dish up. Sprinkle on the sugar and sesame seeds.

A simple and delightful sweet or snack, with a light, spongy batter. The use of beaten egg whites as batter is known as *kaoli* in Chinese culinary terminology.

LITTLE YELLOW CHICKS

Water pastry:
280 g (10 oz) strong white flour
80 g (3 oz) lard (or white vegetable fat)
4 fl oz water

Oil pastry:
230 g (8 oz) strong white flour
110 g (4 oz) lard (or white vegetable fat)

Filling:
170 g (6 oz) red-bean paste
1 beaten egg for brushing

some black sesame seeds for eyes

1. Divide the red-bean paste into 30 equal portions.
2. *Make the water pastry*: sift the flour, and add the lard and 110 ml (4 fl oz) of water. Use your hands to mix it into a dough. Divide into 30 portions, and leave to rest for 30 minutes.
3. *Make the oil pastry*: sift the flour, add the lard, and mix by hand into a dough. Do not overmix. Divide into 30, and leave to rest for 30 minutes.
4. Take a piece of water pastry, flatten it with the hand, place a piece of oil pastry on it, and wrap up the oil pastry into a ball. Flatten with the hand, then with the rolling pin roll into an oblong about 10 cm (4 in) long. Use your hand to roll the oblong into a cylindrical shape. Stand it upright and press gently with the hand to flatten. Roll it again by hand into a cylindrical shape. Stand it upright again and press gently down with the hand, forming a thick disc.
5. Put a ball of bean paste in the centre and wrap into a ball. With your fingers shape it into an oval. Shape a bird's head and then a tail, pinching it flat with tweezers. In the same way, make a pair of wings. Put a black sesame seed on each side of the head for the eyes, and press in lightly. Make 30 chicks.
6. Brush the head and the back of each chick with beaten egg. Let the egg dry, and brush again. Let them dry again. Preheat the oven to

warm, 160°C (325°F, gas mark 3). Put the chicks on a baking sheet, and bake for about 20 minutes. Take out and cool on a rack.

These delightful little chicks are usually served in a woven basket with a handle.

LOTUS-PASTE RABBITS

Water pastry:
280 g (10 oz) strong white flour
80 g (3 oz) lard (or white vegetable fat)
4 fl oz water

Oil pastry:
230 g (8 oz) strong white flour
110 g (4 oz) lard (or white vegetable fat)

Filling:
170 g (6 oz) lotus-seed paste (or red-bean paste)
a little red colouring for the eyes

1. Divide the lotus-seed paste into 30 equal portions. (For the preparation of this paste, see page 225).
2. Make the water pastry as described in the previous recipe (step 2). Divide into 30 portions, and leave to rest for 30 minutes.
3. Make the oil pastry as described in the previous recipe (step 3). Divide into 30 portions, and leave to rest for 30 minutes.
4. Roll the portions of pastry together and shape them as described in the previous recipe (step 4), finishing up with a thick disc.
5. Put a ball of lotus paste in the centre and wrap up, gathering the edges together. Shape the gathered part into a long tapered end about 4 cm (1½ in) long. Press this tapered extension flat with a finger on the pastry board. Slit this flattened part with a sharp knife or razor, forming two long ears (see illustration A). Press the ears back on to the body. Shape the head and mouth with the fingers (illustration B). Dot the eyes with a skewer dipped in red colouring.

6. With a pair of small scissors or razor, make a little snip from the top on the backside and shape into a bob tail. Make 30 rabbits.
7. Preheat the oven to warm, 160°C (325°F, gas mark 3). Put the rabbits on a baking sheet, and bake for 18 to 20 minutes. Take out and cool on a rack.

These little rabbits are charming things for children and adults alike. The pastry is flaky and crisp and a pale creamy white. They may be kept for a week in an airtight tin.

A

B

NEW YEAR CAKE – *NIANGAO*

450 g (1 lb) glutinous rice flour
450 g (1 lb) brown sugar
lard or white vegetable fat to grease tin

1. Stir the sugar in 280 ml (10 fl oz) of hot water till dissolved to a syrup.
2. Sift the flour into a mixing bowl. Stir in the syrup gradually. Mix to a smooth batter consistency.
3. Pour into a greased 20 cm (8 in) cake tin. Steam in a wok or steaming basket on medium heat for about $1\frac{1}{2}$ to 2 hours. This cake can never be overcooked; the colour improves with prolonged cooking.

This is the classic New Year cake which is made weeks in advance and in great numbers. They are steamed, cooled, aired and re-steamed; and the flavour improves with time. To eat, they are sliced 0.6 cm ($\frac{1}{4}$ in) thick with a length of strong cotton thread rather than a knife as they can be quite sticky, and pan fried plain or coated in egg, or steamed to reheat. They are as good as a snack or breakfast with tea or coffee.

NEW YEAR DUMPLINGS – *TANGYUAN*

230 g (8 oz) glutinous rice flour

Filling:
60 g (2 oz) black sesame seeds (toasted and crushed)
60 g (2 oz) pork fat (boiled and minced)
60 g (2 oz) sugar

Syrup:
60 g (4 oz) sugar
1 slice ginger (bruised)

1. Mix together the ingredients for the filling, and divide into 20 balls. Put them in the refrigerator to firm.
2. Mix enough cold water into the flour to make a pliable dough. Divide into 20 equal portions.
3. Take a portion of the dough, roll between the palms into a ball and shape into a flat disc about 4.5 cm (1¾ in) across. Put a sesame ball on it, wrap up and roll into a ball. Make 20 in this way.
4. Bring a pot of water to the boil, and drop in the dumplings several at a time keeping the water on the boil all the time. When cooked they float to the top. Pick them out with a perforated spoon and put them in a bowl of cold water.
5. Bring 570 ml (1 pt) of water, and the sugar and ginger to the boil, lower the heat and simmer for a few minutes till well flavoured. Drain the dumplings and put them into this syrup. Heat through and pour into a bowl. Serve hot or at room temperature.

These dumplings are eaten for breakfast, or as a snack or dessert, on the fifteenth (last) day of the New Year festival. Peanuts, lotus-seed paste and red-bean paste are some alternative fillings. Very often in some areas the dumplings are almond-sized and unfilled, but with one half coloured red or pink.

PAN-FRIED RICE CAKES (HENAN)

230 g (8 oz) glutinous rice

Filling:
110 g (4 oz) red-bean paste, or lotus-seed or red-date paste)
60 g (2 oz) sugar (optional)
cornflour for dusting
3 tbsp peanut oil

1. Wash the rice and steam for 20 minutes, or cook as ordinary rice.

Cool. Pound into a soft dough with a pestle and mortar; oil the pestle if sticky.

2. Divide the red-bean paste into 16 equal portions. (For the preparation of pastes, see pages 225 and 226.)
3. Dust the pastry board with some cornflour, place the cooked rice dough on it, form it into a cylindrical shape, and divide this into 16 equal pieces. Shape each into a round with the fingers; dip your fingers in cornflour if sticky. Put a portion of the filling in the centre and gather in the edges to close. Roll between the palms into a ball and press lightly to flatten. Make 16 in this way.
4. Put a flat-bottomed frying pan on medium heat, and add the oil. Put in the rice cakes. Cook till they turn a pale yellow on both sides. Lower the heat if the pan gets too hot. Take out, drain well on kitchen paper and, if you like, sprinkle with sugar.

A truly delightful cake for a dessert or a snack.

RED-BEAN PUDDING (FUJIAN)

230 g (8 oz) red beans (aduki beans)
170 g (6 oz) glutinous rice flour
170 g (6 oz) rice flour
230 g (8 oz) rock sugar (or granulated sugar)
60 g (2 oz) lard (optional)
2.5 cm (1 in) piece dried tangerine peel (optional)

1. Pick over the beans, rinse well in several changes of water, and drain. Put in 850 ml (1½ pt) of cold water and bring to the boil, then add the peel. Lower the heat and simmer till the beans are so tender that they disintegrate. Take off the heat, and discard the peel. Stir in the sugar till it dissolves. Add the lard, if used.
2. Sift the flours on to the bean mixture. Mix till it has the smooth consistency of a thick flowing batter. Pour the mixture into a greased 20 cm (8 in) cake tin, and steam in the wok on medium heat for about 1½ to 2 hours. To test if it is done, stick in a chopstick; if it comes out clean, the pudding is ready. Cool and cut into 1.3 cm (½ in) thick slices. Steam to reheat.

This is a popular snack in Fujian and Formosa. It is delicious pan fried till a crisp crust forms on both sides.

RICE CUP CAKES

230 g (8 oz) rice flour
230 g (8 oz) sugar (white or brown)

213

15 g (½ oz) fresh yeast or 1 tsp dried yeast
red colouring

1. Dissolve the sugar in 280 ml (10 fl oz) of tepid water. Dissolve the yeast in the syrup.
2. Gradually mix the yeasted syrup into the rice flour. It should be of a batter consistency. Leave in a warm place for 30 minutes or longer, stirring once or twice. When it begins to thicken and bubble it is ready for steaming.
3. Grease 12 dariole moulds or Chinese tea cups; fill each to three-quarters full. Place the cups in a tin and steam in a wok on high heat for 30 minutes. The cakes should split at the top. To see if they are fully cooked, stick in a skewer; if it comes out clean, the cake is done. Take out and dot each in the centre with the red colouring, using a chopstick.

This is a ubiquitous cake on feast days and at the New Year celebrations. The split at the top of the cakes augurs well for all. Sometimes half the batter is coloured pink before steaming.

SILVER WOOD EAR AND FRESH FRUIT SALAD (ZHEJIANG)

7 g (¼ oz) dried silver wood ears (soaked)
fresh mixed fruits: 1 pear, 1 apple, 1 banana, 1 orange or mandarin
110 g (4 oz) sugar
2 tsp cornflour with a little water
½ tsp cassia-flower sugar (or vanilla sugar)

1. Put the soaked and cleaned silver wood ears (see page 227) in a pot with 425 ml (15 fl oz) water, cover and simmer on the stove for about 1 hour. Drain and reserve the juice.
2. Cut the fruits into tiny cubes, the size of garden peas.
3. Add the sugar to the reserved juice with 230 ml (8 fl oz) water, and put on a low heat to dissolve the sugar. Put in the fruits and bring to the boil. Thicken with the cornflour and water mixture. Pour into a serving bowl, and cover with the silver wood ears. Sprinkle on the cassia-flower sugar (for the preparation of this, see page 222).

This is considered a nutritious sweet. The wood ears and the juice are slightly jellied. If a crunchy texture is preferred, cook the wood ears for 30 minutes only.

STEAMED EIGHT TREASURE PEARS (SHANDONG)

6 large firm pears (about 1.1 kg or 2½ lb)

Filling:
60 g (2 oz) glutinous rice
30 g (1 oz) dried persimmon (soaked)
15 g (½ oz) dried longan (rinsed)
15 g (½ oz) crystallized melon
30 g (1 oz) red dates (stoned)
15 g (½ oz) walnuts (blanched and skinned)
80 g (3 oz) cassia-flower sugar (or vanilla sugar)
15 g (½ oz) pumpkin seeds (shelled)
15 g (½ oz) lard

Syrup:
30 g (2 oz) cassia-flower sugar (or vanilla sugar)

1. Rinse the rice, add 80 ml (3 fl oz) of water and steam till cooked.
2. Dice the fruits and nuts to mung-bean size. Mix together all the ingredients for the filling.
3. Rinse and peel the pears, cut off 2.5 cm (1 in) from the tops and reserve to make covers. Core them, scald both parts in boiling water, drain and dry.
4. Fill the pears with the fruit mixture, and cover with the tops. Place them in a dish, and steam in the wok for about 20 to 25 minutes on high heat. Take out.
5. Bring 30 g (1 oz) of cassia-flower sugar and 30 ml (1 oz) water to the boil, and pour over the pears.

This dessert is served hot or cold in Shandong, the land of apples and pears. Choose firm William pears.

STEAMED SILVER WOOD EARS IN COCONUT (GUANGDONG)

1 large coconut in the shell
15 g (½ oz) dried silver wood ears (soaked)
110 g (4 oz) rock sugar (crushed)

1. Shave and scrub the coconut, wash and dry. Saw off the top one-fifth of the way down to make a cover, and drain away the coconut water from the main part.
2. Dissolve the rock sugar in 230 ml (8 fl oz) of boiling water and pour into the coconut container. Cover the coconut with its top, stand it in a bowl and steam in the wok for 1 hour.
3. Add the prepared silver wood ears (see page 227) and steam for another hour.

This is a summer sweet from the subtropical island of Hainan off the coast of southern China. As the coconuts here are rather small, individual ones may be used instead.

SWEET CRISPY WALNUTS (YUNNAN)

230 g (8 oz) walnuts (shelled)
60 g (2 oz) rock sugar (or sugar)
1 tsp rose-petal sugar (or vanilla sugar)
570 ml (1 pt) peanut oil

1. Pour boiling water over the walnuts. Remove the skins, with a toothpick starting from the flat side, rinse and drain.
2. Deep fry the walnuts till slightly crisp. Drain well.
3. Crush the rock sugar and dissolve in 60 ml (2 fl oz) of water. Boil till bubbles appear all over and it becomes syrupy. Put in the walnuts and stir well. Sprinkle on the rose-petal sugar (for the preparation of this, see page 226), and take out.

Fragrant and crisp, this makes an excellent accompaniment to after dinner coffee or drinks.

Savoury Snacks

CHARSIU BAO – STEAMED BREAD BUNS (GUANGDONG)

Bread dough:
900 g (2 lb) strong white bread flour
20 g (¾ oz) fresh yeast or 1 tsp dried yeast
60 g (2 oz) sugar
1 egg
2 tbsp milk

Filling:
230 g (8 oz) Cantonese barbecued pork, charsiu *(see page 130) (diced)*
2 tbsp oyster sauce
1 tbsp light soya sauce
2 tbsp sugar
1 tbsp cornflour
2 tbsp water
2 stalks spring onion whites (chopped)

1. Mix the yeast with the tepid water and let stand till frothy. Sieve 680 g (1½ lb) of the flour, make a well in the middle, and pour in the

216

yeast mixture. Mix to a smooth dough and leave to rise till doubled in size.

2. Cut 30 squares, about 5×5 cm (2×2 in) from greaseproof paper. Mix together all the ingredients for the filling, and set aside.
3. When the dough has risen, mix in the sugar, egg, milk and the rest of the flour, using your hands. Knead till smooth and use immediately.
4. Roll the dough into a cylinder, and cut into 30 equal portions. Take one portion and shape with your fingers to a round of about 8 cm (3 in) in diameter. Put a portion of the filling in the centre, gather in the edges and pinch them together. Place on a square of greaseproof paper, pinched side up.
5. Place them, well spaced out, in a steaming basket or steamer, and immediately steam for 8 minutes on high heat. Take out and leave on a cake cooling tray. To reheat, steam for a few minutes.

These buns have a Cantonese filling, but the same dough may be used for any *bao*. For sweet *bao*, fill with red-bean paste or lotus-seed paste. It is important to have the steamer boiling when filling the buns, as they must be cooked as soon as they are made; no proving is required.

DAPO NOODLES (GUANGDONG)

450 g (1 lb) fresh egg noodles
230 g (8 oz) lean beef (braising or fillet steak)

Seasoning:
3 cloves garlic
2 tbsp fish sauce
570 ml (1 pt) strong clear stock
4 tbsp cooking oil

2 stalks spring onions
pepper

1. Remove any visible fat or gristle from the beef. Mince, not too finely. Bought beef mince is not suitable.
2. Heat the wok, and put in 2 tbsp of oil. Cook half the garlic till golden and pour into a small bowl.
3. Put in the rest of the oil and the garlic. When this is fragrant, stir fry the beef mince till it loses its pink colour. Stir in the fish sauce and 2 tbsp stock. Take out, and put in a bowl.
4. Boil the noodles *al dente*. Boil each portion separately, take out with a mesh wire strainer, and dip in hot water to rinse. Shake dry, and place in individual bowls. Toss in 2 tsp of the garlic oil immediately.

217

5. Bring the stock to the boil. Put a portion of the beef into each noodle bowl. Ladle on some hot stock, and sprinkle on the onions and pepper. Serve hot.

This may be breakfast or lunch, or a snack. If preferred it may be eaten dry, without the soup. Choose the fine variety of noodle; only fresh ones are suitable.

GUOTIE DUMPLINGS (BEIJING)

Pastry:
170 g (6 oz) strong white flour
80 ml (3 fl oz) boiling water

Pork filling:
110 g (4 oz) pork mince
60 g (2 oz) yellow chives, or celery or Chinese 'celery' cabbage (chopped)
1 tbsp sesame oil
½ tsp salt
1 tbsp light soya sauce
1 stalk spring onion (chopped)
1 slice ginger (minced)
1 tsp cornflour with a little water

3 tbsp cooking oil

1. Make a well in the flour, and pour in the boiling water. Mix with a wooden spoon, then knead to a smooth pliable dough and leave to rest for 30 minutes, covered with an overturned bowl.
2. Mix together all the ingredients for the filling, and divide into 24 to 30 portions. If celery or Chinese 'celery' cabbage is used, rub in a pinch of salt, rinse and squeeze dry before mixing.
3. Divide the dough into 24 to 30 pieces. Take a piece of the dough, shape into a round of about 5 cm (2 in) diameter, and put a portion of the filling on it. Fold into a semicircle and pinch to close. Make some pleats on the curved edge and press together.
4. Heat the oil in a flat-bottomed frying pan on medium heat, and put in the dumplings pinched side up, neatly arranged to cover the whole pan. Cook till the bottoms of the dumplings are golden. Pour in about 100 ml (3½ fl oz) of hot water. Cover and cook till dry, about 5 to 6 minutes. Take them out and place on a plate golden side up.

This is a breakfast or snack in Beijing. The dumplings may be dropped into boiling water and cooked till they float, when they are ready.

PRAWN NOODLES (FUJIAN)

450 g (1 lb) thick, round egg noodles (fresh or dried)
230 g (8 oz) fresh prawns (shelled and deveined) or shelled cooked prawns
110 g (4 oz) belly pork (boiled)
60 g (2 oz) Chinese chives (cut into 2.5 cm or 1 in lengths)
110 g (4 oz) mung-bean sprouts

Seasoning:
1 tbsp salted soya bean paste
1 tbsp light soya sauce
½ tsp sugar
2 shallots (skinned and sliced)

3 tbsp cooking oil
280 ml (10 fl oz) stock
a few coriander leaves (chopped)
pepper

1. Remove the soiled ends of the mung-bean sprouts. Rinse and drain. Cut the belly pork into matchsticks.
2. Boil the noodles *al dente*, and drain. Refresh in cold water and drain thoroughly.
3. Heat the wok on high, put in 1 tbsp of oil, stir fry the prawns till pink, and take out. Put in another 1 tbsp oil, stir fry the chives and mung-bean sprouts with a pinch of salt for 1 minute, and take out.
4. Put in the rest of the oil, reduce the heat, fry the shallots till fragrant and lightly coloured, and take out. Add the pork to the oil, stir fry for 1 minute, and put in the paste. Continue frying till fragrant. Pour in the stock, soya sauce and sugar. Cover, and cook for 2 minutes.
5. Stir in the noodles, and bring to the boil. Mix in the prawns, chives, and sprouts. Dish up immediately, and serve sprinkled with pepper and coriander leaves.

A firm favourite from Fujian, this may be eaten as a snack or lunch; or even at a birthday dinner.

Radishes

SAVOURY CHINESE RADISH PUDDING (GUANGDONG)

450 g (1 lb) Chinese radish (mouli)
230 g (8 oz) rice flour
60 g (2 oz) dried shrimps (soaked and lightly pounded)
6 caps winter mushrooms (soaked and diced)

110 g (4 oz) Chinese sausages (diced) or streaky bacon (derinded and shredded)

Seasoning:
2 shallots (skinned and sliced) or garlic (minced)
1 tsp salt
2 tsp sugar
pepper to taste

1 tbsp lard or cooking oil + more to grease tin
1 stalk spring onion (chopped)

1. Peel and grate the radish.
2. Heat the wok, put in the lard, stir fry the shallots till fragrant. Add the shrimps and mushrooms and, when fragrant, stir in the sausages and take off the heat. If bacon is used, crisp it first in the wok before adding the shrimps and mushrooms.
3. Mix the flour with 280 ml (10 fl oz) water to make a thick batter. Add the grated radish and the seasoning and mix well. Adjust the flour or water if necessary to keep the texture smooth and thick. Pour into a greased 25 cm (10 in) cake tin, and sprinkle on the shrimps, mushrooms and sausages. Steam in the wok for 1½ hours on medium heat. To test, stick in a chopstick; if it comes out clean, the pudding is cooked.
4. Take out, and sprinkle with chopped spring onion. Cool and cut into diamond-shaped pieces about 6×4 cm (2½×1½ in).

This pudding may be oven baked in a *bain-marie*. For a snack or breakfast it is cut into 1.3 cm (½ in) thick slices and pan fried till a crisp crust forms on both sides, or re-steamed for 5 minutes. The toppings vary from place to place; some have only shrimps and onions.

Taro

SAVOURY TARO PUDDING (GUANGDONG)

450 g (1 lb) taro
230 g (8 oz) rice flour
60 g (2 oz) dried shrimps (soaked and lightly pounded)
110 g (4 oz) streaky bacon (derinded and shredded)
6 caps winter mushrooms (soaked and diced)

Seasoning:
1 tsp five-spice powder
1 tsp salt
2 tsp sugar
pepper to taste

1 clove garlic (minced)
2 tbsp lard or cooking oil
celery leaves or spring onion (chopped)

1. Scrub the taro under the tap with a stiff brush. Boil it whole till softened; pierce with a skewer to test. Cool in cold water, and cut into *julienne* strips.
2. Heat the wok, put in the lard, stir fry the garlic till fragrant, add the shredded bacon and fry till crisp, put in the shrimps and mushrooms and stir fry till fragrant. Take out one-third of the contents, and set aside. Add the taro to the wok and pour in 570 ml (1 pint) of water. Bring to the boil, stir in the rest of the seasoning, cover and cook on medium heat till well flavoured, a few minutes. Take off the heat. Cool slightly.
3. Gradually stir in the flour to make a soft, thick paste, adjusting the water and flour if necessary. Spread into a greased cake tin, – 23 cm (9 in) is best – level and smooth, and sprinkle on the reserved bacon mixture. Steam in the wok on medium heat for $1\frac{1}{2}$ hours. Take out, and sprinkle on the chopped celery leaves or spring onions. Serve hot or cold, cut into 6×4 cm ($2\frac{1}{2}$×$1\frac{1}{2}$ in) diamond-shaped pieces.

For a snack or breakfast, the cold pudding is cut into 2.5 cm (1 in) thick slices and pan fried till a crisp crust forms on both sides, or steamed for 5 minutes to heat through. In China a Chinese preserved pork or sausage rather than bacon is the usual ingredient. In South-East Asia, a finely chopped red chilli is sprinkled on with the celery leaves, and pork is often omitted. The pudding may be oven baked in a *bain-marie*.

Preparation of Some Chinese Ingredients

Birds's nests: pour cold water over to cover and let them soak, usually overnight, till softened and swollen. Rinse them in many changes of cold water, handling gently: do not break them or wash them away. Transfer them into a white bowl, and pour in cold water until they are floating. As both the bird's nests and the bowl are white, any down can easily be seen. Pick out the pieces of down one by one with a pair of tweezers. The cleaned bird's nests are transparent and white rather like soaked mung-bean vermicelli. They are now ready for further cooking, steaming in soup which can be either sweet or savoury. If they are not required immediately, keep them in cold water in a cool part of the refrigerator or in a cool place, in which case change the water once a day. They may be kept for a couple of days.

Caramel: add 170 ml (6 fl oz) cold water to 570 g (1¼ lb) granulated sugar. Boil on low heat till it turns red and bubbles appear, remove from heat, then add a little boiling water, about 110 ml (4 fl oz). Cool and keep in a bottle. This is used in the colouring of dark red dishes. To make in smaller quantity: bring 110 g (4 oz) granulated sugar and 30 ml (1 fl oz) water to the boil in a thick saucepan and cook for 1 to 2 minutes. When the water evaporates turn the heat to low and continue cooking until the colour changes to brown and smoke appears, then remove from the heat and add 30 ml (1 fl oz) boiling water.

Cassia-flower sugar: mix some dried cassia flowers (sweet-scented osmanthus) or buds with granulated sugar and leave to steep as in the making of vanilla sugar. (Cassia flowers are available in some Asian spice shops, as they are also used in Indian and Arab cookery.)

Chilli oil: put 30 g (1 oz) chilli powder in a china or enamelled container. Heat 140 ml (5 fl oz) of peanut oil (or any good vegetable oil) in the wok till bubbles appear, add in a slice of bruised ginger and 1 stalk spring onion and cook till the onion is brown. Discard both onion and ginger. Take the oil off the heat and let it cool slightly so that the chilli powder does not get burnt and lose its flavour. Pour the slightly cooled oil on to the chilli powder and stir to mix well. When the oil becomes clear it is ready. Cool completely and bottle. The proportion of oil to chilli is 5 to 1.

Cuttlefish or squid (dried): soak the dried cuttlefish (or squid) in cold water for 1 to 2 hours. Remove the membranes. Rinse and put in clean cold water to cover and add 1 tsp of lye water (see page 69). Soak till well swollen and spongy to the touch, for several hours or overnight. The length of soaking depends on the use of the fish, but soak only as long as necessary: over-soaking dissipates some of the taste. Rinse in several changes of water to remove any trace of lye water. If not required immediately, put in cold water in the fridge. After soaking, dried cuttlefish or squid increases about 4 times in volume. Score across the underside (bone side diagonally, with the knife at a slant of about 45°, and then turn it round and score the other way, forming a criss-cross design. Then cut it into two lengthwise and slice into bite size pieces (see illustration on page 174.)

Fermented glutinous rice: cook 450 g (1 lb) of glutinous rice as you would ordinary rice. Let it cool completely. Pound a ball of Chinese wine yeast (called 'yeast cake' or 'wine cake') to powder. Sprinkle cooled boiled water on the cooled rice and mix in the powdered yeast. Put the rice into a carefully washed large-mouthed jar big enough to hold the rice and a third over; it should have a plastic or cork stopper, not a metal one. Leave it in a warm place, about 25°C (80°F). The temperature should not be too hot, or the alcoholic content would be too high. If too cool, the rice wine would turn sour. In China the jar is covered with quilted material. The fermented rice wine jar follows the seasons; when the people put on four layers of clothes, it also needs four. This is the rule of thumb as regards temperature. After two days the fermentation is visible, with little bubbles moving between the rice grains. After the initial fermentation in the warmth it is removed to a dark, cool, dry place to store. It keeps for months. The storage life depends on the cleanliness of the jar, which must be free of grease or salt. As time goes on there will be more liquid than rice. As little as 230 g (8 oz) of rice may be used, for which only half a ball of yeast is needed.

Five-spice powder salt: heat a thick frying pan or wok on medium, and dry fry 2 tbsp of salt until it crackles. Add in 1 tsp of five-spice powder. Turn off the heat and stir fry briefly. Cool and keep in an airtight bottle. It is better to make a small amount when required, or the spices lose their strength.

Garlic: whole garlic is crushed with the back of the chopper and the skin slipped off before it is finely minced, thinly sliced or shredded.

Ginger: always peeled and then thinly sliced, or shredded into fine threads; or bruised and minced finely; or left whole and bruised for the stock pot and other slow-cooked dishes (use a slice about 2.5 cm (1 in) long and wide, and about 0.2 cm (1/10 in) thick.

Ginger juice or spring onion juice: pound or mince ginger or spring onion, add in some water and squeeze. The proportion of water to ginger or spring onion is about equal.

Ginger wine: as above, but use wine instead of water.

Guoba (dried cooked rice): originally this was cooked rice that had stuck to the bottom of the rice pot; *guoba* means just that. When cooking on a wood or charcoal fire there is less precise control over the heat, and very often a hard piece of cooked rice is left at the bottom of the pot and can be eased and lifted out in one piece, a round disc of hard cooked rice. In the frugal Chinese manner this is dried, then deep fried in hot oil and served as an accompaniment (in the form of 'rice crispies') to hot soups or meat dishes in a sauce. There are various ways of making this deliberately, but by far the easiest way is, as it was, when dishing up rice to leave a circle of rice about 2 cm (¾ in) thick at the bottom of the pot. Add in a little water to moisten, and press it down with a potato masher. Put the pot back on a low heat and cook till the rice circle is hardened into one piece and a pale golden underneath. The circle may break, but the small bits may be used in smoking food. Cool and keep in an airtight tin. *Guoba* keeps indefinitely if really dried until it looks transparent. If need be, dry further in a turned-off hot oven.

Hairweed: pour boiling water over to cover, and let stand for 10 minutes. Drain, and rinse in several changes of water till there is no trace of earth or sand. Discard any dry leaves or grass. Boil it in water with a slice of bruised ginger and 1 tbsp of rice wine for about 20 minutes. Drain, discard the ginger, cool and squeeze out the water till quite dry. Mix in a little oil and squeeze again. It is now ready for further cooking. It may now be added to a soup or braised dishes and cooked for another 20 minutes.

Hongqu (dried fermented red rice) water: a medicinal preparation, used for tonic food cooking and as a red colouring. Tie 1 tbsp in a piece of muslin and boil in 200 ml (7 fl oz) of water. For a smaller quantity, soak 1 or 2 tsp in a little hot water, mash well and strain.

Jellyfish (salted): rinse in several changes of cold water. Quarter, pile neatly, roll up tightly and shred very finely. Pour hot water (not boiling) onto the shredded jellyfish for 30 seconds. Rinse thoroughly in cold water, squeezing out the water each time. Soak in fresh cold water for at least 30 minutes or till required. On contact with hot water they shrink dramatically, but revive after re-soaking in cold water.

Lotus seeds (dried): these are usually skinned. Soak them in boiling water for 30 minutes or longer, depending on the recipe. If boiled in a soup, they may be put straight into the pot with the meat and water and cooked for an hour or so. If used as a paste or in a dessert, they are either boiled or steamed after soaking, till tender. Some dried lotus seeds are unblanched. To remove the skins, boil them in water in which lye water (1 tsp to 570 ml or 1 pt water; see page 69) has been added. Simmer on low heat for 10 minutes or till the skin can easily be rubbed off. Rinse well in cold water. Remove the bitter green heart by pushing through a toothpick from one end of the seed.

Lotus-seed paste: boil or steam pre-soaked lotus seeds till they become tender and disintegrate. Drain and sieve. Cook the paste in a little oil in the wok, stir frying till the paste is dry. Add sugar to taste, stir well till the sugar dissolves, take out, cool and use as required. The paste may be frozen.

Mung-bean vermicelli: pour boiling water over to cover, let stand for 10 minutes. Drain and rinse in cold water, then drain again. If not required immediately it may be left soaking in cold water. Sometimes a recipe calls for deep-fried vermicelli; put the dry vermicelli (without rinsing) into hot oil for 30 seconds, take out and drain.

Mustard sauce: this is a dip for meat, dumplings and seafood at the table. The flavour is better if made in large quantity. It may be made in advance and kept in an airtight jar. Gradually mix a little boiled tepid water with 4 tbsp of dry mustard to make a thin paste. Cover and let it stand for 30 minutes for the flavour to develop. Stir in ½ tsp of salt and 1 tsp of vinegar. Salt and vinegar would inhibit the development of flavour if added earlier. Recipe on p. 120.

Persimmons (dried): pour boiling water over to cover. Soak till softened, about 15 minutes. Remove the seeds, and slice or dice before cooking.

Pickles: cucumber, radishes, carrot, Chinese white radish (mouli), sweet red pepper, hot red pepper, white salad cabbage and underripe papaya are among the usual ingredients. Prepare the vegetables by deseeding or peeling where appropriate. Cut them into *julienne* strips, wedges or slices. Rub them with some salt and marinate for 20 minutes. When the water begins to run out, rinse them thoroughly under the cold tap, and gently squeeze dry. Marinate in a mixture of white wine vinegar, sugar and salt to taste.

Pig's trotters: do not wash. Burn off the hair over a naked flame (candle or gas stove). Scrub under the cold tap. The skin may be slightly blackened, but no matter. Bring to the boil enough water to cover with 1 tbsp of salt, and put in the trotters. Boil for 10 minutes on high heat. Drain and scrub under the hot tap, or in a bowl of hot water. Rinse in cold water. Now they are ready for further cooking. This process of boiling and scrubbing is essential to remove any hair or dirt, and above all the odour.

Red-bean paste: boil 450 g (1 lb) of red beans (aduki beans) till they disintegrate. Put in a fine sieve. Wash in cold water in a large clean bowl. Discard the husks in the sieve. Let the water in the bowl settle, pour away any clear water. Put the rest (water and purée) into a muslin bag. Squeeze out the water as much as you can, tie the bag and put it under a weight till all excess water is pressed out. Heat the wok, put in a little oil, stir fry on low heat to remove excess moisture from the paste, and add sugar to taste. Mix well; when the sugar dissolves remove from the wok, cool and use as required. The paste may be frozen. A simpler way is to drain the beans (or cook till almost dry) and blend in a food processor, then cook the paste husks and all.

Red dates (dried jujubes): pour boiling water over to cover, and soak for 10 minutes or till well swollen. Cut open and remove the stones. Boil in soup or braise with meat.

Red-date paste: boil 450 g (1 lb) of red dates till tender, about 15 minutes. Drain, stone and sieve them. Mix in sugar to taste and use as filling. The paste may be frozen.

Rose-petal sugar: mix some dried rose petals with granulated sugar and leave to steep. The petals may be used together with the sugar. Dried rose petals are available from apothecaries specializing in herbs and spices.

Scallops (dried): rinse, and soak in cold water to cover for 2 hours. Add rice wine and steam with the soaking liquor till tender, about 30 minutes. Set aside in the liquor till required. Before cooking, break the scallops with the fingers into fine shreds in the juice. Use both the steaming juice and the scallops in the cooking, at the same time.

Sea cucumbers: pour boiling water over them and let them soak overnight. Change the water, take out the softened ones and slit open the undersides with a pair of sharp kitchen scissors. Remove the sand and innards. Simmer hard ones for a few minutes and leave soaking in the hot water till they are soft enough to be opened. The longer they are soaked, the larger they become. If the inside is not spotlessly clean, the sea cucumber will not expand well. When all are softened and cleaned, keep them in cold water in the refrigerator. They keep here for at least a week if the water is changed daily. Just before cooking, boil them with a slice of ginger and a stalk of spring onion for 20 minutes. Drain and use as required.

Shark's fin (dried and processed): soak in warm water for 30 minutes. Bring to the boil in cold water to cover with a slice of ginger and a stalk of spring onion. Lower the heat and simmer for 2 hours. After the first 30 minutes discard the ginger and the onion, and change the water now and every 30 minutes. To test if it is done, press a piece between the index finger and the thumb; if it breaks easily, it is ready. Drain, rinse in cold water and drain again. It is now ready to be cooked in a soup or stir fried in an omelette.

Shrimps (dried): discard any loose shells and grit, and remove any shell still on the shrimps. Pour hot water over, soak for 2 or 3 minutes, drain, and rinse in cold water. Pour hot water over to cover, and soak for 5 more minutes. Drain and reserve the soaking liquor, pound, mince or leave the shrimps whole as required in the recipe. Reserve the soaking liquor and add to the cooking.

Sichuan pepper salt: dry fry (without oil) 6 tbsp of salt with 4 tbsp of Sichuan peppercorns till fragrant. Take off the heat, and when cool grind into powder. Keep in an airtight bottle. The proportion of salt to Sichuan peppercorns is 3 to 2.

Sichuan pepper water: bring to the boil 30 g (1 oz) of Sichuan peppercorns in 570 ml (1 pt) of water and add 30 g (1 oz) of peeled and bruised ginger. Reduce to half by boiling. Strain off the spices. Cool and keep in a bottle. For a smaller amount, soak some crushed Sichuan peppercorns in hot water for 10 minutes. Strain and use as required.

Silver wood ears (dried): soak in cold water for 30 minutes or till well swollen. Snip off any yellow, stained or woody bits with a pair of scissors. Rinse well, cover in cold water and bring to the boil on high heat. Turn off the heat and let stand, covered, for 1 hour. Drain and use as required, or soak in cold water till needed. (See also Wood ears, below.)

Spinach juice: mince some spinach leaves, and squeeze out the juice. There is no need to add water. Make the quantity required for colouring.

Spring onions:
Shredded: cut into 5 cm (2 in) lengths and slice lengthwise into strands. Use as a garnish and in steamed dishes.
Sliced: cut into 4 cm (1½ in) lengths; for stir-fried dishes.
Diagonally cut: cut diagonally into 4 cm (1½ in) lengths; for stir-fried dishes.
Chopped: cut into 0.6 cm (¼ in) rounds; for seasoning the cooking oil, as in stir frying, or as a garnish in soup and other dishes.
Whole: discard any soiled leaves, cut off the roots and trim the ends.
  Bruise lightly and tie in a knot for easy removal in slow-cooked dishes.
Spring onion brushes: cut spring onion whites into 8 cm (3 in) lengths. Make slashes in both ends with a sharp paring knife. Place in a bowl of

cold water in the refrigerator so that both ends open out like a brush. These are decorative as a garnish, and useful as a brush for dipping in sauces, as in the eating of the Mandarin pancakes with Beijing duck or roast meat dishes in northern China.

Spring onion juice: see ginger juice.

Squid (dried): see cuttlefish.

Stocks:

Ordinary stock: simmer a chicken carcase (with the breast and leg meat taken off) with giblets and neck and 450 g (1 lb) of pork bones or pork barbecue spareribs, chopped up, and a slice of peeled and bruised ginger, 2 stalks spring onion and 1 tsp salt in 2.8 l (5 pt) of water for 1 hour. Strain.

Milk stock: this is a meat stock with a thick and milky look. The milkiness is obtained by boiling a chicken carcase with 450 g (1 lb) of belly pork and 450 g (1 lb) of pork bones in 2.8 l (5 pt) of water with a slice of peeled and bruised ginger and 2 stalks of spring onion. Bring to the boil on high heat, skim, cover and boil on medium heat till the meat falls off, about 1 to $1\frac{1}{2}$ hours. Strain. The rule is that from 1 lb of ingredients there should be 1 pt of stock – a bit more than 1 litre from 1 kg.

Strong chicken stock: Bring to the boil one 1.4 kg (3 lb) chicken in 2.8 l (5 pt) of water with a slice of peeled and bruised ginger, 2 stalks spring onion and 1 tsp salt. Skim and simmer, with the lid slightly ajar so that the stock is crystal clear, for 1 hour. Strain.

Vegetable (or vegetarian) stock: put some sliced bamboo shoots, some winter mushrooms and soya bean sprouts in a pot; cover with twice the volume of water. Bring to the boil on high heat, reduce the heat to low, cover and simmer for 30 minutes or more; the longer it is simmered the better.

Winter mushroom stock: rinse some winter mushrooms, including stalks, and bring to the boil in water. Reduce the heat, cover and simmer till the water is well flavoured, at least 30 minutes. This stock is mainly for vegetarian cooking.

Sweet salted soya bean paste: grind 450 g (1 lb) salted soya beans and mix with 450 g (1 lb) of sugar. Stir well and steam for 2 hours. Take out and stir in 80 g (3 oz) of sesame oil. This keeps well in an airtight bottle in a cool, dry place. It is used both in cooking and as a dip at table.

Wheat gluten: to obtain about 170 g (6 oz) of wheat gluten, use 450 to 680 g (1 to $1\frac{1}{2}$ lb) of strong white flour and 1 tbsp of salt. Put the flour and salt in a mixing bowl, and add enough water to mix into a soft dough. Knead to a very smooth dough. Continue kneading till the dough is elastic. Cover with a tea cloth and leave to rest for at least 1 hour in a warm place. Put the rested dough in a fine sieve over a large bowl with some cold water and wash the dough, squeezing gently as you would a sponge. When the water is white with flour, pour it away (or save the wheat starch for dumplings). Put in some fresh water and wash the dough again. Continue till the water is clear, showing that all the starch is washed out. (If during the washing the dough should separate, add some more salt to the dough and knead till sticky, then continue washing.) What is left is raw gluten. Leave it to rest for 30 minutes before cooking. To cook, spread out in a cake tin, in a layer about 1.3 cm ($\frac{1}{2}$ in) thick, and steam on high heat for about 1 hour. Cool and cut into slices, ready for further cooking. If a fried gluten is required, after steaming, cooling and slicing, deep fry in hot oil till golden. A recipe may call for a raw or a cooked gluten. Raw gluten may be boiled, steamed or deep fried. It may be made into small balls, about the size of walnuts, which take about 5 minutes to boil. They float to the top of the water when cooked. To deep fry, cook on low heat till golden, then raise the heat briefly before taking them out, to colour them. Press them down with a mesh wire strainer to submerge in the oil briefly in order to cook through. When cooked, they puff up to three times their original size. Gluten tastes quite similar to a soya product, but is slightly sweet and has a tender, resilient texture.

Winter mushrooms (dried): rinse in cold water. Pour boiling water over to cover, and put a little saucer over them to weigh them down. Let stand for 5 minutes. Drain and reserve the water for cooking. Cut off and discard the stalks. Slice, shred, dice or leave whole as required in the recipe. Strain the soaking liquor through a piece of muslin.

Wood ears (dried): pour boiling water over to cover, and let stand for 5 minutes. Drain, and rinse in cold water. Cut off any woody parts. Rub them with some salt. Rinse in cold water. Repeat till there is no trace of sand or earth and no 'woody' odour. Soak in cold water till required.

Chronology

Periods	Dynasties or administrations	Dates
Prehistoric: Neolithic		7000–1500 BC
Beginning of historical times	Shang	1500–1027 BC
	Chou	1027–256 BC
Imperial	Qin	221–206 BC
	Han	202 BC–AD 220
	Qi	550–589
	Tang	618–906
	Song	906–1279
	Yuan (Mongols)	1279–1368
	Ming	1368–1644
	Qing (Manchus)	1644–1912
Modern	Republic	1912–1949
	People's Republic	1949 onwards

Guide to Pinyin

Pinyin	Wade system
bao	pao
cai	ts'ai
chang	ch'ang
dan	tan
fang	fang
fen	fên
guo	kuo
hong	hung
ji	chi
jiu	chiu
kong	k'ung
lian	lien
long	lung
mian	mien
pai	p'ai
pei	p'ei
ping	p'ing
qi	chi
qian	chíen
qing	ch'ing
ran	jan
re	je
ruan	juan
se	sê
shi	shih
si	sǔ, szû, ssǔ
song	sung
ta	t'a
tang	t'ang
wen	wên
xi	hsi
xian	sian

Pinyin	Wade system
xiao	hsiao
xue	hsueh, hsuo
yong	yung
you	yu
yuan	yuen
za	tsa
zai	tsai
zha	cha
zhong	chung
zong	tsung
zui	tsui

Index

Note: references to recipes are marked in bold type.

abalone: as *yin* food, 13; soup, 39;
   dried, 52–3; use, 71, **in oyster
   sauce**, 159
aduki beans, red, 57
Afghanistan, 28
Africa, East, 23
agar-agar, 53
alcoholic drinks, 2, 22; *see also* beer;
   lager; wine
almonds: 66; **almond *doufu***, 204–5
America, 7, 10, 23
Amoy *see* Xiamen
anchovies, dried, 52
angled luffa: as folk remedy, 14;
   preparation of, 72–3
Anhui province, 36, 40, 42, 46
ape's lips, 15
apples, 41, 87
Arabia, 25
aromatic rice, 48; *see also* rice
Asia, Central, 5, 28
Asia, South-East, 23, 43
aubergine (eggplant): as *yin* food, 14;
   in Dapo cooking, 38; preparation
   of, 73; **stuffed**, 176–7; **stir-fried
   with salted yolks**, 177–8
Australia, 21

baijiu (white wine), 31–2; *see also* wine
bamboo shoots: consumption of, 2,
   66; properties of, 14
bamboo-tube tea, 28
banana: 87; **Kaoli**, 208–9
barbecue sauce *see sacha-jiang*
barley, 2
basket, steaming, 93
beans, 2; *see also* individual varieties
bean curd, 58–9; *see also doufu*; soya
bear's paws: properties of, 15; in

Yunnan cooking, 39, 41
bêche de mer *see* sea cucumber
beef: consumption of, 2, 72; in
   Chaozhan cooking, 38; **braised
   with *dangkui***, 121–2; **braised with
   spiced brisket**, 122–3; **Chaozhu
   beef fire-pot**, 123–4; **dry stir-fried
   with celery**, 124; **oxtail in tomato
   sauce**, 124–5
beer, Tsingtao, 31
Beijing, 7–8, 36, 40–42
beverages: consumption of, 2; types
   22–35; *see also* alcoholic drinks
bird's nest: properties of, 15;
   consumption of, 44, 53; **soup**, 187–
   8; preparation of, 222
blachan, 10
black rice, 48; *see also* rice
black vinegar, 60; *see also* vinegar
boar, 2
boiling (*zhu*), 96–7
Borneo, 10
boxthorn leaves, 15–16, 74
braised tea, 27
braising (*men*), 101
bream, 2, 52
brick tea, 26–7
broad beans, 57; **and bamboo shoots**,
   183–4
Buddha's hands: properties of, 16;
   preparation of, 74; consumption of,
   87
Buddhism: influence on diet, 6; and
   tea drinking, 23; and vegetarian
   cookery, 41–2
buns, steamed, 24
butter, 47

cabbage *see* Chinese 'celery' cabbage

233

cakes: consumption of, 4, 24; Fujian, 38; rice, 43; recipes, 204–16; *see also* hubing; pilo
Cambodia (Champa), 5
camel, 4, 15
candy flossing (*basi*), 110
Canton *see* Guangzhou
Cantonese cooking: in North America, 10; *tim sum*, 24; characterized, 37–8
caramel, 64, 222
cardamoms, 62
carp: consumption of, 2, 70; tail, 15; in vinegar, 40
cashew nuts, 66
cassia bark, 62
cassia flowers: 62; sugar, 222
cassia tea, 26
Catherine of Braganza, 23
celery: properties of, 16; as flavouring, 62; preparation of, 74–5
cereals: as basis of diet, 1; *see also* individual cereals
chakua see under cucumbers
Champa *see* Cambodia
Chang-an *see* Xian
Chaozhou cooking, 38, 156–7, 123
Charles II, King of England, 23
Charsiu Bao (steamed bread buns), 216–17
cherry and broad-bean salad, 206
chestnuts, 66
chestnuts, water *see* water chestnuts
chicken: consumption of, 2, 72; and *yang* food, 12; in Hunan cooking, 38; tangerine stir–fried, 39; 'clay', 40; fat, 47; **bang–bang**, 113; **and mung-bean salad**, 114–15; **drunken**, 115–16; **soya sauce**, 116-17; **strange–flavour**, 117; **white steeped**, 117–18; **crispy drumsticks**, 144–5; **hot and spicy**, 145-6; **spicy chicken in pumpkin**, 146; **spicy steamed**, 147; **steamed slippery**, 147; **tangerine peel**, 148; **Yunnan qi-guo**, 148–9; *see also* poultry
chillis: consumption of, 10; in Dapo cooking, 38; in Sichuan cooking, 38–9; in Yunnan cooking, 40; dried, 62
chilli oil, 51, 222–3
chilli sauce, 50
Chinese bread, 128
Chinese caterpillar fungus: properties

of, 16; consumption of, 68–9
Chinese 'celery' cabbage: properties of, 16; in Shandong cooking, 41; preserved (*dongcai*), 55; preparation of, 75–6
Chinese chives: properties of, 16; preparation of, 76–7
Chinese cole, 66, 77
Chinese kale, 77
Chinese radish, 77–8; *see also* radish
Chinese spinach, 78; *see also* spinach
Chinese yellow chives, 78–9
Chinese yellow flowering vegetable, 79
Chinese wolfberries: properties of, 16–17; consumption of, 69
Chinese wolfberry wine, 35
ching po leung see 'nourishing and cooling soup'
chives, 2; *see also* Chinese chives; Chinese yellow chives
'chop-suey' *see zacui*
choppers, 91–2
chopping block, 92
chopsticks, long, 92
Chou period: cooking in, 1-2; and vegetarian diet, 41; and preserved vegetables, 54
chrysanthemum leaves, 79-80
chrysanthemum wine, 34
Chu Yuanchang, Emperor, 7
chungcai see under turnips
chunjiu (spring wine), 30; *see also* wine
cicada, 15
clams, 71
clay roasting (*nikao*), 108
cloves, 62
cockles, 71
coconut milk, 10
cold mixing (*ban*), 109
colourings, 63–4
cooking, regional, 36–45
cooking vessels: development of, 1
cooked stir frying (*suchao*), 106
coriander, 62
crab: as *yin* food, 12; in 'lion's head', 40; consumption of, 71; **scrambled eggs with**, 159–60; **stir-fried with ginger and spring onion**, 160–61
crackling tea *see* toasted tea
crispy and smooth method (*cuiliu*), 104
crisp deep frying (*suzha*), 103
crunchy deep frying (*cuizha*), 103

cucumbers: pickled, 55; *chakua*, 55; consumption of, 80–81

'cut and cook' method, 1

cutting techniques, 88–91

cuttlefish: dried, 53; consumption of, 72; preparation, 223; soup, 201

dairy products, 39; *see also koumiss*; milk

dangkui, 62, 69, 122

Dapo cooking: 38; **noodles**, 217–18

dark soya sauce, 50–51

'dates', red or black *see under* jujubes

deep frying (*zha*), 102

deer: tail, 39; consumption of, 41

desserts, recipes for, 204–16

diet: and health, 7, 12–21; Lee Shizhen on, 8

ding (cooking vessel), 1

direct steaming (*zheng*), 99-101

distilling (*ao*), 98

dog, 2

dongcai see under Chinese 'celery' cabbage

doufu: development of, 4; in Beijing cooking, 41; consumption of, 58; **Hakka *Jongtaufu* – stuffed**, 178–9; ***Mapo***, 180–81; **pan-fried**, 181; **snowflake**, 182–3

doujiang see soya-bean milk

Dreams of the Red Chambers, The, 8

dried salted black soya beans, 51

dried seafood *see under* seafood

dried persimmon wine, 34

drunken pickling (*zuiyau*), 109

dry deep frying (*kanzha*), 103

dry stir frying (*kanchao*), 107

dried wheat gluten, 48–9; *see also* wheat gluten

duck: consumption of, 2, 72; Beijing, 10, 39; and Chinese caterpillar fungus, 16; in Fujian cooking, 38; in Hunan cooking, 38; tea-smoked, 39; Yunnan roast, 39; wild, 40–41; fat, 47; pressed, 64; **Cantonese red steeped**, 113–14; **Hangzhou steeped**, 118; **Beijing**, 149–50; ***Congcao***, 151; **five-spice**, 151–2; **Nanjing salt-water**, 152–3; **spicy crispy**, 153–4; ***suzhou***, 154–5; **tea-smoked**, 155–6; *see also* poultry

dumplings: 24, 43; **New Year**, 212; **Guotie**, 218; *see also hakaw; siumai*

eggs: duck, 56; fermented (*pitan*), 57

egg rolls: **steamed egg purses**, 174–5; **steamed egg rolls and cabbage**, 175–6

eggplant *see* aubergine

elephant's trunk, 39, 41

England, 23

Europe, 21; *see also* individual countries

fast boiling (*cuan*), 97

fennel seeds, 62

fermented rice pickling (*zaoyan*), 109–10

festivals, cooking for, 42–5

figs: properties of, 17; consumption, 67, 87

fig wine, 33

fish: consumption of, 1–2; Cantonese, 37–8; in Dapo cooking, 38; salted, 52; fresh, 70–72; **chrysanthemum**, 161–2; **clear-steamed**, 162; **slices in fermented glutinous rice**, 163; **mock crab**, 163–4; **grape**, 164–5; **squirrel**, 165–6; **steamed in the snow**, 167–8; **West Lake vinegar**, 168–9; *see also* individual species

fish gravy, 50

fish maws, dried, 52

fish air bladders, dried, 52

five-spice powder, 62, 223

flaky deep frying (*songzha*), 103–4

Floating Life, A, 8

flour, 48–9; *see also* individual varieties

flower-scented teas, 26; *see also* individual varieties

Formosa, 26, 37–8

France, 23

frog, 40–41

frost coating (*guashuang*), 110

fruit, 2, 87; *see also* individual fruits

fruit juice, 2

frying, 12, 102–7; *see also* rice, fried

fry-stewing (*shao*), 102

Fujian province, 26, 36–8, 42, 44–5, 71, 79

Fuzhou cooking, 38

galangal: consumption of, 10; as flavouring, 62–3; with duck, 152

game, 41, 72; *see also* individual birds and animals

garlic: consumption of, 2; in Sichuan cooking, 38; in Shandong cooking, 40–41, as flavouring, 63; preparation of, 223

geng (stew), 2
ginger: consumption of, 2; green, 18; young, pickled, 55; as flavouring, 63; **lotus root and ginger salad**, 119–20; preparation of, 223–4
ginger juice, 224
ginger wine, 224
Gingko nuts, 66
ginseng, 4
glutinous millet, 2; *see also* millet
glutinous rice, 48; *see also* rice
glutinous rice flour, 49
goose: consumption of, 2, 72; feet, 8; in Chaozhu cooking, 38; **Chaozhu steamed**, 156–7
gourd; consumption of 2, 66; as *yin* food, 12, 15; bitter, 15, 38, 73–4; **stuffed bitter**, 185; *see also* angled luffa
Grand Canal, 7
grapes, 2, 87
Great Wall, the, 54
green tea, 26
grouper, 70
Guangdong, 13, 16, 26, 30, 36–8, 54, 56, 71, 79
Guangsi, 27
Guangzhou (Canton), 9, 37, 41–2; *see also* Cantonese cooking
'gunpowder' tea, 26
guoba (dried cooked rice), 224

Hainan island, 37–8, 54
hairweed: properties of, 18; dried, 54; preparation of, 224
hakaw, 24
Hakkas *see kejia, jongtaufu*
ham, 39–40, 64–5
Han dynasty: and development of cooking, 2, 9, 12; and tea drinking, 23
Hangzhou, 5, 23, 40, 42, 118
haw (*shanzha*), 87
Hawaii, 10
health *see under* diet
heavy soya sauce, 50
Hebei province, 36, 40, 46
heizao see jujube
hemp seed, 2
Henan province, 36, 40
herbs, 61–3
Hoisin sauce, 50
Holland, 23
honey, 60
honeyed syrup coating (*mizhi*), 110

Hong Kong, 24
hongqu see red rice
Hongqu (dried red fermented rice water), 224
hongcha jun (red tea fungus), 25
hongzao see jujube
hors d'oeuvres, cold, 111
horse, consumption of, 2
hot salading (*qiang*), 109
hot salted soya bean paste, 51
hsiangyou see sesame oil
hsieu (cooking vessel), 1
Hu Sihui, *Principles of Correct Diet*, 7
huangjiu, 32; *see also* wine
Hubei province, 82–3
hubing, 4
huiguan ('clan hostels'), 8
Hunan province, 26–7, 36, 38–40, 47

India, 5, 23
indirect steaming, 98
Indochina, 4
ingredients, 46–87, 222–9; *see also* individual foods

Japan, 23, 25
jasmine blossom, 39
jasmine tea, 26, 39
jelly fungus *see* silver wood ears
jellyfish, salted: 53; **in mustard sauce**, 120; **salad**, 120–21; preparation of, 224
Jiangsu province, 29, 36, 40
Jinhua ham, 65
jiu see wine
jongtaufu, 38, 178–9
jujube: consumption of, 2, 87; red and black 'dates', 19, 67, 226; paste, 39

Kaifeng, 5
kanlan, 87
kaoliang (sorghum), 10, 32
kaolingju, 32
kejia (Hakkas), 38
kelp, dried, 54
kidney: **slices in sesame sauce**, 118–19; **'litchi'**, 133–4
kidney beans, 2
koumiss, 7, 30
Kublai Khan, 7, 30, 39
Kuizhou, 27, 32
kumquats, 87

lager: Great Wall, 31; Tsingtao, 31
lamb: 'all-lamb banquet', 40; **iced**

cubes, 125–6; **fire pot**, 126–7; **Mongolian grill**, 127–8; **quick-fried with spring onion**, 129
lard, 38–9, 47
laver, purple (*nori; tzecai*), 54
Lee Shizhen, 8, 31, 79
leeks: consumption of, 40–41, 81; pickled, 55
legumes, 57; *see also* individual varieties
lemon grass, 10
lentils, 2
light soya sauce, 51
lily: buds, 10; flowers, dried, 17, 67; bulbs, dried, 69
'lion's head', 40; crab meat, 131
liquorice root, 63
litchis: consumption of, 29, 87; in Cantonese cooking, 38
little yellow chicks, 209–10
lobsters, 71
Lohancai – 'soft immortal food', 179–80
lohankuo and dehydrated cole soup mix, 68
long beans, 81–2; **dry-fried**, 184–5
long-grain rice, 48; *see also* rice
longans: dried, 17, 67; in Cantonese cooking, 38; consumption of, 87
Longjing tea, 23, 26, 28
loquat (*pipa*), 87
Loshan, 39
lotus flowers, 39
lotus-paste rabbits, 210–11
lotus roots: consumption of, 2, 66, 82–3; in Shandong cooking, 41; **and ginger salad**, 119–20; **honeyed cake**, 207–8
lotus seeds, 67, 224–5
lu-chong see stag's reproductive organs
lye water, 69, 223, 224–5

maggots, 39–40
maize, 7
Malaysia, 10, 43
maltose: properties of, 18; consumption of, 60
Manchuria, 10
mango, 87
manners, in eating, 44–5
Manual for Salvation from Famine, 82
Manual for the Common People, A, 54
Maofoong tea, 23
maotai wine, 32; *see also* wine

mat, pot, 92
Mawangdui, 2
meat: consumption of, 1–2, 72; fatty, 12; dumplings, 24; preserved, 38, 64–5; *see also* individual meats
medicinal wines, 33–5; *see also* Chinese wolfberry wine; chrysanthemum wine; dried persimmon wine, fig wine; red date (jujube) wine
meeting (*hui*), 97–8
meikancai see under 'red-in-the-snow'
melon: consumption of, 2; winter, 12–13, 21, 86–7; fuzzy, 38; crystallized, 69
methods, 95–110; *see also* individual cooking methods, e.g. braising, frying, etc.
milk, 4 *see also* koumiss
millet: as staple crop, 1; consumption of, 2–3, 10; wine, 28; *sanshao*, 31
Ming dynasty, 7–8, 37
Ming Huang, Emperor, 29–30
Ming Shih-Tsung, Emperor, 20
mint leaves, 63
mixed spices, 63
Mongolia, Inner, 27, 36, 40, 47
Mongols: diet of, 6–8; and *koumiss*, 30
monosodium glutamate, 60–61
mung beans: consumption of, 57; **chicken and mung-bean salad**, 114–15; preparation of, 225
mushrooms: consumption of, 10; winter, 21, 68, 229; **button with crab-meat sauce**, 186
mussels, dried, 53, 71
mustard greens, sour and salted, 56
mustard seed, 2, 225
mutton, 2, 4; *see also* lamb
myrobalan, 4

New Year Cake, 211
New Zealand, 21
nightstock flowers, with chicken, 39
noodles: invention of, 3; crispy, 10; varieties, 65–6
nori see laver, purple
'nourishing and cooling soup' (*ching po leung*), 68
'nutritious soup mixture', 68
nuts, 38

oils and fats, 46–7
oil-fried tea, 27–8
oil soaking (*youjin*), 104

oil splashing (*youfa*), 104
opium, 9
oranges, 2, 87
orchid tea, 26
oysters: in Fujian cooking, 38; dried,
53; **omelette**, 169; **soft-fried oyster
and crab-meat omelette**, 169–70
oyster sauce, 49

pachiaw see star anise seed
pan baking (*guotie*), 107
pan braising (*guota*), 107
pancakes: mandarin, 10; oyster, 38
pan frying (*jian*), 107
panther's womb, 15
papaya: in Cantonese cooking, 38;
consumption of, 83, 87
paper-parcel deep frying (*zhibaozha*),
103
pastes, 49–51; *see also* individual
varieties
pau, 24
peaches, 2, 87
peanuts: consumption of, 7, 57; and
yang food, 12
peanut oil, 47
pears: consumption of, 2; in
Shandong cooking, 41, 87; **steamed
eight treasure**, 215
peas, 57
Pen-Cao-Yen-I ('Discourses upon
Pharmaceutical Natural History'),
79
peppercorns (*fagara*): Sichuan, 38;
white, 63
perch, 2
Persia, 4
persimmons: consumption of, 2, 87;
properties of, 18–19; dried, 69;
preparation of, 225
pheasant: consumption of, 2; in
Yunnan cooking, 40–41
'phoenix marrow', 15
pickle: Chinese mixed, 55;
preparation of, 225
pickling with salt (*yenyan*), 109
pigeon, 72
pigs: raising of, 1; killing, 2–3;
sucking, 8; trotters, 13, 19, 225–6,;
bladder, 19; head, 39; **trotters in
black vinegar**, 134–5; *see also* pork
pilo, 4
pine nuts, 67
pineapple: in Cantonese cooking, 38;
consumption of, 87

pipa see loquat
pitan see under eggs
plain deep frying (*qinzha*), 103
plums: consumption of, 2, 87;
suanmei, 56
plum sauce, 50
plunging and rinsing (*shua*), 97
pocai, 64, 83–4
Polo, Marco, 7
pomelo, 87
pomelo tea, 26
pomfret, 70
pork: consumption of, 2, 7, 72; sweet
and sour, 10; and Buddha's hands,
16; in Dapo cooking, 38; in Hunan
cooking, 38; in Yunnan cooking, 39;
preserved, 64; **Anhui meat balls,**
129–30; *Charsui* – **Cantonese
barbecued,** 130–31; **crab meat lion's
head,** 131–2; **five-spice rolls,** 132–3;
with fish flavour, 135–6; **steamed in
fermented rice,** 136; **red-cooked
pork knuckle and hairweed,** 136–7;
red crispy, 137–8; **rock-sugar pork
knuckle,** 138–9; **spare ribs steamed
in salted black beans,** 139; **steamed
in fermented bean curd,** 139–40;
steamed sandwiched, 140–41;
tungpo, 141; **white sliced,** 142;
wrinkled, 142–3; **Yunwu smoked,**
143–4
pots, cooking, 92
poultry: in Sichuan cooking, 38;
consumption of, 72
prawns: dumplings, 24; Longjing tea
with, 28, 40; consumption of, 71;
saltwater, 121; **Longjing tea,** 170–1;
pan-fried cakes, 171–2; **steamed
rolls,** 172–3; **noodles,** 219
preparation: and *xuzhi*, 8–9; stages of,
88–94
preserved tea, 28
Pu-erh tea, 23, 25
pumpkin seeds, as snacks, 24
purple rice, 48; *see also* rice

Qia-Ming, *Essential Knowledge of
Eating and Drinking*, 8
qi-guo, 39, 100, 148–9
Qingdao, 41
Qin dynasty, 22–4, 30, 41
Qu-yuan, 43
quail: consumption of, 2, 41; **in sweet
and sour sauce,** 157–8
quickfrying (*bao*), 105

quick frying and stir frying in sauce (*peng*), 107
quick frying in oil (*youbao*), 105
quick frying in salted soya bean paste (*jianbao*), 105
quick frying in spring onions (*congbao*), 105
quick-thickened gravy method (*liu*), 104

rabbit: 40–41; **hot and spicy**, 158–9
radish, salted, 55–6; *see also* **savoury Chinese radish pudding**
rape: consumption of, 2; seed oil, 46
rats, bamboo, 39
raw stir frying (*senchao*), 106
recao, 36
red bean paste: consumption of, 10; preparation of, 226
red-bean pudding, 213
red date (jujube) wine, 34–5
red fermented bean curd, 51
'red-in-the-snow' (*xualihong*): preserved, 55; fermented (*meikancai*), 55
red rice (*hongqu*), 64
red snapper, 70
red tea, 25–6
red tea fungus *see hongcha jun*
red (Zhejiang) vinegar, 60
restaurants: development of, 5, 8; opium in, 9; contemporary, 10; MSG in, 60–61; *see also* tea houses
rice: consumption of, 2–3, 7; growing of, 10; fried, 10; white, porridge, 21; cakes, 43; varieties of, 47–8; fermented, 56, 69; **eight treasures**, 206–7; **pan-fried rice cakes**, 212–13; **rice cup cakes**, 213–14; fermented glutinous, 223
rice flour 49
roasting in the oven (*kao*), 107–8
rose petals, 62, 226
rose tea, 26
Russia, 23

sacha-jiang (barbecue sauce), 50, 123
salad: **chicken and mung bean**, 114–15; **lotus root and ginger**, 119–20; **salted jellyfish**, 120–21; **cherry and broad-bean**, 206; **fruit, in rock-sugar syrup**, 207; **silver wood ear and fresh fruit**, 214
salt, 4, 60
salted black soya beans, 51

salt roasting (*yenchi*), 108
salted soya beans, 51
salted soya bean paste, 51
Samarkand, 4
San Francisco, 10
sanshao, 31
saucepan, double, 92
sauces, 49–51; *see also* individual varieties
sausages, 64
savoury Chinese radish pudding, 219–20
scallops, 72, 226
Scholars, The, 8
sea bass, 70
sea carp, 70
sea cucumbers (bêche de mer; sea slug; trepang): properties of, 19–20; dried, 53; consumption of, 72; preparation of, 226
sea scallops, dried, 53
seal slug *see* sea cucumber
sea snails, 72
seafood: dried, 52–4; fresh, 70–72
seasoning, 37, 59–61
seaweed, dried, 54; *see also* individual varieties
senyou see vegetable oil
sesame oil (*hsiangyou*): properties of, 20; cooking with, 46, 51
sesame seeds: consumption of, 10, 67; properties of, 20
Shaanxi province, 36, 40
shallots: consumption of, 2; as flavouring, 63
Shandong province, 25, 31, 36, 40, 46, 82
Shang dynasty, 28
Shanghai, 36, 42
Shanxi province, 36, 40
shanzha see haw
shaobing, 24, 41
shaojiu (white wine), 33; *see also* wine
shaoxingjiu, 32, 40; *see also* wine
shark's fin: consumption of, 5, 44, 52; preparation of, 226–7
Shen Nung, Emperor, 22
shihyu, 4
shrimps: mini, dried, 53; (ordinary) dried, 53; preparation of, 227
shrimp paste: *blachan*, 10; in cooking, 49
shrimp sauce, 50
Sichuan chilli paste, 51
Sichuan pepper salt, 227

Sichuan pepper water, 227
Sichuan peppercorns, 63
Sichuan province, 22–3, 30, 36, 38–40, 46–7, 54
Sichuan preserved vegetable (zhacai), 56
silver fish, dried, 52
silver wood ears (jelly fungus): properties of, 20; consumption of, 67–8; **and fresh fruit salad**, 214; **steamed in coconut**, 215–16; preparation of, 227; *see also* wood ears
Singapore, 10, 24, 43
simmering (*dun*), 98
siumai, 24
snakes, 41
slippery and smooth method (*hualiu*), 104–5
slippery stir frying (*huachao*), 106–7
slow braising (*pa*), 102
smoked vegetarian duck, 181–2
smoking (*xun*), 108
snacks, savoury: recipes, 216–19
soft and smooth method (*ruanliu*), 105
soft deep frying (*ruanzha*), 103
Song dynasty, 5–6, 10, 30, 39, 40
sorghum *see kaoliang*
soup: **bird's nest**, 187–8; **Cantonese beef ball**, 188–9; **casseroled fish**, 189–90; **chicken steamed with wolfberries**, 190; **chrysanthemum fire-pot**, 191–2; **clear scallop**, 192; **duck bundles**, 192–3; *egg furong*, 193–4; **gluten meat-ball**, 194–5; **hot and sour** *doufu*, 195; **hot and sour fish broth**, 195–6; **hot and sour sea-cucumber**, 196–7; **hot-water Chinese 'celery' cabbage**, 197; **liver custard**, 197–8; **lotus speedpod**, 198–9; **milky fish-head**, 199; **mock bird's nest**, 199–200; *pocai* **dumplings and cuttlefish**, 201–2; **red braised shark's fin**, 202; **shark's fin and crab-meat**, 203; **wine cup** *doufu*, 203–4
soup mixtures, 68
'soup mixture', 68
South-East Asia *see* Asia, South-East
soya: consumption of, 2–3, 57; bean curd, 4, 10, 38, 41; bean paste, 41, 50–51; products, 58–9
soya-bean milk (*doujiang*), 58
soya-bean paste, sweet salted, 228
soya sauces, 50–51, 64

spices, 61–3
spinach juice, 227
spirits: from millet, 31; from sorghum, 32
spring onions: properties of, 20; in Shandong cooking, 40–41; as flavouring, 63; **quick fried lamb with spring onions**, 129; juice, 224
spring rolls, 24
squid: dried, 53; consumption of, 72; **hot and sour**, 173; preparation of, 223, 228
stag's reproductive organs (*lu-chong*), 21
star anise seed (*pachiaw*), 63
starch, 61
steamed bread buns *see charsiu bao*
steamed lotus-leaf buns, 156
steamers, 92
steaming (*zhengai dun*), 98–101
stewing in a thick sauce (*jiang*), 109
steeping (*lu*), 108
strainers, 91
stewing (*wei*), 102
stir frying (*chao*), 105–6
stocks, preparation of, 228
strawberries, 87
Su Tungpo, 6, 39, 44
suanmei see under plums
sugar, 4, 59–60; *see also* sweeteners
sulphur, 4
sunflower cold platter, 112–13
Swatow mustard greens, 84
sweets, 39
sweet potatoes, 7, 10, 84–5
sweet salted soya-bean paste, 51
sweeteners, 4

tacai, 36
tahini, 46, 51
Tang dynasty, 3–5, 9, 22–3, 28–30, 42
tangerines, 87
tangerine peel, dried, 62
Taoism: influence on diet, 6; and vegetarian cookery, 41–2
taro: consumption of, 2, 85; **savoury pudding**, 220–21
Te Tsung, Emperor, 42
tea: varieties, 22–8; as colouring, 63; *see also* individual varieties
tea houses, 23–4
tea oil, 47
Teochiu cooking, 38
Tianjin, 42
Tibet, 23, 26, 47, 54

tien-sin, 36
toasted tea (crackling tea), 27
tobacco, 7
tomatoes, 64
tonic foods, 4, 39, 41; *see also under* diet
trepang *see* sea cucumber
Turfan, 28
Turkestan, 4
turnips: pickled, 56; *chungcai*, 56
tzecai see laver, purple

utensils, 91–4

veal, 4, 72
vegetables: as basis of diet, 1, 72–87; preserved, 54–6; **Hunan pickled**, 174; *see also* individual vegetables
vegetable oil (senyou), 46
vegetarian cookery, 41–2
vegetarian goose, 183
venison, 2
vermicelli, 10; *see also* noodles
vinegar: black rice, 13; Zhenjiang, 40; as seasoning, 60

waiting (*kay*), 101–2
walnuts: 67; **sweet crispy**, 216
Wang Mang, Emperor, 3, 41
water chestnuts: consumption of, 2, 85–6; and *yin* food, 12
water spinach, 86
watercress, dried, 68
Weihai, 41
West Lake, 5, 40
wheat, 2, 10
wheat flour, 48
wheat gluten: **sweet and sour vegetarian spare ribs**, 186–7;

preparation of, 228–9
wheat starch, 49
white fermented bean curd, 51
white wine vinegar, 60
wild flowers, 40
wine: 28–35, 61; grape, 28; longan, 17; millet, 2, 28, 32; rice, 2, 32; wheat, 2; *see also* individual varieties
wok, 9, 93–4
wood ears: consumption of, 10, 68; properties of, 21; preparation of, 229; *see also* silver wood ears
Wuloong tea, 25–6
Wunchen, Princess, 23

Xiamen (Amoy), 42
Xian (Chang-an), 4
Xinjiang Uygur Autonomous Region, 27, 47, 54
xuelihong see 'red-in-the-snow'
xuzhi see under preparation

yam: knotty, 18, 69; **candied**, 205
yang food, 12–21
Yangkuifei wine, 29–30
Yangtze river, 6, 10, 23, 40, 54
Yantai, 41
yeast wine, 69
yin food, 12–21, 33
Yuan dynasty, 30
Yuan Mei, *Sui-Yuan Shitan*, 8–9
Yunnan province, 23, 27–8, 36, 38–40, 47, 65
Yunwu tea, 23
zacui ('chop-suey'), 9
zhacai see Sichuan preserved vegetable
Zhejiang province, 26–7, 36, 40, 79
Zhejiang vinegar, 60
zhulan tea, 26